Benjamin Kutsyuruba

Teachers' Work in Times of Uncertainty

Benjamin Kutsyuruba

Teachers' Work in Times of Uncertainty

Post-Soviet Change and Teacher Collaboration

VDM Verlag Dr. Müller

Impressum/Imprint (nur für Deutschland/ only for Germany)

Bibliografische Information der Deutschen Nationalbibliothek: Die Deutsche Nationalbibliothek verzeichnet diese Publikation in der Deutschen Nationalbibliografie; detaillierte bibliografische Daten sind im Internet über http://dnb.d-nb.de abrufbar.

Alle in diesem Buch genannten Marken und Produktnamen unterliegen warenzeichen-, marken- oder patentrechtlichem Schutz bzw. sind Warenzeichen oder eingetragene Warenzeichen der jeweiligen Inhaber. Die Wiedergabe von Marken, Produktnamen, Gebrauchsnamen, Handelsnamen, Warenbezeichnungen u.s.w. in diesem Werk berechtigt auch ohne besondere Kennzeichnung nicht zu der Annahme, dass solche Namen im Sinne der Warenzeichen- und Markenschutzgesetzgebung als frei zu betrachten wären und daher von jedermann benutzt werden dürften.

Coverbild: www.purestockx.com

Verlag: VDM Verlag Dr. Müller Aktiengesellschaft & Co. KG
Dudweiler Landstr. 125 a, 66123 Saarbrücken, Deutschland
Telefon +49 681 9100-698, Telefax +49 681 9100-988, Email: info@vdm-verlag.de
Zugl.: Saskatoon, University of Saskatchewan, Diss., 2008

Herstellung in Deutschland:
Schaltungsdienst Lange o.H.G., Zehrensdorfer Str. 11, D-12277 Berlin
Books on Demand GmbH, Gutenbergring 53, D-22848 Norderstedt
Reha GmbH, Dudweiler Landstr. 99, D- 66123 Saarbrücken
ISBN: 978-3-639-07783-4

Imprint (only for USA, GB)

Bibliographic information published by the Deutsche Nationalbibliothek: The Deutsche Nationalbibliothek lists this publication in the Deutsche Nationalbibliografie; detailed bibliographic data are available in the Internet at http://dnb.d-nb.de.

Any brand names and product names mentioned in this book are subject to trademark, brand or patent protection and are trademarks or registered trademarks of their respective holders. The use of brand names, product names, common names, trade names, product descriptions etc. even without
a particular marking in this works is in no way to be construed to mean that such names may be regarded as unrestricted in respect of trademark and brand protection legislation and could thus be used by anyone.

Cover image: www.purestockx.com

Publisher:
VDM Verlag Dr. Müller Aktiengesellschaft & Co. KG
Dudweiler Landstr. 125 a, 66123 Saarbrücken, Germany
Phone +49 681 9100-698, Fax +49 681 9100-988, Email: info@vdm-verlag.de

Produced in USA and UK by:
Lightning Source Inc., 1246 Heil Quaker Blvd., La Vergne, TN 37086, USA
Lightning Source UK Ltd., Chapter House, Pitfield, Kiln Farm, Milton Keynes, MK11 3LW, GB
BookSurge, 7290 B. Investment Drive, North Charleston, SC 29418, USA
ISBN: 978-3-639-07783-4

To My Beautiful Wife Olichka – The Love of My Life!

To Our Little Bundle of Joy, Kevin!

To My Parents, Venedykt and Oryssya Kutsyuruba –
I Could Never Wish for Better Parents!
It's a Blessing to Have Parents like You!

ACKNOWLEDGEMENTS

The completion of this book would be impossible without the support and encouragement of many special people, to whom I extend my sincerest gratitude. I would like to thank my dissertation advisor, Dr. Patrick Renihan, whose expertise, advice, and guidance were of invaluable help throughout the PhD program. His encouragement, his understanding, his humor, and most of all, his patience, are greatly appreciated. I am truly grateful for his mentorship and dedication. Special thanks to the committee members, especially Dr. Larry Sackney for support, recommendations, and suggestions during the PhD program, as well as his advice regarding the process of transforming my dissertation into a book. Many thanks to others who participated in the study and book project by giving their time and advice. Most importantly, I have been greatly supported by family and friends. I would like to express my deepest appreciation to my parents, who did not have an opportunity to achieve their educational goals to the fullest extent due to repressions and oppression from the Soviet regime, but always encouraged and supported my educational pursuits, no matter the cost and personal sacrifice. I am forever grateful and I thank you sincerely. I would also like to thank my relatives and friends for their prayers and support. My greatest gratitude to my wife Olichka, whose love, understanding, encouragement, support, and unselfish sacrifices have allowed me to achieve my goals. I am truly blessed beyond measure to have you in my life! Finally, thanks to God, for His love, His grace, and His countless blessings.

CONTENTS

CHAPTER 3

CHAPTER 4

CHAPTER 5

CHAPTER 6

CHAPTER 7

CHAPTER 8

CHAPTER 9

PREFACE

The collapse of the Soviet Union marked a critical turning point in the development of Ukraine's national identity. The period of independence of Ukraine became characterized by significant changes at the societal level. Few organizations reflected the complexities and contradictions of societal changes as poignantly as schools. This book describes educators' experiences in a context of large-scale philosophical, ideological, social, political, and economic changes of the post-Soviet era, and the teachers' interpretation of the impact of related changes upon teacher collaboration in Ukrainian schools within the period of independence. Utilizing constructive postmodernism framework, this book examines teacher collaboration through micropolitical and cultural perspectives. Ultimately, this book focuses on the two-fold process of collaborative school culture development in times of uncertainty and radical change and highlights the need for better understanding of the role of teachers' lives outside of school in the process of establishing collaborative relationships in their work. It is my hope that this book will inform senior educational administrators and policy makers about the ways in which schools may better respond to teachers' needs in times of societal changes and will serve as a reference for planning reform policies related to teacher collaboration in schools.

Chapter 1

INTRODUCTION:
SOCIETY IN TRANSITION

Work of hundreds of thousands of teachers of schools ... in [the] direction of new approaches to training of students [and preparing] them for life and activities in a democratic, legal and European state – independent Ukraine – will promote [the progress of the education system] ... (Ministry of Education of Ukraine, 1999, p. 83)

The breakup of the Soviet Union was a critical turning point in the development of Ukraine's national identity. The collapse of the Soviet Union and declaration of independence in 1991 had an impact on its society. The most frequently noted were the political, economic, and social changes. Disintegration of the USSR and the appearance of a group of independent states caused severe political and social crises, economic decline, and decrease of living standards in these countries (Ministry of Education of Ukraine, 1999). Before 1991, "Soviet Ukraine was no more than part of an authoritarian, oppressive empire" (Pascual & Pifer, 2002, p. 176). After the declaration of independence, Ukraine chose a path which balanced political democratization of the society, economic reform, and social stability (Dyczok, 2000). Ukraine's initial goals were to disengage from the former centralized command system, assert control over economic processes on its territory, introduce market reforms, and end its previous isolation from the global economy. Reforms in the political arena, decline in demographics, rising cost of health care, growing unemployment, and environmental damage were some of the issues the newly formed country had to face.

All of these issues greatly affected education (Zhulynsky, 1997). The collapse of the Soviet Union in 1991 provided an opportunity for researchers to study education in depth as the country made a transition from totalitarian Marxist-Leninist ideology to democracy and pluralism. The transition is not yet complete; the struggle still continues between the forces of progress and pluralism on one side and bureaucratic totalitarian forces on the other (Kononenko & Holowinsky, 2001). The recent political and social developments, following the President's Elections in December, 2004, revealed the ongoing struggle between these forces in Ukrainian society.

According to Golarz and Golarz (1995), schools have historically been a reflection of the larger society of which they are a part. The ways in which schools function have been influenced by the values and belief systems of each school's surrounding community, especially by the professional educators and leaders who directly develop and maintain each system of education. The systems of values and beliefs that influence the relationships of people within schools are certain to change during the periods when society is in transition. Ukraine's political and cultural changes have resulted in a collapse of a former system of values and beliefs and created a need for a new system (Kononenko & Holowinsky, 2001). This need prompted the post-Soviet Ukrainian society to move from the modernist Soviet era into a new era characterized by postmodern views.

For much of the 20th century, the dominant view of society and organizations was grounded in the *modernist* perspective. This orientation was derived from Weber's (1947) theories of organizations, which were based on rationality. Weber's theories and worldview have extended far beyond organizations to become firmly entrenched in all aspects of life (Sackney & Mitchell, 2002). Turner (1990) characterized modernity as:

> the consequence of a process of modernization, by which the social world comes under the domination of asceticism, secularization, the universalistic claims of instrumental

rationality, the differentiation of the various spheres of the lifeworld, the bureaucratization of economic, political and military practices, and the growing monetarization of values. (p. 6)

These developments aligned with a modernist age, in which reason was believed to be capable of creating a unifying structure of thought and knowledge. Modernist thought has not only driven general organizational and social theories, but it also has dominated the theories that have been used to structure educational systems (Sackney & Mitchell, 2002), emphasizing order, accountability, structure, systemization, linear development, and control in schools. Rather than education being viewed at the forefront of social change, it was viewed as the stabilizing force that socialized individuals and groups into an awareness and acceptance of their place in the social and organizational orders.

The societal order in the former Soviet Union was characterized by the dominance of modernist views, which began to give way to postmodernist perspectives with the introduction of *perestroika* [restructuring] and *glasnost* [openness] in the 1990s (Lahusen & Kuperman, 1993), the period of social and cultural openness instituted by Mikhail Gorbachev to revitalize the Soviet system. The post-Soviet Ukraine faced the new, unexplored terrain of postmodernism. Postmodernity is a social condition in which economic, political, organizational, and personal lives become organized around very difference principles than those of modernity (Hargreaves, 1994). In education, "the vector of changes focused on transition from the 'Soviet school' model to the democratic European one" (Ministry of Education of Ukraine, 1999, p. 3). The existing educational system, characterized by uniform requirements, centralized planning and administration, faced new challenges. Centralized financing and management of education, authoritarian pedagogy noticeably gave way to the elements of decentralization and pedagogy of cooperation (Ministry of Education of Ukraine, 1999). Schools, like other areas of social life, were caught on the cusp of a new era:

... one between a modernist paradigm (characterized by professional values such as responsibility, meditative role, and concern for bottom-line results) and the postmodern pattern (with swift currents of institutional changes marked by decentralization, pluralistic demands from multiple voices, and school system redesign). (Maxcy, 1994, p. 3)

One of the core requisites of the postmodern society became the ability to collaborate, on both a large (society) and small (school) scale (Fullan, 1993). The push for more collaborative relationships in postmodern society had a great impact on education, too. Collaboration turned into an articulating and integrating principle of action, planning, culture, development, organization and research. Collaborative decision-making and problem solving became "a cornerstone of postmodern organizations" (Hargreaves, 1994, p. 17). School members needed to develop the ability to collaborate in order for their schools to function well in the world of evolving postmodern views.

This book has been written out of conviction that collaborative relationships and culture are necessary for Ukrainian society to face the changing realities of the new era. Specifically, it is concerned with the development of collaborative cultures in schools. Teacher collaboration and collegiality have been presented as having many virtues (Hargreaves, 1994) and as a critical component when undergoing any changes within schools (Little, 1982). Collaboration and collegiality take *teacher professional growth* beyond personal reflection or dependence on outside experts to a point where teachers can learn from each other, sharing and developing their expertise together (Lieberman & Miller, 1984). The confidence that comes with collegial sharing and support leads to greater readiness to experiment and take risks, and with it a commitment to continuous improvement among teachers as a recognized part of their professional responsibility (Hargreaves, 1994). In this sense, collaboration and collegiality are seen as forming vital bridges between teacher development and school improvement. Shulman (1989) argued that collaboration is absolutely necessary if we wish teaching to be of the highest order. When collaboration takes the form of shared decision-making and staff consultation, it is seen as playing an important role in *school improvement* and *school effectiveness* (Meadows & Saltzman, 2002; Rosenholtz, 1989).

Collaboration and collegiality are also viewed as ways of securing effective implementation of externally introduced change (Fullan & Stiegelbauer, 1991).

The need for collaborative relationships and culture in schools was indicated by high-school teachers in Ukraine in my study of supervision and professional development (Kutsyuruba, 2003). This finding and my past experiences as a school teacher in Ukraine encouraged me to inquire into the area of collaboration in Ukrainian schools during the times of post-Soviet transition. Being one of the core requisites of the postmodern age, is collaboration a wide-spread practice among teachers in Ukrainian schools? What are the professional teacher relationships like in Ukrainian schools? Did relationships between school members change or do they continue to reflect a top-down, centralized model of schooling characteristic of educational systems in the Soviet Union? How did post-Soviet societal changes affect education? Did societal changes have any impact on teacher collaboration in Ukrainian schools? Can a collaborative culture in Ukrainian schools be developed *instrumentally* or do certain conditions *enable* its development? Questions of this nature required study, and the unprecedented post-Soviet societal changes in Ukraine provided a case in point.

The Study

The purpose of the study described in this book was to examine teachers' perceptions of the impact of societal changes on teacher collaboration in schools within the period of independence of Ukraine (1991 – 2005). This study provided a description of teacher experiences in a context of large-scale philosophical, ideological, social, political, and economic changes of the post-Soviet era, and the teachers' interpretation of the impact of related changes upon teacher collaboration in Ukrainian schools.

Several research questions gave focus to the study. They were divided into two subgroups. First, questions inquiring into teachers' perceptions of the nature of post-Soviet societal changes: *What are teachers' perceptions of the nature of post-Soviet societal changes? What is the perceived general impact of post-Soviet societal changes on Ukrainian schools?* Second, questions regarding the impacts on teacher collaboration: *What is the nature and state of teacher collaboration in Ukrainian schools? What are teachers' perceptions of the impact of external societal changes on collaboration among teachers? What are the internal practices that influence teacher collaboration in schools?*

A study of this nature is of value for several reasons. While the move toward collegiality, cooperation, and collaboration in schools is certainly present in the educational literature, very little is known about how societal changes affect professional interaction and collaborative relationships of teachers. There is academic significance to this study, as few descriptions and analyses of this kind are offered to schools as they grapple with the issues caused by societal changes. The reflections and insights from teachers involved in this study provide new knowledge on what these experiences are like and how they compare and contrast with what is presently known and documented about collaboration in the literature. In conditions of rapid and radical change, collaboration becomes an articulating and integrating principle of action, planning, culture, development, organization, and research (Hargreaves, 1994).

The significance of this study is also found in its ability to inform policy makers in their understanding of how schools may better respond to teachers' needs in times of societal changes. It expands the knowledge base from which school administrators, teachers, and leaders may view societal changes in the context of education. This study also provides policy makers with a source of reference for planning reform policies related to teacher collaboration in schools.

This study should add to a better understanding of relationships between macropolitics of society and micropolitics of organizational life in schools. By connecting these perspectives, we can better understand the complexity and often misguided and even damaging effects of large-scale policies that are created without input from individual school contexts (Marshall & Gerstl-Pepin, 2005). Moreover, schools cannot be understood without understanding the environment or larger social contexts in which they operate. This study draws connections between these perspectives to better understand the nature of teacher collaboration in schools.

A study of this nature should add to the clarity required by the Ukrainian society to implement reforms in education during the period of transition from the "Soviet school" model to the democratic European one. According to Ministry of Education of Ukraine National Report (1999), there was social and political consensus concerning the necessity to concentrate common efforts on the development of educational sphere, improvement of student preparation, and increasing the level of teacher qualification in Ukraine. "Although significant positive changes were carried out in this period, unfortunately not all provisions of the strategic plans of the development of education in Ukraine were implemented" (p. 78). Incomplete fulfillment of the plan of reforms was believed to be caused by the external factors, such as the negative effect of economic and social crises and other phenomena of the transitive period. This study provides a rich description of teachers' perceptions of the impact of these and other societal changes on schools and situates teacher collaboration as the necessary component for the reforms in education in Ukraine. It is my hope that the findings of this study will encourage the Ministry of Education, Boards of Education, school administrators, and teachers in Ukraine to pay closer attention to collaborative relationships in Ukrainian schools.

The study tries to establish better connections between theory and practice of education in Ukraine. Due to insufficient research conducted in the area of collaboration in Ukraine, in conceptualizing this study I relied on my experiences with collaboration during my teaching career in Ukrainian schools. As well, anecdotal description obtained from the professionals in Chernivtsi, Ukraine indicated the lack of research in this area. In part, this study is grounded on some of the findings that pertained to teacher collaboration from my previous research (Kutsyuruba, 2003). This study is instrumental in providing academic descriptions of the experiences with collaboration in Ukrainian schools. The insights and descriptions shared by the teachers in this study help to fill the gap between theory and practice in the area of teacher collaboration in Ukraine.

Overview of the Book

Thus far I introduced the reader to the notion of teacher collaboration and described the context of post-Soviet societal changes in Ukraine in relation to teacher collaboration and the reasons for the investigation of these issues at this time. In addition, I presented the purpose, research questions, and significance of the study detailed in this book. In Chapter Two, I review some of the current literature pertaining to the period of transition in Ukraine, the notion of postmodernism, and description of teacher collaboration from the dual lenses of organizational culture and micropolitics. The research methodology and design, research methods, and analysis of the data used in the study are detailed in Chapter Three. The findings obtained from the data analysis are grouped and presented in five chapters. Chapter Four presents the findings related to teachers' perceptions of the nature of post-Soviet societal changes, while Chapter Five discusses the impact of those changes on schools in general. The descriptions of nature of teacher collaboration follow in Chapter Six. Chapters Seven and Eight respectively present teachers' perceptions of the external and internal factors that influence collaboration among teachers in Ukrainian schools. In Chapter Nine, I provide the summary of the study, discussion of the major themes emerging from the findings, and implications for theory, practice, policy, and methodology.

Chapter 2

PERSPECTIVES ON COLLABORATION:
A REVIEW OF THE LITERATURE

One of the emergent and most promising metaparadigms of the postmodern age is that of collaboration as an articulating and integrating principle of action, planning, culture, development, organization and research. (Hargreaves, 1994, p. 245)

In this chapter, I provide a theoretical overview of the nature of collaboration in schools from a constructive postmodernism framework utilizing cultural and micropolitical perspectives. First, I present an overview of issues concerning changes in society and education during the period of post-Soviet transition in Ukraine. Subsequently, I discuss the use of a constructive postmodernism framework an analytical tool for the discussion of collaboration in the context of post-Soviet change, following which I present the definition, characteristics, benefits, and challenges of teacher collaboration. In order to view schools as cultures, I apply a lens of organizational culture perspective to schools, discussing the nature, functions, and elements of school culture, as well as, power relationships within school cultures. To better grasp the deep meaning of collaborative interactions in schools, I use the micropolitical perspective. After explicating the cultural and micropolitical nature of collaboration in schools, I turn to the discussion of various types of school culture as they pertain to teacher collaboration in schools. Furthermore, I analyze the potential for collaboration in Ukrainian schools, utilizing the notion of *the collective* that prevailed in Soviet system of education. The chapter concludes with the initial conceptual framework for the study, which describes the interaction of key theoretical concepts.

Education in the Period of Transition in Ukraine

Following the collapse of the Soviet Union, Ukrainian society was caught amidst the rapid and radical change. What are the characteristics of "a changing society"? Batelaan and Gundare (2000) outlined the main characteristics of the changing society in Central and Eastern Europe:

- The change in Central and Eastern Europe from a more (the East) or less (the West) state controlled economy into a market economy;
- The change from a more or less centralized society into a decentralized society;
- The change from a society based on the national state as organizing principle, to a society based on multinational networks;
- The change from an industrial society into an information society;
- The change from a mono-cultural/egalitarian society in terms of values (particularly with reference to religion, family, and social relations) into a multicultural society, diverse in terms of values. (p. S31)

Changing societies in the countries of the former Eastern bloc were not characterized by more or less gradual process as it was in Western Europe, but by a revolutionary change. Moreover, ideological transformations were documented by many researchers in the countries of former USSR and eastern Europe (Urban, 1992). Democratic tradition of Western European nations had always valued individual responsibility, whereas the Soviet system emphasized collective responsibility and collective values (Batelaan & Gundare, 2000; Kubicek, 2002).

Few organizations reflect the complexities and contradictions of societal changes as poignantly as schools. In Ukraine, given the critical importance of education and close control the state wielded over it, the system of education was one of the first institutions to undergo rapid and radical reform following independence (Wanner, 1998). After the proclamation of independence of Ukraine in 1991 and declaration of its intention to transform into a democratic state with the regulated market economy, the strategic plans of changes in education were submitted to this nation-wide purpose of transformation (Ministry of Education of Ukraine, 1999). Development of a detailed plan of reforming and transforming the system of education from the "Soviet" into the national one became one of the main priorities of the government and new top officials of the Ministry of Education. Educational reforms represented a compromise reached among divergent groups wielding zones of influence in the government. As Wanner (1998) noted, by targeting education for reform, political leaders capitalized on the potential of education to articulate and instill new norms of social and cultural behavior in the newly established country.

At the beginning of the independence period, an influential blueprint for education, written by a commission from the Ministry of Education and released in 1992, outlined how the educational system should be reformed to reflect changing political and social realities. The report claimed that post-Soviet educational reform intended to eliminate the "authoritarian pedagogy put in place by a totalitarian state which led to the suppression of natural talents and capabilities and interests of all participants in the educational process" (Ministry of Education of Ukraine, 1992, p. 3). In place of *uniformity* and *collectivism*, propagated by the Soviet education, the commission asserted that the educational system must strive to develop *individuality*, *nationality*, and *morality* among students and teachers in schools. Wanner (1998) concluded that educational policymakers advocated pursuing an educational program through an individualist approach by cultivating individuality at the same time that it encouraged conformity to a national identity. By emphasizing such individuality and conformity to national identity, reforms encouraged "an awareness of differences in experiences, memories, and identities" (p. 82).

Except for this report, there was no systematic assessment of the needs of education reform in the first few years of independence, because politicians were preoccupied with the immediate needs of political and economic reform (Dyczok, 2000). The following years became the period of stagnation and partial losses of the achievements of the initial reforms (Ministry of Education of Ukraine, 1999). By 1996, a new Education Law was passed and government commissions were established to prepare policy documents on structural and substantive reform to the education system. However, the pace of change and reforms was slow, "since many educators and education administrators [were] products of the previous education system and not familiar with alternative models" (Dyczok, 2000, p. 98). As Wanner (1998) found, the formal, structural aspects of Soviet education were easier to reform than the practices instilled by the values of the Soviet system.

Analyzing the evolution of the educational reform efforts in Ukraine within the 1990-1999 period, the Ministry of Education (1999) concluded that although significant positive changes were carried out in this period, unfortunately, not all provisions of the strategic plans of the development of education in Ukraine were implemented. Among the positive outcomes were the democratization and decentralization of management and financing, deideologization of education, occurrence of institutions promoting the development of democracy and formation of a market economy, decrease of ideological pressure, and acceptance of pluralist perspectives in the society (pp. 78-80). The most significant areas of regress or absence of positive changes were a lack of attention to development and implementation of new social ideology, partial transition to the new paradigm of education, and fragmentary character of reforms in the system of education (pp. 78-79). In general, the system of education received necessary state and public support, but the economic crisis, significant decrease of the gross national product, and cuts to educational budgets negatively affected education.

Teachers found themselves in the middle of the reform and were directly impacted by its outcomes. Economic crisis, inflation, and social instability caused falling wages and significant delays in payments. Teachers needed to search for additional earnings or other forms of maintenance for their existence, which resulted in the deterioration of quality of teaching and deprofessionalization. They were frequently called upon to do unwanted or menial tasks well below what they were trained for, simply to keep the school functioning (Wanner, 1998). Teachers had less time and opportunities for individual professional development, studying of new sources of educational information, and performance of additional measures to increase student achievement (Ministry of Education of Ukraine, 1999).

The professional relationships in schools were significantly affected by the transitive character of education. Despite the gains of the education reforms, the bureaucratic relationships between school members still reflected relationships characteristic of the educational system in the Soviet Union. The emerging individualism in Ukrainian society, with its emphasis on individual liberty, rights, and interests, may be one of the factors that forced teachers to work in isolation, resulting in conservatism and resistance to innovation. I believe, an attempt to answer the question, "Can teacher collaboration be *planned* or does it *emerge?*" which I asked myself before commencing on this study, may shed some light on the nature and current state of teacher collaboration in Ukrainian schools. The expanded question is, "Can teacher collaboration be developed *instrumentally* or do certain conditions *enable* its development?" I assume collaborative relationships between teachers in Ukrainian schools require both *planning* and certain societal *conditions* to develop. Collaboration will not just happen overnight; there need to be certain mechanisms and a theoretical foundation in schools, as well as certain conditions in place in Ukrainian society for collaboration to develop.

It is from this point that I discuss the theoretical basis for postmodern, cultural, and micropolitical perspective on collaboration. As most of the literature on collaboration reflects a Western perspective, applying the main concepts of collaboration to the Ukrainian context may be difficult. However, the lack of research in this area in Ukraine and an attempt to switch to the democratic European education model prompted the use of Western theoretical perspective to present a necessary background for the discussion. In order to provide a better understanding of the notion under study, and for the purposes of clarification of terms, I now turn to the discussion of the characteristics of the postmodern perspective.

The Postmodern Perspective

One of the challenges facing postmodernists is the lack of clear definition of postmodernism itself. Aronowitz and Giroux (1991) stated that in keeping with the multiplicity of differences that it celebrates, postmodernism is not only subject to different ideological appropriations, but it is also marked by a wide variety of interpretations. While it is possible to identify a number of streams in postmodern social theory, there is little agreement in the discourse about the meaning of key concepts, constructs, and terms (Turner, 1990). According to Giroux (1994), postmodernism is a "shifting signifier" (p. 51); that is, its nature is dynamic rather than static in its meaning and does not have a firm definition. As Hargreaves (1994) framed it, the prefix "post" suggests, there is more clarity about what we are moving beyond than what we are moving towards. A postmodern worldview is thus contrasted with something that has gone before, and to define *postmodern* is impossible without exploring its relationship to and contrast with *modern*.

In addition to the contested definitions, a number of debates on postmodernism as construct can be found in the literature. One of the debates centers on whether postmodernism is an epoch or epistemology (Biesta, 1995). A second debate turns on the historical location of postmodernism and the question of whether it is reactionary or progressive (Sackney & Mitchell, 2002); that is, whether we view postmodernism as anti-modern or beyond modernism (Turner, 1990). In order to embrace the discussion of these two major debates and use postmodernism as an analytical tool, postmodernism needs to be presented within a framework, at least for the purposes of the following analysis and discussion. For this reason, I utilize the broader framework of postmodernism (Furman, 1998), that presents it as three types of social theory: *descriptive* social theory, *normative* or *constructive* social theory, and *oppositional* or *deconstructive* social theory. Although the classification of postmodern perspectives is only a heuristic device for analysis, and cannot be claimed to be completely precise or comprehensive (Furman, 1998), it provides insights into the notion of postmodernism and what it can bring into personal, social, and organizational lives.

Postmodernism – Era or Epistemology?

On the first debate, Furman (1998) argued that as *descriptive* social theory, postmodernism describes and interprets the conditions of the age of postmodernism that are becoming prevalent in our social world. These conditions are the global information revolution, the increased mobility and travel, the international monetary and trade systems that created an interdependent global economy, and political uncertainty with the decline of nation-state as a separate political and economic entity. People are aware as never before that there are multiple ways of living, thinking, and believing in the world, all with claims to legitimacy and none with a valid claim to superiority or hegemony. Furman (1998) asserted:

> We realize that across national and cultural boundaries, we are inextricably connected to and dependent on others who may be quite different from us. Thus, beyond describing the tangible conditions of the postmodern era, descriptive postmodernism gives us some inkling of the changes that are occurring in how we think as humans in society. (p. 305)

The view of postmodernism as descriptive social theory helps us make sense of the world we live in and our reactions to this world; a world in which our viewpoint shifts from parochial to global, and a world in which we are inescapably aware of otherness. The central feature of such a postmodern worldview becomes "the collapse of belief", the "growing suspicion that all belief systems – all ideas about human reality – are social constructions" (W. T. Anderson, 1990, p. 3). Viewing postmodernism as descriptive social theory allows understanding that postmodernist thinking represents a general shift in how we think about the world we live in and our place in it.

This leads us to the perspective that postmodernism can be viewed both as a cultural form or social era that follows modernism and as an epistemology or a method of cultural production that conceptualizes how we perceive, experience, and understand the world (Sackney & Mitchell, 2002). The postmodern view is that *epistemology*, which is the study of how we know or what we know to be true, always precedes *ontology*, which is what we see and what we believe to be real. This perspective contrasts with *positivist* assumptions, where *ontology* is believed to precede *epistemology*, where facts reflect reality, and where truth claims mirror reality (Evers & Lakomski, 1996). As Scheurich (1994) argued, social or postmodern realism is the unabashed recognition that all epistemology, ontology, and the ways of thinking that yield such categories as epistemology and ontology are socially conditioned and historically relative or contextual. Sackney and Mitchell (2002) also argued that postmodernism represents a historical movement into a different ontological era, and that it is grounded on a different epistemological orientation. This new orientation is disenchanted with approaches that attempt to homogenize and explain human nature, society, or the foundation of knowledge (Sackney et al., 1999).

The usefulness of this debate for the following discussion lies in the fact that we live in a world with varying levels of postmodernist thinking. Ukraine has moved from a modern era of foundational truth and unified perspective into a society of plurality, diversity, and interdependence in social, political, and economic realms. This new era requires new ways of thinking and recognition of otherness from schools as well. Descriptive postmodernism informs our understanding of the social context of schooling and how schools confront this issue. Giroux (1994) raised an important issue, whether or not schools have remained intractably modernist in the midst of an increasingly postmodern world. Another issue is whether schools should discard all the good that was gained in modernist era and start anew, or whether they should build upon the previously formed foundation. The second debate in postmodernism may help to provide clarity for this issue.

Postmodernism – Deconstructive or Constructive?

For the second debate, the reactive or progressive nature of postmodernism, Furman (1998) differentiated between postmodernism as *oppositional* or *deconstructive* social theory and postmodernism as *normative* or *constructive* social theory. The former interpretation of postmodernism, as *deconstructive* or *oppositional*, is most commonly used in education literature. As a *deconstructive* theory, postmodernism is oppositional to modernism, and seeks to deconstruct the modernist paradigm through a series of negations drawing on the works of Foucault (1980; 1982), Derrida (1973), and Lyotard (1984). These include the negation of epistemic certainty, foundational knowledge, and objective reason. It seeks to expose the internal contradictions of metanarratives by deconstructing modern notions of truth, language, knowledge, and power (Slattery, 1995). Deconstructive postmodernism has also been called the *cold-blooded* postmodernism (C. Henry, 1995). According to this view, there cannot be any shared values or universally agreed facts, because no truth exists, outside ourselves, to be discovered. In this form, postmodernism denies the contributions of modernist theoretical frameworks and research agendas in education without offering constructive alternatives.

Postmodernism as a normative social theory is *constructive postmodernism* (Furman, 1998). According to this perspective, in spite of its rather reactive label, postmodernism is not anti-modern. Rather, postmodernism has moved beyond its origins to develop a nature that, although tentative, tenuous, and troublesome to some extent, is stubbornly unique and clearly distinct from modernity (Sackney & Mitchell, 2002). Unlike the *deconstructive* postmodern perspective, *constructive* or *normative* postmodernism does not seek the wholesale negation of all features of pre-modern or modern societies, but seeks to incorporate the best of these into a more balanced entity.

Rather than negating the possibility of any worldview, constructive postmodernism seeks to build a new worldview, a way to live in harmony with nature and with each other as the postmodern age unfolds. This normative perspective takes on a prescriptive tone in attempting to provide direction for the shaping of the emergent postmodern world culture (Furman, 1998). Of value to the present discussion is the point that constructive postmodernism includes the sense of relationships between people as *cooperative* rather than *competitive* and *coercive*, respecting the wisdom of all cultures, viewing the world as an organism rather than a machine, and regarding persons as interdependent rather than isolated (Center for a Postmodern World, 1990).

Researchers described constructive postmodernism as the *warm-hearted* (C. Henry, 1995) or *friendly* postmodernism (Nielsen, 1993). This view indicated that while the sensate self exists without any transcendent, scientific, or subjective authority, resulting in denial of shared truths and values, a shared "content or common sense" (C. Henry, 1995, p. 39) is practiced to provide some escape from unrelieved relativism. Nielsen (1993) also claimed that, despite fundamental differences, temporary progress can be made by reconstructing emotional and cognitive bridges for mutual problem solving. Locating postmodernism as after-modernism rather than as anti-modernism clears the way for new political and social strategies that can embrace difference, diversity, pluralism, and incommensurability (Turner, 1990). It also expands our ability to appreciate otherness in a pluralistic and increasingly global society (Sackney & Mitchell, 2002).

The second debate may be extremely useful for the practice of collaboration among teachers in schools. A modernist view called for a type of collaboration in schools that focused on sameness, unified school culture, articulation of common visions and values, unity of views, common platform for educators and other members of schools, to name a few (Fullan, 1993; Furman, 1998). Deconstructive postmodernism, at its extreme, seems to negate the possibility of any unity altogether. However, its perspective cannot be discarded as irrelevant for the discussion of collaborative relationships in school. As Furman (1998) suggested, deconstructive postmodernism can serve as a critical tool for examining efforts to build collaborative cultures or communities in schools by providing cautions in regard to the unwitting use of modernist perspectives and point out the mismatch between the modernist school and postmodernist society. Unlike deconstructive postmodernism, that negates the possibility of any collaboration, and modernism, that emphasizes collaboration through sameness, constructive postmodernism adopts the view that collaboration is based on the "feeling of responsibility to cooperate with others who may be different. The center [of collaboration] is shifted from sameness to two new ideas: acceptance of otherness and cooperation within difference" (Furman, 1998, p. 307). Constructive postmodernism seems to adopt the achievements of the modernist perspective in the area of collaboration and apply a new lens, defining it as a network of persons who may differ but who are interdependent. It is from this constructive postmodern perspective that I try to analyze the characteristics and potential for developing collaboration in Ukrainian schools.

The preceding review provides an important backdrop to the use of a postmodern epistemology as a framework for discussing collaboration in schools. Taken together, the insights from postmodern debates challenged the way the concept of collaboration was applied in education and suggested new directions and metaphors for schools within a postmodern context. One of the metaphors that employed the postmodern perspective was the notion of schools as *cultures*. A postmodern conceptualization of school culture added some conceptual detail that was missing in an overly bounded and integrated view of culture (M. E. Henry, 1993). This view was criticized for creating "beautiful structures" and assuming "homogeneous culture so that individual versions are more or less identical" (Gerholm, 1988, p. 191). Ideal models of social structure, proposed by functionalism and various types of structuralism, gave way to multi-perspective views on culture. Postmodernists viewed culture as a process, paradoxically fragmented and characterized by a plurality of perspectives, adding a significant and new dimension to the existing notion of culture. Respect for diversity, otherness, multiple perspectives, and interdependence among school professionals represented the move towards collaborative cultures in schools. In the recent decades, collaborative school cultures became a popular notion in the literature (Deal & Peterson, 1999; Firestone & Seashore Louis, 1999; Fullan, 1993; Fullan & Hargreaves, 1996; Hargreaves, 1994; Little, 2002; Rosenholtz, 1989). Though a more detailed theoretical overview of collaborative cultures is presented in the later sections of this chapter, it is necessary to describe the essence of collaboration in schools early within this study. The following section reviews the major characteristics of teacher collaboration in schools.

Collaboration

One of the core requisites of the postmodern society became the ability to collaborate, on both a large (society) and small (school) scale (Fullan, 1993). Collaboration has become "an articulating and integrating principle of action, planning, culture, development, organization and research" (Hargreaves, 1994, p. 245). Collaborative decision-making and problem solving became "a cornerstone of postmodern organizations" (p. 17). The push for more collaborative relationships in postmodern society had a great impact on education, too. School members needed to develop the ability to collaborate in order for their schools to function well in the world of evolving postmodern views.

What Is Collaboration?

The term *collaboration* has become something of an educational buzzword (Friend & Cook, 2000). However, despite all the current discussion about collaboration, not many clear definitions of it have been presented. Researchers (Friend & Cook, 2000; Hargreaves, 1994) noted that the term collaboration is often discussed as if it is widely understood, sometimes carelessly used, and occasionally misapplied. Collaboration has mistakenly been treated as a synonym for other concepts such as teams, consultation, problem solving, and committee meetings. In terms of specific initiatives, collaboration and collegiality often take the form of team teaching, collaborative planning, peer coaching, mentor relationships, professional dialogue and collaborative action research, to name a few. "What most authors seem to agree on is that collaboration includes working together in a supportive and mutually beneficial relationship" (Friend & Cook, 2000, p. 5). Beyond teachers working and talking together in one way or another, there is little else that these many different activities and initiatives have in common (Hargreaves, 1994). Little (1990) described this factor as *joint work*, that requires closer interdependence between teachers and their colleagues and more mutual adjustments at the level of practice. This can be evidenced when teachers work together, share knowledge, contribute ideas, and develop plans of achieving educational and organizational goals (Cavanagh & Dellar, 1996).

In the process of joint work, collaboration involves shared creation (Schrage, 1990). Communication, cooperation, and coordination are notions which are used to describe joint work, but do not go far enough to describe the process of collaboration. Schrage (1990) distinguished collaboration by the genuine desire of the participants to solve a problem or create something new. Individuals that are cooperating, communicating, or coordinating are not collaborating. Creating a shared understanding is simply a different task than exchanging information and interacting for individual or shared interests. The investment that participants bring to a collaborative process distinguishes it from other levels of working together. Meaningful collaboration arises out of genuine interests or purposes held in common and creates *interdependence* among participants (Little, 2002; Nias, Southworth, & Yeomans, 1989).

Friend and Cook (2000) outlined a definition of collaboration that encompasses essential elements universal to the interpersonal collaboration that occurs in schools: "Interpersonal collaboration is a style for direct interaction between at least two coequal parties voluntarily engaged in shared decision making as they work toward a common goal" (p. 6). They argued that defining collaboration as a style enables us to distinguish the nature of the interpersonal relationship, that is, collaboration, occurring during shared interactions from the activities themselves, for example, teaming or problem solving. What this definition of collaboration conveys is *how* the activity is occurring, that is, the nature of the interpersonal relationship occurring during the interaction and the ways in which individuals communicate with each other.

Characteristics of Collaboration

Considered alone, the definition only hints at the subtleties of collaboration. In order to explain the basic definition of collaboration more fully, Friend and Cook (2000) identified several characteristics of collaboration. According to these authors, collaboration between teachers and their colleagues

- is voluntary. It is not possible to force people to use a particular style in their interactions with others. School professionals have to choose to carry out collaborative activities;
- *requires parity among participants.* Parity is a situation in which each person's contribution to an interaction is equally valued, and each person has equal power in decision making;
- *is based on mutual goals.* Professionals do not need to share many or all goals in order to collaborate, just one that is specific and important enough to maintain their shared commitment;
- *depends on shared responsibility for participation and decision making.* Parity creates the basis for the required shared responsibility for decisions. Even though school professionals may not divide the tasks equally or participate fully in each task for the sake of efficiency, they equally participate in the critical decision making involved in the activity;
- *includes sharing resources.* It should be a given that each individual participating in a collaborative activity has resources to contribute that are valuable for reaching the shared goal. Contributing resources, whether they are time, availability, knowledge, materials, or others, assists in the development of sense of ownership;
- *requires shared accountability for outcomes.* Whether the results of collaboration are positive or negative, all the participating individuals are accountable for the outcomes. (pp. 6-11)

Hargreaves (1994) added to the description of characteristics of collaboration, stating that collaborative relationships tend to be

- *spontaneous.* They may be administratively supported and facilitated, but ultimately, collaborative working relationships evolve from and are sustained through the teaching community itself;
- *development-oriented.* Within collaboration, teachers work together primarily to develop initiatives of their own, or to work on externally supported or mandated initiatives to which they themselves have a commitment;
- *pervasive across time and space.* Working together is not often a scheduled activity that can be fixed as taking place at a designated time in a designated place;
- *unpredictable.* Because teachers have discretion and control over what will be developed, the outcomes of collaboration are often uncertain and not easily predicted. (pp. 192-193)

In addition to characteristics just noted, Friend and Cook (2000) proposed that several characteristics of collaboration can have multiple functions – they can be both prerequisites for as well as outcomes of collaboration: attitudes and beliefs supportive of a collaborative approach, mutual trust, and a sense of community.

Benefits of Collaboration

In a postmodern world, in which problems are unpredictable, solutions are unclear, and expectations are intensifying, the promise of collaboration is extensive and diverse (Hargreaves, 1994). As Peterson and Brietzke (1994) argued, strong collegial relationships enhance productivity, staff development, and school improvement efforts. Collegiality increases the capacity for change and improvement, because collegial relationships provide powerful sources of stimulation, motivation, and new ideas for teachers (Lieberman & Miller, 1984; Rosenholtz, 1989). In the extensive overview of the claimed benefits of collaborative relationships in schools, Hargreaves (1994) found in his research that greater collaboration

- *provides moral support.* Collaboration strengthens resolve, permits vulnerabilities to be shared and aired, and carries people through those failures and frustrations that accompany change;
- *increases efficiency.* Collaboration eliminates duplication and removes redundancy;
- *improves effectiveness.* Collaboration improves the quality of student learning by improving the quality of teacher's teaching. Collaboration encourages risk-taking, greater diversity in teaching strategies, and improved senses of efficacy among teachers;
- *reduces overload.* Collaboration permits sharing of the burdens and pressures that come from intensified work demands and accelerated change;
- *establishes boundaries.* Collaboration reduces uncertainty and limits excesses of guilt by setting commonly agreed boundaries around what can be reasonably achieved;
- *promotes political assertiveness and confidence.* Collaboration, in its strongest forms, enables teachers to interact more confidently and assertively with their surrounding systems and the multiplicity of reasonable and unreasonable innovations and reforms that come from them. Collaboration strengthens teachers' confidence to adopt externally introduced innovations, the wisdom to delay them and the moral fortitude to resist them;
- *promotes teacher reflection.* Collaboration in dialogue and action provides sources of feedback and comparison that prompt teachers to reflect on their own practice;
- *increases responsiveness to change.* Collaboration pools the collected knowledge, expertise and capacities of the teacher workforce to enable it to respond quickly to changing constraints and opportunities in the surrounding environment;

- *promotes teacher learning*. Collaboration increases teachers' opportunities to learn from each other;
- *leads to continuous improvement*. Collaboration encourages teachers to see change not as a task to be completed, but as an unending process of continuous improvement. (pp. 245-247)

In their study, Louis, Marks, and Kruse (1996) found that collaboration makes a strong contribution to the quality of teachers' work lives and to the formation of *professional communities*. Characteristics of professional communities included collaboration and related concepts such as shared norms and values, a collective focus on student learning, deprivatized practice, and reflective dialogue. Putnam and Borko (1997) termed communities of teachers working collaboratively as "discourse communities" (p. 1247). These collaborative communities provide opportunities for teachers to reflect deeply and critically on their own teaching practice, on the content they teach, and on the experiences and backgrounds of the students. Working with other teachers within a context of mutual respect, but a context that also encourages a productive level of debate, challenge, and conflict, has the potential to invigorate teaching with increased intellectual stimulation (Putnam & Borko, 1997). "Engaging with one another in this way can support the risk taking and struggle entailed in transforming [teachers'] practice" (Tschannen-Moran, 2001, p. 311). Increased trust, mutual respect, and development of expertise are among other most frequently mentioned outcomes of teacher collaboration (Little, 1990; Rosenholtz, 1989; Tschannen-Moran, 2001).

Challenges of Collaboration

Despite the promises and benefits of collaboration, it remains not without its challenges and criticisms. "Notwithstanding its immense and very real promise…, collaboration carries with it great dangers also, in ways that can be wasteful, harmful and unproductive for teachers…" (Hargreaves, 1994, p. 247). Most critiques of collaboration and collegiality focused on difficulties of implementation, in particular, the issues of time for teachers to work together and the issues concerning the unfamiliarity that teachers have with the collegial role (Hargreaves, 1991). From the results of their research, Leonard and Leonard (2001) discussed a number of inhibitors, or barriers, to implementing collaboration in schools, such as time management, teacher efficacy constraints, fragmented vision, team competitiveness, and conflict management. Furthermore, as Friend and Cooke (2000) noted, the physical structure of schools, with its design for isolation of teachers, has many drawbacks for creating collaborative schools.

Other dilemmas concern the meaning of collaboration. As it was mentioned above, collaboration is often discussed as if it is widely understood. Researchers also cautioned against accepting uncritically the taken for granted "goodness" of increased teacher collaboration (Johnson, 2003). Fullan (1993) recognized the advantages of "many people working together insightfully on the solution and committing themselves to concentrated action together" (p. 34), but warned against pushing collaboration to the extremes. In this condition, it has inherent dangers of groupthink, "the uncritical conformity to the group, unthinking acceptance of the latest solution, suppression of individual dissent" (Fullan, 1993, p. 34). Collaborative relationships are indeed powerful, but unless they are focused on the right things they may end up being powerfully wrong (Fullan, 2001). "People can collaborate to do the wrong things, as well as the right things; and by collaborating too closely they can miss danger signals and learning opportunities" (Fullan, 1993, p. 34).

Hargreaves (1994) found that collaboration can be comfortable and complacent, confined to safer, less controversial areas of teachers' work, consolidating rather than challenging existing practices. It can also be administratively captured, contained, and controlled in ways that make it stilted, unproductive, and wasteful of teachers' energies and efforts. Describing this form of collaboration, Cooper (1988) asked,

Whose culture is it anyway? If teachers are told what to be professional about, how, where and with whom to collaborate, and what blueprint of professional conduct to follow, then the culture that evolves will be foreign to the setting. They will once again have "received" a culture. (p. 47)

Collaboration can become cooptation (as in collaboration with the enemy) when it is used as an administrative and political ruse to secure teachers' compliance with and commitment to decisions made by others. In this way, collaboration involves micropolitical dimensions of school life, such as power and influence-based interactions of the participants who lack micropolitical competence and skills (Ball, 1987; Blase, 1998; Hargreaves, 1991, 1994; Johnson, 2003).

The above mentioned benefits and challenges of collaboration set a necessary background for a more detailed discussion of collaboration and collegiality in schools. Most often, discussions about and advocacy or critique of collaboration have largely taken place within a single conceptual or disciplinary framework or lens (Hargreaves, 1994; Pounder, 1998). "However, because collaboration may increase the complexity of organizing and managing, a single lens, framework, or disciplinary approach is an inadequate aid to understanding such complex organizational phenomena" (Pounder, 1998, pp. 1-2). Hence, in the following section, utilizing a postmodern epistemology, I present the major characteristics of collaboration through two lenses: organizational culture perspective and micropolitical perspective.

Dual Lenses on Collaboration

Schools are no longer simply institutions, but viable living organisms, human creations with unlimited possibilities (M. E. Henry, 1993). What can be seen in schools is how people behave. In an attempt to understand how schools function, it is necessary to describe the characteristics of the school as an organization, knowing that although there are similarities among schools, they also differ in how they cope with various factors of school life (Dalin, Kleekamp, & Rolff, 1993). Thus, it is pivotal to describe and understand the nature of human relationships in schools. For these purposes, I will proceed with the description of an organizational culture perspective that emphasizes what is shared and held in common in human relationships: values, beliefs, norms, and habits. I will also present the micropolitical perspective on human relationships that deals with the use of power, control, conflict, and cooperation to achieve preferred outcomes and highlights differences over similarities among people in educational settings.

Organizational Culture Perspective

Organizational theory has attempted to demonstrate the usefulness of multiple views of how and why organizations function the way they do. Within these multiple approaches to organizational analysis, one of the most controversial of the organizational theory perspectives is that of organizational culture (Deal & Kennedy, 1982; Ott, 1989). According to Ott (1989), the organizational culture perspective is a way of looking at and thinking about behavior of and in organizations. The cultural perspective "means the use of organizational culture as a frame of reference for the way one looks at, attempts to understand, and works with organizations" (Ott, 1989, p. 1).

This organizational perspective represented a break from the functionalist tradition in educational administration (Greenfield, 1984) and became a counterculture within organization theory (Ott, 1989). Its assumptions, theories, and approaches are very "different from those of the dominant structural and systems perspectives" (Ott, 1989, p. 2). Ott stated that in structural and systems perspectives of organization theory, organizations are assumed to be institutions whose primary purposes are to accomplish established goals, set by people in positions of authority. Within these perspectives, the personal preferences of organizational members are restrained by systems of formal rules, by power and authority, and by norms of rational behavior. In the organizational culture perspective, the personal preferences of organizational members are not restrained by these systems. Instead, they are controlled by cultural norms, values, beliefs, and assumptions. According to Ott (1989), "In order to understand or predict how an organization will behave under different circumstances, one must know what its patterns of basic assumptions are – its organizational culture" (p. 3).

What is school culture? Pragmatically, culture is an informal understanding of the "way we do things around here" or the "force that keeps the herd moving roughly in the western direction" (Deal & Kennedy, 1983). In order to capture this "powerful, pervasive, and notoriously elusive force" (Deal & Peterson, 1999, p. 2), a variety of notions, such as "climate", "ethos", "morale" and "saga" was used by researchers. Geertz (1973) contributed to the current understanding of the term, arguing that culture represents a historically transmitted pattern of meaning. These patterns of meaning are expressed explicitly, through symbols, and implicitly, in our taken-for-granted beliefs. Explicit expression of culture lies in the school's own unwritten rules and traditions, norms, and expectations: "the way people act, how they dress, what they talk about and avoid talking about, whether they seek out colleagues for help or don't, and how teachers feel about their work and their students" (Deal & Peterson, 1999). Beneath the conscious awareness of everyday life in schools, there is a stream of implicit thought and activity. Deal and Peterson (1990) noted that this invisible flow of taken-for-granted beliefs and assumptions gives meaning to people's actions and shapes their interpretations of the world. They added, "this deeper structure of life in organizations is reflected and transmitted through symbolic language and expressive action. Culture consists of the stable, underlying social meanings that shape beliefs and behavior over time" (p. 7).

Elements of school culture. Deal and Peterson (1990) referred to culture as deep patterns of values, beliefs, and traditions that have been formed over the course of the school's history. Heckman (1993) stated that culture in schools lies in the commonly held beliefs of teachers, students, and principals. Deal and Kennedy (1983) also added that other elements, such as heroes and heroines, rituals and ceremonies, and an informal network of priests and priestesses, storytellers, spies and gossips, are equally important. Shared values and beliefs are the soul of culture, but rituals and ceremonies provide tangible opportunities for values to be reinforced, heroes to be celebrated, and symbols to be displayed and exchanged. School cultures are reinforced and transformed by the network priests and priestesses, who worry about the values; storytellers whose stories carry the values and reinforce the heroes and heroines; and spies and gossips, who remind everyone that schools are human organizations.

According to Stolp and Smith (1995), school culture can be defined as "historically transmitted patterns of meaning that include the norms, values, beliefs, traditions and myths, understood, maybe in varying degrees, by members of the school community" (p. 13). Some aspects, however, are not necessarily apparent even to those who work in the school. These are the assumptions that come to be taken for granted and eventually drop out of awareness (Schein, 1985). Those hidden assumptions continue to shape how people think about their work, relate to their colleagues, define their mission, and derive their sense of identity (Stolp & Smith, 1995).

Schein (1992) provided one of the most widely recognized definitions of school culture, defining it as:

> A pattern of shared basic assumptions that the group learned as it solved its problems of external adaptation and internal integration, that has worked well enough to be considered valid and, therefore to be taught to new members as the correct way to perceive, think, and feel in relation to those problems. (p. 12)

In order to avoid conceptual confusion of the notions, Schein (1985; 1992) distinguished three basic levels of the organizational culture: *artifacts, espoused values,* and *basic assumptions.* According to Schein (1985), *artifacts* are an organization's physical and social environment, observable manifestations, its language, products, and artistic creations. In order to understand the meanings of artifacts, it is necessary to live in the cultural environment long enough. Artifacts are easy to apprehend, but difficult to interpret without knowledge of the deeper levels. *Espoused values* are statements and beliefs about the way things are done in an organization and how people are supposed to behave. The espoused values are still subject to rational analysis, so that what is said may contradict what is believed. *Basic underlying assumptions* are difficult to express. They can be so deeply rooted in an organization that they can become taken for granted, setting strong communal guidelines for the actions that provide continuity and stability in rapidly changing situations. Thus, school cultures are complex networks of shared norms, values, beliefs, assumptions, traditions and rituals that have been constructed over time by students, teachers, parents, and administrators, and shape how people think, feel, and act, as they work together and deal with problems and accomplishments (Deal & Peterson, 1990; Schein, 1985). In Figure 1, I attempt to bring together various discussions in the literature regarding the nature and functions of school culture and present them as a synthesis in a graphic manner.

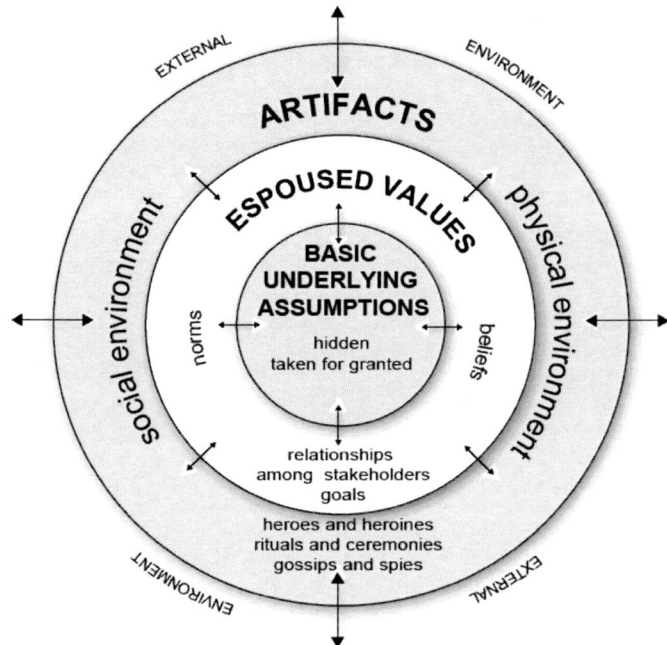

Figure 1. School culture.

Functions of culture in schools. A formal definition of school culture can tell us what culture is, but it does not tell us how culture arises in a school, and more important, how it survives and develops. In order to understand the dynamics of school culture, it is necessary to explore its functions (Deal & Kennedy, 1983; Deal & Peterson, 1999; Schein, 1985). For Schein (1985), the best way to understand this dynamic process of culture is to draw on group formation and leadership theories of the organizations.

Schein (1985) argued that the process of culture formation is identical with the process of group formation in that the very essence of group identity – the shared patterns of thought, belief, feelings, and values that result from shared experiences and common learning – is what turns out to be the culture of that group. "Without a group there can be no culture, and without some degree of culture we are really talking about an aggregate of people, not a 'group'" (p. 50). Thus, according to

Schein, culture formation and group development are two facets of the same process, and are the result of leadership activities.

Schein (1985) continued that it is necessary to understand how the individual intentions of the leaders of an organization, their own definitions of the situation, their assumptions and values come to be a shared, and consequently, a validated set of definitions to be used by other members of organization in similar situations. These intentions and definitions are analyzed into an external and internal set of issues.

The external issues deal with the leader's and the group's definition of the environment and survival in it. The internal issues draw upon the leader's and group's definition of how to organize relationships among the group members "to permit survival in the defined environment through effective performance and the creation of internal comfort" (Schein, 1985, p. 51). External and internal issues are mutually interdependent. Environment initially influences the formation of the culture. Once the culture is present in the sense of shared assumptions, these assumptions influence what will be perceived and defined as the environment for this culture.

The issues or problems of external adaptation specify the coping cycle that any system must be able to maintain in relation to its changing environment. Among the external adaptation issues, Schein (1985) mentioned shared understanding of core mission and strategies, goal setting, means used to attain the goals, measurement of the goal fulfillment, and correction strategies in case the goals are not being met. The culture of the group will also be influenced by its mode of building and maintaining itself, its processes of internal integration. The internal issues are seen by Schein to include common language and conceptual categories; group boundaries and criteria for inclusion and exclusion; power and status; intimacy, friendship, and love; rewards and punishment; and ideology and "religion" (p. 66).

Deal and Kennedy (1983) discussed external and internal issues of strong school cultures. In many schools, teachers do not know what is expected of them nor do they understand how their actions are related to school-wide efforts. When different individuals' interests pull the school in several directions, it is hard to see what happens to beliefs, standards, motivation, effort, consistency, and other ingredients essential to teaching and learning. "Strong cultures provide the internal cohesion that makes it easier for teachers to teach; students to learn; and for parents, administrators, and others to contribute to the instructional process" (p. 15).

Deal and Kennedy (1983) continued that externally, schools are judged by appearance as much as by results. Internal disagreements, mixed signals, unfavorable stories, and the lack of effectiveness make it difficult to secure the faith and support of external groups. "Through shared values, heroes and heroines, rituals and ceremonies, and a supportive informal network, a school can communicate its identity to outside groups and get them involved" (Deal & Kennedy, 1983, p. 15). Both external and internal issues are crucial in shaping the school's culture.

School culture and postmodern conceptualization of power. Discussing the culture of the school, one generally refers to the system of meaning-making in the organization and the process by which problems are solved (Sackney et al., 1999). The culture metaphor is important for the postmodern organization, because the development of a unitary, but inclusive culture can bring order to the behavior of people inside the organization. Order or consensus in a postmodern organization is created through institutional dialogue which is defined by the use of influence rather than power (Clegg, 1990). Meaning is achieved through collaborative effort when the dialogue operates from trust and respect. Consequently, organizational sense-making relies more upon building the relationships, meanings, and connections than on structures and rules (Sackney et al., 1999). Structures, rules, and top-down authority are the characteristics of modernist organizations. Power, in the postmodern view, is manifested through language, metaphors, symbols, norms, values, and underlying assumptions, that is, through the elements of school culture. Power resides with individuals: "It is not vested in the top of the organization, but rather evolves from the dynamic collaborative activities of the group as they confront the problems in their work" (Sackney et al., 1999, p. 47).

By decentering and breaking top-down power structures within schools, postmodernism stresses otherness, difference, and diversity. Sackney et al. (1999) argued that diversity is held together by a combination of strong cultures and information networks. The world of flexibility with no clear center or location of power requires a collaborative culture to hold together the decentralized parts. As problems are resolved, solutions are supported by the continual process of cultural construction, deconstruction, and reconstruction. "These behaviors become inculcated into the norms, values and assumptions as the 'correct' way to behave" (p. 45). Through the process of social interaction the new behaviors become articulated as the culture of the school.

Cultures of teaching. This study is concerned mainly with the school culture in relation to teachers, that is, teacher cultures or *cultures of teaching* (Hargreaves, 1994). As Hargreaves posited, these cultures "comprise beliefs, values, habits and assumed ways of doing things among communities of teachers who have had to deal with similar demands and constraints over many years" (p. 165). Cultures of teaching help give meaning, support, and identity to teachers, their work, and relationships between them and their colleagues. According to Waller (1932), teacher cultures are among the most educationally significant aspects of teachers' lives and work, as they provide a vital context for teacher development and for the ways that teachers teach.

There are two important dimensions of teacher cultures: content and form. "The *content* [emphasis in original] of teacher cultures consists of the substantive attitudes, values, beliefs, habits, assumptions and ways of doing things that are shared within a particular teacher group" (Hargreaves, 1994, pp. 165-166). The content of the teacher cultures is the "way we do things around here" or the "force that keeps the herd moving roughly in the western direction" (Deal & Kennedy, 1983). Hargreaves (1994) continued that the *form* of teacher cultures consists of the "*characteristic patterns of relationships* and *forms of association* [emphasis in original] between members of those cultures" (p. 166) and can be found in how relations between teachers and their colleagues are articulated. In order to understand the nature of teacher cultures, it is important to look at both the *content* and the *form*. Relations between teachers and their colleagues, or the form of their culture, change over time, and it is through this form that the content of the culture is realized, reproduced, and redefined. It is from this point of view that I will discuss the relationship of organizational culture perspective to collaboration later in this chapter.

Summary. Looking at collaboration from an organizational culture perspective allows embracing the complexity of school cultures. Culture is a powerful, pervasive and notoriously elusive force that permeates every aspect of the school life and shapes beliefs and behavior in schools. It is composed of explicit and implicit shared norms, values, beliefs, and assumptions that shape how people think, feel, and act in schools. School culture is a complex network of ceremonies and rituals that have been constructed over time by all stakeholders in the process of schooling. School culture is shaped under the influence of both external and internal environments of the schools. In the process of development, it becomes the system of meaning-making in organizations and the process by which problems are solved. From a postmodern perspective, sense-making in schools relies more upon building the relationships, meanings, and connections between people than on structures and rules. A culture of teaching, as a part of broader school culture, gives meaning, support, and identity to teachers, their work, and relationships with others in schools. Within the context of multiple perspectives, otherness, difference, and diversity, collaborative culture becomes the force that holds together the decentralized parts of the school.

Micropolitical Perspective

A second perspective on human relationships is the micropolitical perspective. One needs to utilize this framework to gain a better understanding of the school culture that shapes how people think, feel, and act. Micropolitical approach can "serve as a lens for examining the daily lives of the individuals most affected by education policy: people who work in and around schools" (Marshall & Gerstl-Pepin, 2005, p. 101). As Marshall and Gerstl-Pepin powerfully noted,

Everyone engages in micropolitics, even those who say they hate politics. Micropolitical analyses examine politics at the interpersonal level. Power in micropolitical arenas is often informal and understood, not elected, named, or appointed. Inequitable power relations relating to policy and politics are examined at an individual and/or local level. Micropolitical analyses examine political interaction in micro-arenas, such as classrooms, corridors, offices, and lounges. (p. 102)

In other words, micropolitics "offers a new lens for understanding [collaboration] ... in schools by uncovering power, influence, conflict, and negotiating processes between individuals and groups within school organizations" (Achinstein, 2002, p. 423). Micropolitical perspective is based on the need to understand the politics embedded in individual schools. In the following sections, the role of politics in organizational life with the focus on micropolitics in educational setting will be discussed.

Politics and organizations. A specific focus on the politics within organizations first emerged in the 1960s in studies of public administration and management. The early work in micropolitics began as a direct challenge to popular apolitical theories of organization developed by Fayol (1949), Taylor (1947), and Weber (1947). The leaders of this challenge were early apolitical theorists, such as Burns (1961), Cyert and March (1963), Pettigrew (1973), and Strauss (1962), who saw serious limitations inherent in apolitical models of organizations. Their main concerns dealt with such issues as division of labor, allocation of resources and incentives, and hierarchical task specialization that apolitical models espoused to prevent political activity and to ensure organizational consensus. Apolitical models were criticized as biased toward technical rationality failing, therefore, to account for complexity, instability, and conflict within organizations.

The political perspective represented a departure from the traditional rational approaches to studying organizations and grew out of critiques of rational models, which emphasized authority, but neglected power. As well, open systems models were critiqued because of their stress on high levels of consensus in organizations, and their tendency to view conflict as abnormal. Burns (1961), Cyert and March (1963), Pettigrew (1973), and Strauss (1962) acknowledged that the above mentioned issues of apolitical models actually *created* political competition, coalitions, and conflict within organizations. In addition, these political theorists perceived organizations to be heavily involved in political activity through a context of organizational decision making, power and authority structures, disparate goals, and resource allocations (Spaulding, 1995). Critics argued that systems theory tends to assume that individuals in organizations share similar goals (Ball, 1987). Furthermore, these early theorists revealed that members of organizations use political strategies such as coalition building and political exchange to achieve their organizational and personal goals. Critics concluded that rational and systems models tended to ignore the values, ideologies, choices, goals, interests, expertise, history, and motivation of individuals in organizations. This critique prompted the evolution of the micropolitical perspective on organizations. In the following section, a more detailed description of the mentioned above micropolitical perspectives on the organizational theory will be presented.

Micropolitics and organizational theory. The traces of at least four different models have captured the attention of organizational theorists interested in micropolitical perspective. Although different metaphors have been attributed to them, they are widely recognized as depicting organizations as *control systems, natural systems, political systems,* and *interpretive systems* (Mawhinney, 1999b). In the reappraisal of problems and prospects of micropolitical research, Mawhinney (1999b) presented an extensive overview of these models.

At the time when the micropolitical perspective began to evolve in the organizational theory in the 1960s, the research was dominated by *control systems,* and *natural systems,* and the theorists sought to rethink the robustness of these models of organizations (Hault & Walcott, 1990). The control systems model emphasized authority but neglected power in organizations, which were seen as rational tools for achieving maximum predictability of actions and outcomes. A self-reliant, closed, and *mechanistic* nature of these systems became challenged by those who attribute *organic* features similar to those characterizing natural systems. They underscored the imperative of organizational survival in a larger environment, depicting environmental forces as shaping goals, structures, and activities in a way which stresses the functional inter-relatedness and harmony within organizations. "Both control and natural systems models posit a highly integrated view of organizations where questions of human purpose, and of conflicting goals arising from the exercise of that purpose are largely ignored" (Mawhinney, 1999b, p. 162).

The limitations of the control and natural systems models led organizational theorists to a new focus on organizations as *political systems*. Burns (1961) was one of the first organizational theorists who argued against consensus models of organizations and proposed investigating both cooperative and conflictual behavior and regarded political behavior to be a central impetus for social change in organizations. This idea gained further attention in Cyert and March's (1963) work, which examined decision making in organizations and discovered that it occurred within a framework of disparate goals where coalitions are likely to emerge to achieve political goals. In a similar fashion, Pettigrew (1973) stated that decision making cannot be explained without understanding political power and the strategies that individuals and groups use to gain such power. The individual and group strategies, examined by Mangham (1979), revealed that opportunities for individuals to exercise strategic choice will inevitably create conditions of goals conflict within organizations. He argued that, although negotiation among individuals to reach goal consensus will call forth techniques of politics, such as persuasion and bargaining, these strategies could ultimately be the impetus for creation of shared collective meaning among individuals and groups within organizations.

In recent years other organizational theorists have acknowledged the role of dialogue, debate, and coalition formation in forging a sense of collective meaning among organizational members (Mawhinney, 1999b). Bacharach and Lawler (1980) argued that victory in debates generally goes to the coalition that has the most strength. Their approach is distinguished by an emphasis on group-level coalition politics over individual action, and particularly by the use of power to retain or gain control of real or symbolic resources. Bacharach and Lawler (1980) focused on systems of authority and control carried in various organizational roles, which influence the outcomes of bargaining. In their view, organizations are conceptualized as political bargaining systems dominated by networks of coalitions of stakeholders that seek to further their partisan interests. In addition, the tactical use of power by coalitions to retain or obtain control of real or symbolic resources is fundamental to the organizational politics. Pfeffer (1981) supported this point of view, arguing that organizations can be seen as political arenas where shifting coalition and interest groups become winners and losers in their struggle for power and come into conflict.

The interplay between conflict, consensus, and coalitions became the subject of the interpretive approaches to organizational analysis. *Interpretive systems* approaches, found in micropolitical research, have in common a focus on an actor's perspective, but take different orientations toward the nature of cultural systems in organizations (Mawhinney, 1999b). Some interpretive approaches view organizational cultures as integrated entities, emphasizing processes of gaining organization-wide consensus through developing shared values and cognitions. "The assumption that members of an organization can share the same taken-for-granted interpretations has typically been adopted by all focusing on the role of leaders and managers in typifying policy, inducing commitment to it, building organizational community and, thus, coherence" (Mawhinney, 1999b, p. 163).

Other interpretive perspectives acknowledge the lack of consensus that commonly exists across organizational sectors. They focus on the conflicting cultural understandings of different subsystems of actors within organizations. As Mawhinney (1999b) stated, discrepancies among these understandings lead researchers taking this orientation to use a critical-conflict perspective to analyze their findings. Another interpretive orientation, which shares the same tendency, embraces ambiguity as the endemic condition in all organizational cultures. "Whereas the unity view of the interpretive systems assumes consensus is fundamental order in organizations, the ambiguity view sees consensus as fluctuating across issues" (Mawhinney, 1999b, p. 163).

As micropolitical analyses have been particularly eclectic in their conceptual frameworks, educational context has not been left aside. Micropolitics of organizations have influenced the way schools are viewed by researchers. Organizational theorizing from control, natural, and interpretive systems perspectives and inter-perspective dialogue has enriched the body of literature from which educational analysts interested in the organizational dynamics of schools are now able to draw (Mawhinney, 1999b). Educational researchers have benefited from the diversity of conceptual perspectives, considering micropolitical research as a disparate field of study, where "conceptual boundaries and distinctive features await definition" (Malen, 1995, p. 159). Indeed, as Mawhinney (1999b) observed, the accumulated micropolitical research in education, "best characterized by a conceptual pluralism framed from diverse perspectives, offers insights on interrelationships among dimensions of organizational structures, decisions, sources of power, goals, values, purposes and strategies" (p. 164). The following section presents an overview of these micropolitical interrelationships in the educational context.

Micropolitics in educational context. Micropolitical research has emerged as one of the newer thrusts in understanding the complexities of organizational life in schools (Mawhinney, 1999b). In the last few decades, researchers from the United Kingdom, United States, and Canada (G. Anderson, 1991; Bacharach & Mundell, 1993; Ball, 1987; Blase, 1991; Blase & Anderson, 1995; Iannaccone, 1991; Lindle, 1998; Malen, 1995; Marshall & Gerstl-Pepin, 2005; Marshall & Scribner, 1991; Mawhinney, 1999b; Scribner & Layton, 1995; Townsend, 1990) have contributed to the development of micropolitical research in schools. Although the concept of micropolitics has been defined in multiple ways, all variations shared a common interest in investigating "power, influence, and control among individuals and groups in a social context" (Willower, 1991, p. 442).

The micropolitical perspective was first applied to educational organizations by Iannaccone (1975), who examined the interactions of administrators, teachers, and students in California schools in the early 1970s. He described *micropolitics of education* as politics that takes place in and around schools, and defined micropolitics as being concerned with the interactions and political ideologies of social systems of administrators, teachers, and students within school buildings. He labeled these as *internal* organizational subsystems. Micropolitical analysis is also concerned with external system issues of the interaction between professional and lay subsystems, which may be called the *external* systems.

According to Iannaccone (1975), and other educational researchers (Bacharach & Lawler, 1980; Bacharach & Mitchell, 1987), schools should be recognized and understood as political entities where school members (either individual or groups) develop micropolitical strategies in an attempt to achieve their own personal and school's goals. Furthermore, Bacharach and Lawler (1980) and Bacharach and Mitchell (1987) stated that school members often form shared objectives and micropolitical strategies with other school members, i.e., coalitions, in order to achieve successful and preferred decision outcomes. Extending this perspective into their analysis of organizational politics of school life, Bacharach and Mundell (1993) sought to explain the conditions which provoke interest groups to mobilize, to act separately, or to form coalitions in order to achieve a desired organizational outcome. They stated that power, from this perspective is manifested through the overt actions of coalitions seeking to influence decisions. Political action in schools involves the acquisition and exercise of influence, authority, control, and power.

Other educational researchers also applied the developing micropolitical perspective to educational contexts. Hoyle (1988) emphasized the strategies adopted by individuals and groups to use authority and influence to fulfill their interests. The work of Hoyle (1986) and Gronn (1986) revealed that school personnel use both sanctioned and nonsanctioned, overt and covert micropolitical strategies within school organizations. In addition, research showed that a group's use of micropolitical influence can be more powerful than that of an individual (Ball, 1987). Ball also emphasized the prevalent existence of micropolitical strategies of conflict as opposed to micropolitical strategies of cooperation. He viewed schools as arenas for struggle, rife with conflicts because they are poorly coordinated and ideologically diverse.

Unlike Ball (1987), Blase (1991), in his work on educational micropolitics, acknowledged that micropolitical strategies of conflict *coexist* with the micropolitical strategies of cooperation within schools. This view was supported by Townsend (1990) who called for a new micropolitical research agenda that recognizes that cooperation is as important as conflict. School micropolitics were also found to be significantly shaped by the organizational and community factor (Blase, 1991). Furthermore, Blase (1991) stated that school members use micropolitical strategies for purposes of both protection and influence. Micropolitics was considered to pervade the organizational lives of those involved with schools: students, parents, teachers, administrators and support staff, who act jointly to respond to the uncertainty and controversy generated as a result of clash of interests (Mawhinney, 1999b).

In order to put together the various perspectives in the field of micropolitics, Blase (1991) developed a broad-based, working definition of micropolitics:

> Micropolitics refers to the use of formal and informal power by individuals and groups to achieve their goals in organizations. In large part, political actions result from perceived differences between individuals and groups, coupled with the motivation to use power to influence and/or protect. Although such actions are consciously motivated, any action, consciously or unconsciously motivated, may have political "significance" in a given situation. Both cooperative and conflictive actions and processes are part of the realm of micropolitics. Moreover, macro- and micropolitical factors frequently interact. (p. 11)

Blase and Blase (2002) observed that this definition of micropolitics has driven much of the research produced during the past decade and, among other things, includes both legitimate and illegitimate forms of power. Explaining the essence of this definition, they stated that *goals* are interests, preferences, or purposes, and *differences* may be related to needs, values, and ideologies. Consciously motivated actions are intended, calculated, or strategic; unconsciously motivated actions usually include routine, non-decision-making, habitual actions that result from socialization and actions that limit or prevent others' influence. "Political significance includes both conflictive and cooperative-consensual behaviors and is reflected in individual and group behavior as well as organizational structure" (Blase & Blase, 2002, p. 10). Hierarchical authority, policy, and cultural norms, for instance, can be political factors consciously used by administrators to control or influence others. On the other side, they can also be factors that may control or influence others regardless of their use or lack of use by organizational participants.

Amidst the diversity of conceptualizations, similar to conceptual diversity of micropolitical research in organizational theory, micropolitical studies in educational administration tried to clarify some of the interrelationships among factors such as structures, decisions, sources of power, goals, values, purposes and strategies within schools. Marshall and Scribner (1991) attempted to capture this diversity in their analysis of themes found in the research on dimensions of micropolitics of educational administration. They outlined eight central themes in micropolitical research (Marshall & Scribner, 1991, pp. 350-353).

The first common focus of the research, identified by Marshall and Scribner (1991) is on the *ideologies and values of subsystems of teachers and administrators in schools*. This dimension emerged from observations that conflicts arise because of clashes in the political ideologies of teachers, administrators, and students. Conflicts, for instance, arise over the authority of professional expertise, over teacher autonomy, and over parent and student choice. Other micropolitical studies examined the negotiations of *boundaries and turf between administrators and teachers*. This theme reflected the ongoing negotiations between the administrator zone and the teacher zone in the school site. A third theme in micropolitical studies, *maintenance of bureaucratic myths,* stated that school site actors often assert bureaucratic rationality for political ends. Rational assertions of the need to routinize, standardize, and specialize hide more political motives. A fourth aspect in micropolitical studies was that street-level bureaucrats, such as teachers, often *revise and remake policy in site-level implementation*. Teachers in this context are seen as policy brokers. Studies also documented the *mobilization of bias in organizational life*. Bias is often taken for granted, unstated, or ignored. Often the dilemmas arising from conflicts among the common goals or education – equity, choice, efficiency and quality are subverted by micropolitical processes, that "channel values and make one-case-at-a-time microalterations, so that the organization can be preserved by avoiding the major dilemmas" (Marshall & Scribner, 1991, p. 350). The most powerful form of bias mobilization may occur through *reality creation in organizations*. People use power, language, symbols, and interactions to define reality. Those who have the power to determine which issues and questions are seen as normal, relevant and critical and which will be viewed as irrelevant or illogical play the most powerful micropolitical games and define the acceptable reality. Furthermore, the micropolitical issue of *privatization of conflict* arises when conflict is confined within the school walls, or within one subgroup on the site. Finally, Marshall and Scribner (1991) discussed *salient structures and tasks around which people, then leaders, then coalitions and loyalties develop*. We can observe common language, values, priorities, and potential for political power in the situations where subsystems link with each other, either because of intertwining tasks or common ideologies.

Research on these dimensions of the micropolitics of school life have given us a new understanding of organizational dynamics (Mawhinney, 1999b). Research on school micropolitics focused on the strains and tensions stemming from diverse sources of power, rival interests, and intractable conflicts within and around schools, and coalition formation or cooperation of teachers to achieve their interests. Such research attempted to understand how such political phenomena affect the way schools cope with fundamental educational and social issues (Marshall & Scribner, 1991). These issues can be both internal and external to school. This brings us to another trend in the micropolitical research in schools: the interrelationships of external (macro) and internal (micro) politics of organizations (Blase & Blase, 2002; Malen, 1995; Mawhinney, 1999b; Townsend, 1990). In the interest of examining these issues in more detail, I will now turn to a discussion of the challenges in describing macropolitics and micropolitics of education.

Defining macropolitics and micropolitics of education. In general, *politics* refers to decisions related to the allocation of values for a given society or social organization regarding who gets what, when, and how (Blase & Blase, 2002), actors and spectators, coalitions and interest groups (Marshall & Scribner, 1991). Although, traditionally political theorists studied politics from a macro-perspective (Marshall & Scribner, 1991) following Iannaccone's (1975) writings, research of school level politics gained more importance. Researchers (Ball, 1987; Blase, 1991; Blase & Blase, 2002; Marshall & Scribner, 1991) stated, that these two broad perspectives on the politics of education, macropolitics and micropolitics/organizational politics are grounded in similar concepts, such as power, influence, control, conflict/cooperation, strategies, exchange, negotiation, interest groups, values, and ideologies. The term macropolitics typically refers to the school's external relationships and environments at the local, state, and national levels (Willower, 1991), and the interactions of public and private organizations within, between, and among levels (Marshall & Scribner, 1991). As Iannaccone (1975) stated, this larger, external collection of organizations has considerable importance for understanding politics at the school level. Barott and Galvin (1998) recognized that the school is nested in multilevel governmental structures:

> The organizational politics of the building site is the micropolitics of a subunit of a larger complex organization: the school district. In turn, the school district is a local government unit, variously connected to other local governments, as well as to the state and national governments. (p. 312)

Despite this fact, it was not until the early 1990s that politics of education scholars showed increased interest in the consequences and outcomes of decisions at the national, state, and local levels on schools (Boyd, 1991; Marshall & Scribner, 1991). As a result, the field became more policy oriented:

> The burgeoning field of "policy studies" in education quickly called attention to the significance of the implementation process, as policies were put into action. Those actually implementing policy in schools turned out to be the final policy makers, as evidence mounted that they could reshape or resist the intentions of policies adopted at higher levels. From these not entirely surprising revelations, it was only a short jump to the beginning of the systematic study of the dynamics of the "micropolitics" of schools. (Boyd, 1991, p. vii)

Townsend (1990) challenged the robustness of a micro analysis of political phenomena in schools divorced from the macro forces which frame micropolitics of schools. Similar issues were raised by Malen (1995) in her review of the state of micropolitical research. As a result of this movement, with few exceptions, most perspectives on organizational politics and micropolitics in education recognized the importance of external (macro) factors and their influence on schools in general and on its internal political processes and structures in particular (Bacharach & Mundell, 1993; Ball, 1987; Barrot & Galvin, 1998; Blase, 1991; Blase & Anderson, 1995; Blase & Blase, 2002; Iannaccone, 1991). At the same time, Malen (1995) noted that, like the macropolitics of education, there is a lack of consensus on what exactly defines the micropolitics of education. Malen captured the extent of the unresolved conceptual problems this poses. She concluded that the question about macro-micro political tensions remains unanswered, and asked of micropolitics:

> What is the essence of micropolitics? How does it differ from macropolitics? Or does it? Is 'micropolitics' defined by the size of the arena? The level of the system? The unit of analysis...? ....Is it defined by the style of play? (p. 159)

Mawhinney (1999b) claimed that these questions, posed by Malen (1995), deserve our attention, because we know from the past decades of research that micropolitics is not wholly concerned with internal politicking that occurs within organization. Micropolitics also focuses on the interaction of organizations with their environments. "Micropolitical analyses have not always assumed a deterministic stance, rather many depict organizations as manipulating and influencing their environments" (Mawhinney, 1999b, p. 165). Other studies confirmed that macro level factors (or factors external to schools), significantly influence the micropolitical character of schools (Blase, 1991).

Not unexpectedly, as Blase and Blase (2002) stated, many macropolitics of education scholars followed the lead of Iannaccone (1975) in identifying organizational politics/micropolitics with a particular level of the educational system, literally what takes place in and around the school. However, organizational scholars in education (Bacharach & Mundell, 1993; Blase, 1991; Blase & Anderson, 1995; Hoyle, 1986; Marshall & Gerstl-Pepin, 2005), critical theorists in education (Apple, 1982; Freire, 1985), organizational researchers outside of the area of education (Bolman & Deal, 1997; Burns, 1961; Pfeffer, 1981) consistently stated that micropolitics or organizational politics can occur at any level of an organization, system of organizations, or in society at large. According to Bacharach and Mundell (1993), it is too easy for one to simply divide macro and micropolitics in terms of how large the unit of analysis is:

> For example there are those who would maintain that micropolitics can only occur on the school level and does not occur on the school district level. However, it is our contention that micropolitics can occur on numerous levels such as the departmental, school, and district levels. Micropolitics is not defined by its context, but rather by its nature. That is, micropolitics (at all levels) involves the strategic contests among interest groups over different logics of action. (p. 432)

In addition, Pfeffer (1981) stated that structural artifacts of formal organizations, such as structure, policies, programs, curricula, as well as informal dimensions of organization (e.g., culture, social relations), in part result from micropolitical processes. Such processes or structures are considered a precursor to the development of the formal organization itself.

Clearly, micropolitics is defined by its nature; it refers to the immediate, ongoing, dynamic interaction between and among individuals and groups, and such interaction occurs at all levels of public education – the national, state, and local levels (Blase & Blase, 2002). Such micropolitical perspective allows to "examine the political and policy implications of what happens in classrooms and seeks to connect them to broader political, social, and contextual processes occurring at the district, state, federal, and global arenas" (Marshall & Gerstl-Pepin, 2005, p. 102). Macropolitics, on the other hand, can be described as the external factors that impinge on schools micropolitics (Mawhinney, 1999b). These factors can be: the impact of formal legislation on school-based structures, the impact of district-level policy mandates on the relationships among teachers, the impact of community values and beliefs expressed through parental demands on the school, the influence of school district ideology on principal behaviors, and the impact of community demographics on the interactions between administrators and teachers, as documented in many studies (Blase, 1991; Mawhinney, 1999b).

Despite the recognition of macro forces, Mawhinney (1999b) argued, the nature of macro-micro relationships is not well understood, which still poses a conceptual challenge for researchers seeking to understand the micropolitics of organizational life in schools. One way to bring some clarity into this issue is to examine the connection between macro and micropolitical perspectives. As Marshall and Gerstl-Pepin (2005) stated, by connecting these perspectives, we can better understand the complexity and often misguided and even damaging effects of large-scale policies that are created without input from individual school contexts. Another way is to recognize that both within and beyond the school walls, people hold ideological conceptions about the ways that schools should be (Achinstein, 2002). Schools cannot be understood without understanding the environment or larger social contexts in which they operate (G. Anderson, 1991; Ball, 1987). Macropolitics (ideologies found in the larger environment) and micropolitics (ideologies within a community or organization) frequently interact (Ball, 1987; Blase, 1991; Iannaccone, 1975; Malen, 1995). The notion of ideological conceptions will be instrumental in the following discussion of micropolitical perspective on teacher collaboration in schools.

Micropolitics and collaboration. The micropolitical perspective has important implications for the discussion of collaboration and collegiality and the questions we ask about it. Achinstein (2002) noted that micropolitical perspective examines how teachers' communities are shaped by ideology. Ideological stances that represent "educational perspectives and commitments of teachers" (Ball, 1987, p. 281) are a central concern of micropolitics. For teachers, ideology defines the framework of shared values about schooling, education, and students that includes an orientation about student learning and outcomes, notions about school reform and change, and conceptions about relationship between school and society. Ideology as a political process refers to the management of meaning, how teachers make sense of their work and ultimately take action (Ball, 1987).

Hargreaves (1994) argued that micropolitical perspective casts doubt on the widely advocated virtues of collegiality at the classroom level where there are substantial differences in values and beliefs among the teachers involved. As Huberman (1990) argued, because of frequent differences in beliefs and approaches to instruction, teachers might not wish to work collaboratively with their colleagues. These differences often are the result of various ideological stances discussed above.

Micropolitical perspective also raises questions about the rights of individuals and the protection of individuality in the face of a group pressure (Hargreaves, 1994). Sometimes, norms of collegiality in schools are treated as if they were administrative laws of collegiality. This can lead to unfair treatment of those teachers who prefer to work alone and are able to plan better in solitude than together with their colleagues. "The protection of their individuality, and their discretion of judgment, is also a protection of their right to disagree and reflect critically on the value and worth of what it is they are being asked to collaborate about" (p. 191). Thus, the micropolitical perspective raises questions about the implications of collaboration for individuality and solitude, as well as the values that individual teachers hold about education, schooling, and students.

Micropolitical perspective inquires into the circumstances where collaboration becomes cooptation, "as in collaboration with the enemy" (Hargreaves, 1994, p. 191). In this view, collaboration can become a commitment not to developing and realizing teachers' own purposes but to implementing purposes devised by others in schools. Collaboration may become cooptation when teachers commit to the requirements of externally mandated changes without evaluating and understanding their worth and applicability.

Finally, micropolitical perspective encourages us to discriminate between the different forms of collaboration and collegiality, to examine the nature of those forms, and to ask who constitutes those forms and whose interests they serve (Hargreaves, 1991). Spontaneous, unpredictable, and culturally dynamic forms of collaboration are often redefined and reinscribed in more bureaucratically contrived and administratively controlled systems of cooperation, draining such collaboration of its richness, spontaneity, and unpredictability. Thus, micropolitical perspective sensitizes us to the possible existence of different types of collaboration and collegiality among teachers.

Summary. The micropolitical perspective provides another lens for understanding collaboration in schools by uncovering power, influence, conflict, coalitions, and negotiations between individuals and groups within school organizations. Micropolitics deals with the interactions and political ideologies of social systems of administrators, teachers, and students within school buildings. However, it is not limited just to the school level. Micropolitics is also concerned with the use of formal and informal power by individuals and groups to achieve their goals at any levels of organizations, systems of organizations, or in society at large. The micropolitical perspective is focused on the strains and tensions stemming from diverse sources of power, rival interests, intractable conflicts within and around schools, and coalition formation or cooperation of teachers to achieve their interests. It examines the political and policy implications of what happens in classrooms and seeks to connect them to broader political, social, and contextual processes occurring at the district, state, federal, and global arenas. In this context, micropolitical and macropolitical perspectives are closely connected.

The micropolitical perspective has important implications for the discussion of teacher collaboration in schools. It casts doubt on the widely advocated virtues of collegiality in the context where there are substantial differences in values and beliefs among the teachers involved. It also raises questions about treating norms of collegiality as if they were administrative laws of collegiality. Micropolitical perspective inquires into the circumstances where collaboration becomes cooptation, i.e., collaboration with the enemy. Finally, this perspective allows us to differentiate between the different forms of collaboration and to examine the nature of those forms and the interests they serve.

Culture and Micropolitics of Collaboration

Viewing collaboration through two lenses, cultural and micropolitical, allows us to draw a distinction between different types of school cultures according to the nature of collaboration in them. Looking micropolitically, one can observe the

> unfortunate dysfunctions of bureaucracy ... evident in the structure of the school day, in which teachers work in isolation from one another with very little time for building relationships, co-teaching, planning, collaboration, nurturing individual students, professional community building, or participation in decision making. (Marshall & Gerstl-Pepin, 2005, p. 105)

Looking culturally, as Hargreaves (1994) observed, collaboration can be a device to help teachers work together to pursue and review their own purposes as a professional community, or it can be a means to re-inscribe administrative control within persuasive and pervasive discourses of collaboration and partnership. Collaborative culture sometimes takes a form of a safe simulation, which is "more perfect, more harmonious, (and [thus] more controlled) than the reality of collaboration itself" (p. 17). The following sections provide a detailed description of different forms of collaboration in schools.

The Types of School Cultures

Cultures vary considerably from school to school because of different sets of external and internal issues that shape school environments and define behaviors within schools. Many schools exist as isolated workplaces where teachers work largely alone in their rooms, seldom interacting with their colleagues and keeping problems of practice to themselves (Peterson & Brietzke, 1994). However, in other schools teachers regularly engage in professional discourse with colleagues; share ideas, knowledge, and techniques; and practice collaborative problem solving of school and classroom issues (Little, 1982, 1990; Rosenholtz, 1989). There are also school cultures that possess characteristic features of both of these polarities. They may seem collaborative from the outside, but remain isolative, tense, and cliqued from the inside. The characteristics of *non-collaborative*, *pseudo-collaborative*, and *collaborative* cultures (see Figure 2) are presented below.

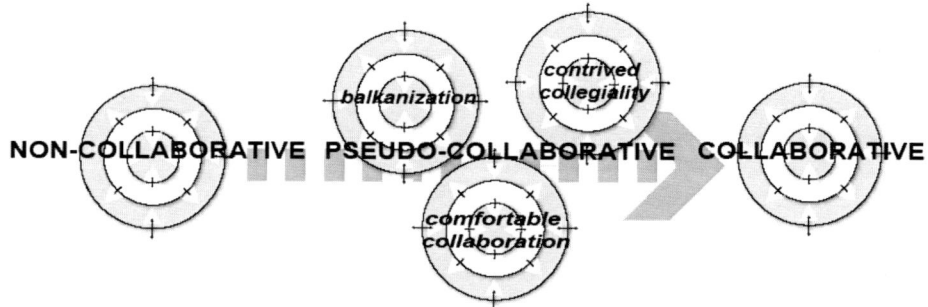

Figure 2. Types of school culture.

Non-collaborative cultures. Lortie (1975) described non-collaborative cultures as being oriented toward individualism (working alone in isolation), conservatism (employing educational approaches that have long traditions), and presentism (focusing on immediate issues, not the long-term development of the schools). As a result, little interaction, collegiality, or collaboration takes place in this type of school culture. Little (1982; 1990) observed, that in these schools teachers feel separated from each other, seldom engaging in conversations, professional sharing, and problem-solving with their peers. In the process of problem solving, teachers either leave each other alone or are at "loggerheads – disagreeing without any inclination or process to solve differences" (Fullan, 1999, p. 33). Schools may intensify isolation by the way they organize time, space, responsibilities, or resources and by permitting a culture of "protective individualism community" (Little, 2002, p. 44).

Pseudo-collaborative cultures. Non-collaborative and collaborative schools represent two extremes of the continuum (see Figure 2). However, most of school cultures usually lie somewhere in between these two opposites, possessing characteristic features of both. These can be referred to as pseudo-collaborative cultures. Fullan and Hargreaves (1996) described three types of school culture that seem collaborative in context, but lack collaborative substance. "The mere existence of collaboration should not be mistaken for a thoroughgoing *culture* [emphasis in original] of it" (p. 52). In such cultures, while teachers associate more closely with some of their colleagues than they do in a culture of individualism, their work lacks deeper collaboration and togetherness. These cultures are described as *balkanization, comfortable collaboration*, and *contrived collegiality* (Fullan & Hargreaves, 1996). When established in schools, they discourage a higher level of professional interaction, collegiality, and pressure to improve.

Balkanization is a culture made up of separate and sometimes competing groups, jockeying for position and supremacy like loosely connected, interdependent city states (Fullan & Hargreaves, 1996). Teachers attach their loyalties and identities to particular groups within the school. They usually group with colleagues with whom they work more closely, spend the most time, and socialize with more often in the staff room. Competition, poor communication, poor integration of groups, and indifference are some of the characteristics of such cultures. This isolation of competing groups discourages the interplay of ideas, solutions and networking of practical knowledge that is characteristic of more collaborative environments.

Collaboration within schools can take a bounded, rather than extended form. This type of culture is called *comfortable collaboration* (Fullan & Hargreaves, 1996). It carefully limits collaboration; teachers stay out of deeper, more extended relationships that could foster problem-solving, exchange of craft knowledge, and professional support. Comfortable collaboration restricts the extent to which teachers can inquire into and advise one another on their practice. This type of collaboration can be thin, superficial, and congenial, with teachers sharing some materials, instructional techniques, and experience, but avoiding deeper discussions of teaching, long-range planning, and the shared purpose of schooling (Peterson & Brietzke, 1994). Huberman (1993) termed such culture as *independent artisanry*. In a school that fosters such a culture, teachers respond readily to requests for help, share materials on occasion, and have access to resources for professional development. However, as Little (2002) stated, in such cultures, it is unlikely to observe deep or sustained collaboration or evidence that teachers are closely familiar with one another's teaching practices. Fullan and Hargreaves (1996) stated that it is a culture that focuses on the immediate, the short-term and the practical to the exclusion of longer-term planning concerns. This type of collaboration is too cozy, but it does not help teachers discover and share deeper knowledge and solve more vexing problems in schools.

Cultures of *contrived collegiality* are characterized by a set of formal, specific, bureaucratic procedures to increase the attention being given to joint teacher planning, consultation and other forms of working together (Fullan & Hargreaves, 1996). This process is double-edged with positive and negative characteristics. At its worst, contrived collegiality can be reduced to a "quick, slick administrative surrogate for collaborative teacher cultures" (p. 58). Formal structures, such as site-based management councils, peer coaching arrangements, and school improvement teams may bring teachers together and foster innovations in organizations. Nevertheless, relying solely on formal structures in organizations, contrived collegiality will not necessarily foster deeper, more substantial, and more productive informal linkages, norms, and shared commitments found in collaborative settings (Peterson & Brietzke, 1994). Contrived collegiality, however, is useful as a preliminary phase in setting up more enduring collaborative relationships among teachers.

Collaborative cultures. Collaborative cultures are the ones which schools should strive for. Collaborative cultures are not characterized as balkanized groups, congenial interaction, or only as structures of shared work. In contrast to these less potent cultures, collaborative cultures are more potent and support a shared sense of purpose, focus on long-term improvement, and support networks of professionals who share problems, ideas, materials, and solutions (Peterson & Brietzke, 1994). They are cultures that support deeper, richer professional interchange among administrators, teachers, students, and parents. In collaborative school cultures, the underlying norms, values, beliefs, and assumptions reinforce and support high levels of collegiality, teamwork, and dialogue about problems of practice.

In a postmodern society, with its complexity and unpredictability, organizations, characterized by flexibility, adaptability, creativity, collaboration, continuous improvement, a positive orientation towards problem-solving and commitment to maximizing their learning capacity are most likely to survive and prosper. Collaborative culture in this context can take a form of a *moving mosaic* (Hargreaves, 1994). A moving mosaic creates a complex web of collegial relationships which extend beyond traditional boundaries and which minimize interpersonal conflicts as teachers recognize that their strength is increased when they work together. Hargreaves (1994) found,

> Warm human relationships of mutual respect and understanding combined with the toleration and even encouragement of debate, discussion and disagreement create flexibility, risk-taking and continuous improvement among the staff which in turn lead to positive results among the students, and positive attitudes among the staff to changes and innovations which might benefit those students. (p. 239)

Teacher collaboration, thus, becomes acceptance of otherness and cooperation within differences (Furman, 1998). The following section describes the essence of collaborative cultures in a more detailed manner.

The Essence of Collaborative School Cultures

In collaborative cultures, teachers share ideas, materials, problems, and solutions in order to foster student learning and growth (Peterson & Brietzke, 1994). While each school is different and unique, there are several common features of collaborative school cultures. The following analysis is a summary of these key characteristics outlined by the researchers:

- Time to work together on significant projects or instructional issues (Peterson, 1997);
- Opportunities for career-long learning and improvement (Rosenholtz, 1989);
- Staff who trust and value sharing expertise, advice, and help from others (Peterson, 1997);
- Decreased sense of powerlessness, uncertainty, and increased sense of efficacy (Lortie, 1975; Rosenholtz, 1989);
- Strong norms of collegiality, cooperation, team teaching, professional development, and shared decision-making (Fullan & Hargreaves, 1996);
- Sense of caring focused on staff as well as students (Peterson, 1997);
- Spontaneous, voluntary, pervasive across time and space, and unpredictable relationships (Hargreaves, 1994);
- Innovation, support, and recognizing the value of dissonance inside and outside the organization (Fullan, 1999);
- Commitment to solving problems of practice and improving instruction, hard work, dedication, collective responsibility, more satisfying and productive work environments, help, trust, openness, and interdependence (Nias et al., 1989); and
- Connections and professional networking with professional associations and other teachers (Peterson, 1997).

As social organizations, schools are characterized by the type of relationships between the people that inhabit them. Schools where teachers remain isolated and uncertain in their classrooms lack professional relationships, discussion, and interaction (Fullan & Hargreaves, 1996). Collaborative schools, on the other hand, are exciting and professionally rewarding places for teachers. They are places where instruction and curriculum are regularly being refined, changed, and developed (Peterson & Brietzke, 1994). Collegial relationships among staff members are an important feature of these schools. School norms and structures in collaborative schools provide the purpose and the opportunity for deeper involvement and interaction on professional issues of importance to teachers.

Little (1990) identified four types of collegial relationships among teachers in schools: scanning and storytelling, help and assistance, sharing, and joint work. The first three are the most common and relatively weak forms of collaboration. Joint work is the strongest form of collaboration that implies and creates stronger independence, shared responsibility, collective commitment and improvement, and greater readiness to participate in the difficult business of review and critique (Fullan & Hargreaves, 1996).

Little (1990) defined joint work as "encounters among teachers that rest on shared responsibility for the work of teaching (interdependence), collective conceptions of autonomy, support for teachers' initiative and leadership with regard to professional practice, and group affiliations grounded in professional work" (p. 517). Joint work provides teachers with opportunities to meet and talk about significant problems of practice. It increases the trust, knowledge, and commitment of staff to each other and to the school. Working together can also establish the foundation for ongoing, in-depth professional growth within the school. Fullan (1993) argued that building a culture that supports teacher development can foster collaboration. Joint work fosters collaboration and mutual interdependence within schools and builds a strong professional culture.

Joint work is the main characteristic that other types, such as non- and pseudo-collaborative school cultures lack. In order to develop a strong collaborative culture, joint work is the most important constituent of a deep and meaningful interaction within the school. The basic functions of the strong, positive, collaborative culture and its effects on schools include fostering school effectiveness and productivity; improving collegial activities, that foster communication and problem-solving practices; fostering successful change and improvement efforts; building commitment and identification of staff, students, and administrators; amplifying the energy, motivation, and vitality of a school staff, students, and community; and, increasing the focus of daily behavior and attention on what is important and valued. Collaborative culture affects every aspect of the school life from the casual interactions in the halls, to the type of instruction that is valued, to the importance of professional development, to the effectiveness of the learning and teaching processes in school.

Summary

Viewing schools through cultural and micropolitical perspectives allows us to differentiate between types of school culture. Cultures may vary from school to school based on different sets of external and internal issues. Depending on the nature of relationships between teachers, schools can have non-collaborative, pseudo-collaborative, and collaborative cultures. Non-collaborative school cultures are characterized by individualism, isolation, conservatism, and presentism. In pseudo-collaborative cultures, such as balkanization, comfortable collaboration, and contrived collegiality, relationships between teachers lack deeper collaboration and togetherness and may be prescribed and imposed on them by administration. Collaborative cultures are the most effective for school communities that want to progress, develop, and change for better. Joint work, collaboration, and collegiality in relationships foster shared norms and commitments in schools. They support deep professional interchange among teachers in a form of a moving mosaic, which extends beyond traditional boundaries and minimizes interpersonal conflicts as teachers recognize that their capacity increases through working together. Collaborative cultures are characterized by interdependence, teamwork, shared decision-making, and commitment of every stakeholder in schools. Developing strong, trusting collaborative cultures in school may help build a foundation for continual growth for students, teachers, and administrators.

The Potential for Collaboration in Ukrainian Schools

A strong collaborative culture, as outlined before, seems to be a necessity for every school. This pertains also to schools in Ukraine. However, before starting to build collaborative cultures, education in Ukraine needed to win a struggle against vestiges of old thinking embedded in

Marxist-Leninist ideology. Possessing unique and specific characteristics, being built on a different ideological foundation, and being situated in the period of transition, the nature of Ukrainian schools necessarily differs from their counterparts in North America and Western Europe. In the following sections, I provide a brief historical and ideological background of education in Ukraine to analyze the potential for collaborative cultures in schools.

Historical and Ideological Background

Reforms in Ukrainian education during the transitional period have been characterized by the struggle between forces of progress towards innovation and forces of a reactionary past (Kononenko & Holowinsky, 2001). The main purpose of education in the former USSR was indoctrination in the communist philosophy and way of life. One of the main dogmas in education was the importance of the *collective* in schools, introduced into the Soviet education and elaborated on by Anton Makarenko, who was considered to be a leading Soviet educator (Kononenko & Holowinsky, 2001). Makarenko (1967), similar to Feldstein (1977), understood the collective as a link within society, and an individual's collective as an integral part of a society in which the collective had evolved as a socio-historical phenomenon. Kononenko and Holowinsky (2001) stated that Soviet educators considered a school collective an integral part of Soviet society, bound organically to other collectives.

The communist political system was based on the Marxist-Leninist *collectivism*, clearly manifested in the Soviet socialization process. Individuals were not allowed personal goals; their behavior was evaluated instead in terms of its relevance to the goals of the *collective*. Makarenko (1967; 1984) asserted that the individual's interests should always be secondary to the interests of the collective and the society. Negating the primacy of the individual, Makarenko (1959) maintained that an individual's personality changes under the influence of the collective. Within the nuclear family, parents were not independent educators of their children; their authority was only the reflection of societal authority. When the needs and values of the family conflicted with those of the society, society always took priority (Keltikangas-Jarvinen & Terav, 1996). As a result, individuals were expected to develop a collective, rather than a personal identity, that emphasized group responsibility for actions (Mal'kova, 1988; Monoszon, 1988). Sukhomlinskii (1981) stated that the goal of Soviet education was to produce a citizen with certain personality characteristics and values, including an obedience to official authority, loyalty to communist homeland, and a sense of social responsibility.

For more than 70 years, teachers in the former Soviet Ukraine were indoctrinated in this totalitarian ideology and applied it to school life and relationships among school members. Makarenko's (1984) educational system, the *Vospitanie* [Upbringing], was considered the only accepted educational practice and was systematically applied to all levels of education throughout the Soviet Union. Its emphasis was on organizing the entire life of the young person within an 'integral educational process', including not only the school but also the family, clubs, public organizations, production collectives and the community as a whole in the service of upbringing of the active and committed communist person (Godon et al., 2004). Another prominent feature of Makarenko's thought was the importance of 'the collective' in the process (including the collective of the school and the cultivation of traditions of collective life). For Makarenko, *vospitanie* takes place in *the collective*, "an association of people for common purposes and activities, having a certain structure of powers and responsibilities and defined interdependent relationships between its members in the overall context of a communist society" (Godon et al., 2004, p. 562). Novikova (1978) summarized the guiding principles of Makarenko's system: Optimal personality development can only occur through productive activity in collectives, i.e., organized groups. Competition between groups, not between individuals, is the mechanism for behavior motivation. Rewards and punishments are given on a group basis, so that the whole group benefits or suffers as a result of individual's conduct. Behavior evaluation, rewards, and punishment are delegates to the members of the collective. The principal methods of social control are public recognition or public

31

criticism. As a result, individuals are "prepared for particular behavioral patterns that will be required of them throughout their lives, a behavioral pattern that is systematically reinforced in all societal settings" (Keltikangas-Jarvinen & Terav, 1996, pp. 716-717).

During the period of transition, where in some areas of education the remnants of Soviet system still prevailed, some reformers began to question the ideological foundations of the Soviet education and its significance for Ukraine. Krasovetsky (1995) provided a critical overview of Makarenko's theory of education in a collective. He argued that education cannot accept a principle of unconditional surrender of individual interests to the interests of a collective; the notion that the decision of a collective must always supersede that of an individual should be rejected; and, the concept of collective responsibility for individual actions should be discarded. As Krasovetsky (1995) pointed out, the concept of collective as a *tool* of education should be rejected, but the idea of a collective as a *condition* should be retained.

Collaboration and the Notion of a Collective

The concept of the collective can be very useful in the discussion of collaboration. From the constructive postmodernism view, this concept can be used to provide a basis for establishing collaborative school cultures in Ukraine. Building or constructing on past achievements, instead of discarding them (which is typical of deconstructive postmodernism), can provide a foundation for "cooperation within difference" (Furman, 1998, p. 307) and "acknowledgement and celebration of otherness" (Slattery, 1995, p. 15). I believe that the *collective* (not as a tool, but as a condition) can be used to provide the necessary foundation for the implementation of collaborative culture in Ukrainian schools for a number of reasons.

First of all, the concept of the *collective* may become a balancing force between *individualism* and *collectivism*. Krasovetsky's (1995) critique of a collective as a tool for education raised the issue regarding the relationships of these notions. As mentioned elsewhere in this chapter, Fullan (1993) described the tension between individualism and collectivism, arguing that they must have equal power in schools. On one hand, driven to the extreme, collectivism can cause *groupthink*, or uncritical conformity to the group and suppression of individual dissent. As a reflection of Makarenko's (1967) teachings, collectivism suppressed individualism in Ukrainian schools, creating groupthink among teachers. The prevalence of collective interests left people powerless. A sense of powerlessness leads people to externalize problems and deny personal responsibility (Senge, 1990). On the other hand, the emphasis on individualism can lead to the *isolation* and *privatism* of school members and establishing non-collaborative schools cultures (Fullan, 1993; Fullan & Hargreaves, 1996; Hargreaves, 1994; Little, 1982; Lortie, 1975). The democratic movement and emerging individualism in Ukrainian society, with its emphasis on individual liberty, rights, and interests, may eventually force teachers to work in isolation, resulting in conservatism and resistance to innovation. Thus, in order to build a strong collaborative culture and create "a feeling of responsibility to cooperate with others who may be different" (Furman, 1998, p. 307), it is necessary to carefully balance individual and collective values, beliefs, and norms of school members.

Secondly, a *collective* may be viewed as the implicit nature of the school culture. The implicit nature consists of deep patterns of values and beliefs that are formed over the course of history and become "the underlying social meanings that shape beliefs and behavior over time" (Deal & Peterson, 1990, p. 7). For more than seventy years, the assumption of a *collective* became so ingrained in the Soviet education, that they came to be taken for granted and continued to shape how teachers thought about their work, related to their colleagues, and behaved in schools. The use of the *collective* with its emphasis on working together can help serve as a platform for establishing strong collaborative cultures in Ukrainian schools. In collaborative schools, the hidden and taken for granted, underlying assumptions reinforce and support high levels of collegiality, team work, and dialogue about problems of practice.

And finally, the notion of a *collective* can provide Ukrainian teachers with the micropolitical *skills* for collaboration. The ability to collaborate is based on the skills for team work, which is a necessary component of postmodern organization (Sackney et al., 1999). The majority of teachers in Ukrainian schools, indoctrinated in the *collective*, possess the necessary predispositions to elaborate on their skills to work together with others in true collaboration. Teachers, as they work together as the *collective*, can develop skills necessary for cooperation, team teaching, shared decision-making, joint problem solving, conflict resolution, improvement of instruction, and establishing connections and professional networking with other teachers (Lortie, 1975; Rosenholtz, 1989). Thus, the *collective* can provide teachers with a framework to start practicing joint work (Little, 1990), through sharing responsibility, interdependence and collective autonomy, which are pivotal for building a strong collaborative culture in Ukrainian schools. It is argued that a *collective* perspective may become an important, but not exclusive concept that will be helpful in establishing collaborative relationships in schools in Ukraine.

Establishing Collaborative School Cultures in Ukraine

In order to conclude the various discussions about the potential for collaboration in Ukrainian schools, I turn back to the question posed at the beginning: "Can a collaborative culture be developed *instrumentally* or do certain conditions *enable* its development?" As argued earlier, Ukrainian schools may require both instrumental shaping and necessary conditions to establish collaborative cultures within them. This argument is presented according to two aspects of the problem.

Shaping collaborative cultures. Looking at the positive characteristics and outcomes of collaborative cultures, one could assume that it does not take much to establish them in schools. However, collaborative cultures are not easy to develop (Fullan & Hargreaves, 1996; Little, 2002). As Rosenholtz (1989) remarked, "Norms of collaboration don't simply just happen. They do not spring spontaneously out of teachers' mutual respect and concern for each other" (p. 44). They are shaped by the ways principals, teachers, and key people reinforce and support underlying norms, values, beliefs, and assumptions over a period of time.

The process of shaping a collaborative school culture involves reading the existing culture and identifying aspects of the underlying norms and assumptions that serve the core mission and meet the needs of the school. Depending on the type of existing culture in the school, the starting points and duration of this process for individual schools in Ukraine in their attempt to build a strong collaborative culture will vary. Schools may start forming strong collaborative cultures by improving team work, teaching norms of collegiality and collective problem-solving to students, fostering communication, and building commitment and identification of all school members.

Shaping a collaborative culture also requires reinforcing and celebrating those aspects that support development of a collaborative culture and changing the folkways and norms that destroy collegiality and collaboration (Deal & Kennedy, 1982; Deal & Peterson, 1999; Schein, 1992). Peterson and Brietzke (1994) added that structures, actions, and relationships that support collaboration and the establishment of a professional community need to be developed to reinforce collaborative cultures. Reviewing and fostering the existing concept of a *collective* that dominated the Soviet education (not as a tool, but as a condition of education), may provide a necessary balance between emerging individualism and prevailing collectivism, foster the implicit underlying assumptions of school cultures, and develop necessary micropolitical skills for collaboration.

Conditions for establishing collaborative cultures. After the collapse of the former Soviet Union, Ukrainian society chose a path of political democratization, reforms, and social stability. However, the struggle between the bureaucratic and democratic forces has not finished. The recent developments in Ukraine proved the society's struggle for real democracy in all aspects of life, including education. Ukrainian society is still in the transition from modernist to postmodernist views. As schools are the reflection of the larger society, education in Ukraine faced the new and unexplored terrain of postmodernism. This terrain, according to Maxcy (1994), is usually marked with decentralization, pluralistic demands for multiple voices, and school system redesign. Moreover, postmodernism requires from society members the ability to collaborate (Fullan, 1993), based on the premises of acceptance of otherness and cooperation within difference (Furman, 1998). Thus, the Ukrainian society may first need to learn to accept otherness and cooperate within difference; then every stakeholder in the school may become aware of the need for collaboration and try their best to work together with others for the school to become a successful organization and meet the educational needs of society-at-large.

Synthesis of the Literature: Initial Conceptual Framework

As this study draws on a diverse array of literature, a review of the conceptual framework is necessary for a better understanding of concepts under study. Miles and Huberman (1984) suggested that the next step after concepts have been discussed is to identify how these concepts are linked together in a theoretical model, or a set of abstract constructs and relationships among them (Denzin & Lincoln, 2000b). Such models are "simplifications of reality, but can be made more or less complicated and may capture all or only a portion of the variance in a given set of data. It is up to the investigator to decide how much a particular model is supposed to describe" (p. 782). The main variables in this study and their interactions are presented in the initial conceptual framework (see Figure 3).

The initial conceptual framework for the study depicts two distinct levels, macro (society) and micro (school), for the discussion of teacher collaboration in schools. The societal changes at the macro level, namely philosophical, ideological, economic, social, and political, are shown as having an impact on teacher collaboration in schools at the micro level. Research literature on micropolitics in education recognized the importance of external (macro) factors and their influence on schools in general and on its internal political processes and structures in particular (Bacharach & Mundell, 1993; Ball, 1987; Barrot & Galvin, 1998; Blase, 1991; Blase & Anderson, 1995; Blase & Blase, 2002; Iannaccone, 1991). The micropolitical perspective and organizational culture perspective are also shown as analytical lenses for teacher collaboration at the micro (school) level.

The development of teacher collaboration in Ukrainian schools is central in this study. I have situated discussion of collaboration within a discourse of postmodernism as a social theory (Furman, 1998). Ukraine has moved from a modern era of foundational truth and unified perspective into a society of plurality, diversity, and interdependence in social, political, and economic realms. This new era requires new ways of thinking and recognition of plurality and multiple perspectives from schools, also. Postmodernism informs our understanding of the social context of schooling and how schools confront this issue. The constructive postmodern perspective (Furman, 1998) provides an analytical tool that facilitates discussion of collaboration in schools. Unlike deconstructive postmodernism, that negates the possibility of any collaboration, and modernism, that emphasizes collaboration through sameness, constructive postmodernism adopts the view that collaboration is based on the feeling of responsibility to cooperate with others who may be different. The emphasis in collaboration has shifted from sameness to acceptance of otherness and cooperation within difference (Furman, 1998). The constructive postmodern perspective allows building upon the existing foundation, adopting the previous achievements in the area of collaboration, and applying a new lens, defining collaboration as a network of persons who may differ but who are interdependent.

The ability to collaborate, on both macro (society) and micro (school) levels, has become one of the core requisites of the postmodern society (Fullan, 1993). Collaboration has become "an articulating and integrating principle of action, planning, culture, development, organization and research" (Hargreaves, 1994, p. 245). Collaboration can be described as joint work (Little, 1982), shared creation (Schrage, 1990), or a style for direct interaction between two coequal parties voluntarily engaged in shared decision-making as they work toward a common goal (Friend & Cook, 2000). Collaborative relationships are voluntary, spontaneous, development-oriented, pervasive across time and space, and unpredictable (Hargreaves, 1994). Collaboration is perceived to be beneficial for teachers in that it provides moral support, reduces overload, increases their efficiency and effectiveness, leads to continuous improvement, increases responsiveness to change (Hargreaves, 1994), improves the quality of professional work life, and forms professional communities (Louis et al., 1996). Most frequently discussed challenges of collaboration are the difficulty of implementation, meaning of collaboration, administrative imposition, and lack of necessary skills.

As collaboration may increase the complexity of organizing and managing, a single lens or framework is inadequate to understand such complex organizational phenomena. I followed the lead of researchers (Hargreaves, 1994; Pounder, 1998), who suggested the use of several conceptual or disciplinary frameworks. The initial conceptual framework (Figure 3) depicts the discussion of teacher collaboration through dual lenses: organizational culture perspective and micropolitical perspective.

Looking at collaboration from an organizational culture perspective (Deal & Kennedy, 1982; Ott, 1989; Schein, 1985) allows embracing the complexity of school cultures. Culture is composed of explicit and implicit shared norms, values, beliefs, and assumptions that shape how people think, feel, and act in schools (Deal & Kennedy, 1982; Schein, 1992; Stolp & Smith, 1995). School culture is a complex network of ceremonies and rituals that have been constructed over time by all stakeholders in the process of schooling (Deal & Peterson, 1999). School culture is shaped under the influence of both external and internal environments of the schools. It becomes the system of meaning-making in organizations and the process by which problems are solved, relying more upon building the relationships, meanings, and connections between people than on structures and rules (Sackney et al., 1999). A culture of teaching (Hargreaves, 1994), as a part of broader school culture, gives meaning, support, and identity to teachers, their work, and relationships with others in schools. Within the context of multiple perspectives, otherness, difference, and diversity, collaborative culture becomes the force that holds together the decentralized parts of the school.

The micropolitical perspective (Bacharach & Mundell, 1993; Ball, 1987; Blase, 1991; Burns, 1961; Hoyle, 1982; Iannaccone, 1975) provides another lens for understanding collaboration in schools by uncovering power, influence, conflict, coalitions, and negotiations between individuals and groups within school organizations. Micropolitics deals with the interactions and political ideologies of social systems of administrators, teachers, and students within school buildings (Iannaccone, 1975). However, it is not limited just to the school level. Micropolitics is also concerned with the use of formal and informal power by individuals and groups to achieve their goals at any levels of organizations, systems of organizations, or in society at large (Blase & Blase, 2002). The micropolitical perspective is focused on the strains and tensions stemming from diverse sources of power, rival interests, intractable conflicts within and around schools, and coalition formation or cooperation of teachers to achieve their interests. It examines the political and policy implications of what happens in classrooms and seeks to connect them to broader political, social, and contextual processes occurring at the district, state, federal, and global arenas (Marshall & Gerstl-Pepin, 2005). In this context, micropolitical and macropolitical perspectives are closely connected.

The micropolitical perspective has important implications for the discussion of teacher collaboration in schools. It examines how teachers' communities are shaped by ideological stances, or educational perspectives and commitments of teachers (Achinstein, 2002). Micropolitics, according to Hargreaves (1994) questions the widely advocated virtues of collegiality in the context where there are substantial differences in values and beliefs of the teachers; raises questions about treating norms of collegiality as administrative laws of collegiality; inquires into the circumstances where collaboration becomes collaboration with the enemy; and allows differentiating between the different forms of collaboration.

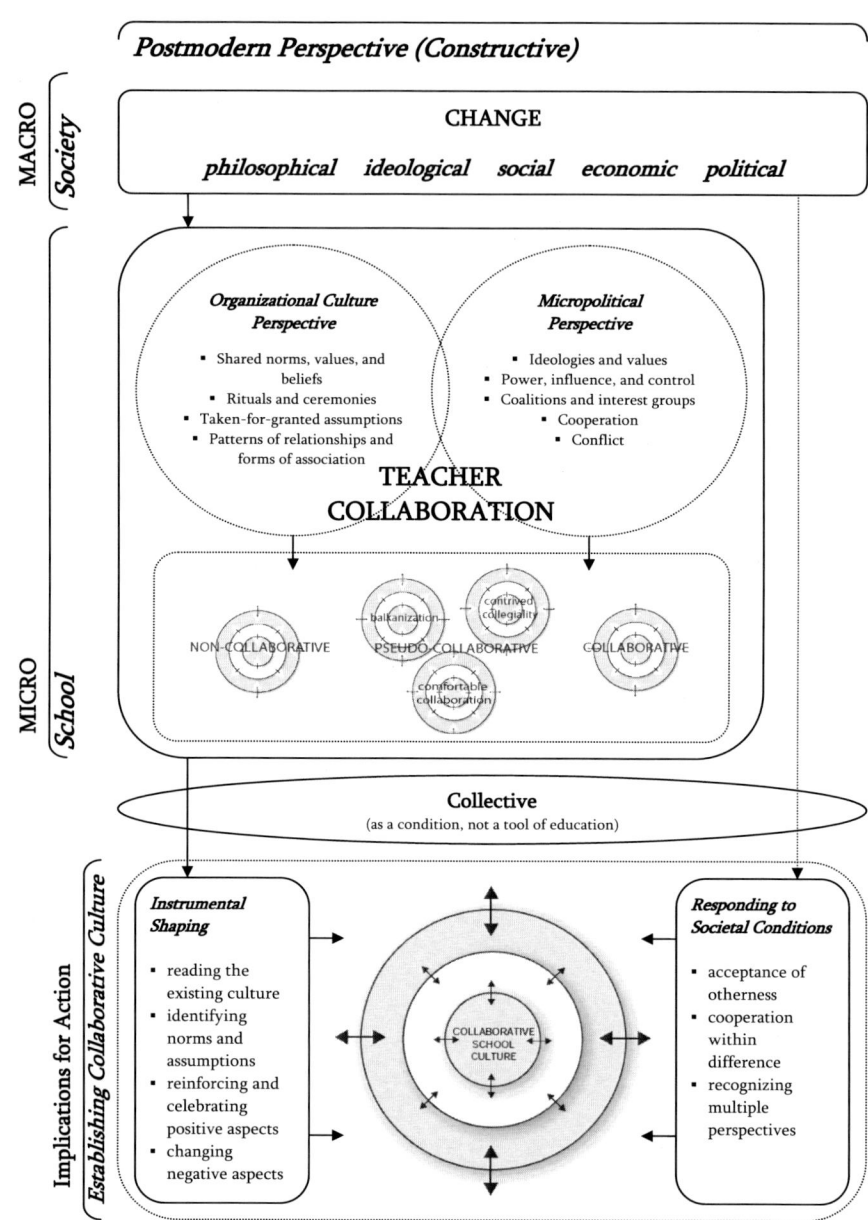

Figure 3. Initial conceptual framework.

36

Cultures may vary from school to school based on different sets of external and internal issues. Depending on the nature of relationships between teachers, schools can have non-collaborative, pseudo-collaborative, and collaborative cultures. Non-collaborative school cultures are characterized by individualism, isolation, conservatism, and presentism (Little, 1982; Lortie, 1975). In pseudo-collaborative cultures, such as balkanization, comfortable collaboration, and contrived collegiality, relationships between teachers lack deeper collaboration and togetherness and may be prescribed and imposed on them by administration (Fullan & Hargreaves, 1996).

Collaborative cultures are characterized by joint work, deep professional interchange, interdependence, teamwork, shared decision-making and commitments of every stakeholder in schools (Hargreaves, 1994; Rosenholtz, 1989). Developing strong, trusting collaborative cultures in school may help build a foundation for continual growth for students, teachers, and administrators.

The development of collaborative school cultures in Ukraine is the basic premise of this study. The concept of the collective (Makarenko, 1967, 1984), pervasive in the Soviet system of education may have an important role in this process. From the constructive postmodernism view, this concept, as a condition, not a tool of education (Krasovetsky, 1995), can serve as a basis for establishing collaborative school cultures in Ukraine. Building or constructing on past achievements, instead of discarding them (which is typical of deconstructive postmodernism), can provide a foundation for cooperation within difference (Furman, 1998) and acknowledgement and celebration of otherness (Slattery, 1995).

The final part of the conceptual framework portrays implications for action in establishing collaborative cultures in Ukrainian schools. It is argued that as a result of societal impact on teachers and their relationships inside and outside of the schools, such cultures may be established by a two-fold process: instrumental shaping and responding to societal conditions. The process of shaping a collaborative school culture involves reading the existing culture, identifying aspects of the underlying norms and assumptions that serve the core mission and meet the needs of the school, reinforcing and celebrating positive aspects that support development of a collaborative culture, and changing the negative norms that destroy collegiality and collaboration (Deal & Kennedy, 1982; Deal & Peterson, 1999; Schein, 1992). As postmodernism requires from society members the ability to collaborate (Fullan, 1993), the society in transition from modernist to postmodernist perspectives needs to learn how to *accept otherness* and *cooperate within difference* (Furman, 1998). As it is shown in the conceptual framework, the instrumental shaping and teachers' responses to the societal conditions may be viewed as main elements in the process of establishing collaborative school cultures in Ukraine.

Summary of the Chapter

This chapter provided a theoretical overview of the nature of collaboration in schools from a postmodern framework utilizing cultural and micropolitical perspectives. An overview of issues concerning education during the period of post-Soviet transition in Ukraine was presented. The constructive postmodernism framework was used as an analytical tool to facilitate discussion of collaboration in schools. It was followed by the definition, characteristics, benefits, and challenges of teacher collaboration. Teacher collaboration was viewed through the dual lenses: the organizational culture perspective and the micropolitical perspective. Following this, the discussion of various types of school culture as they pertain to teacher collaboration in schools was presented. Through the notion of a collective, that prevailed in Soviet system of education, an analysis of the potential for collaboration in Ukrainian schools was discussed. It was argued that establishing collaborative school cultures in Ukraine requires both instrumental shaping and certain conditions in the society. As a synthesis of the reviewed literature, an initial conceptual framework for the study concluded this chapter.

Chapter 3

METHODOLOGY, DATA COLLECTION,
AND DATA ANALYSIS

Some set a great value on method, while others pride themselves on dispensing with method. To be without method is deplorable, but to depend on method entirely is worse. You must first learn to observe the rules faithfully; afterwards, modify them accordingly to your intelligence and capacity. The end of all method is to have no method (Sze & Wang, 1963, p. 17).

Methods selected for the study are very important and require much thinking on part of the researcher. As Schulman (1988) suggested,

To assert that something has method is to claim that there is an order, a regularity, obscure though it may be, which underlies an apparent disorder, thus rendering it meaningful. Method is the attribute which distinguishes research activity from mere observation and speculation.

When adversaries argue about the nature of the world or the best approach to some particular human endeavour, we typically find ourselves evaluating their perspective claims by examining the methods they use to reach their conclusions. There are few subjects that generate as much passion among scientists as arguments over method. (p. 3)

The method should fit the purpose of the research. There are four frames through which research purpose can be achieved. According to Lather (1991) these are: a *positivist* frame through which to describe and predict behaviours, an *interpretive* frame through which to understand meanings, a *critical theory* frame through which to promote emancipation, and a *deconstructionist* frame through which to redefine concepts.

Owens (1982) argued that research design involves a critical decision making process. Researchers choose from two legitimate paradigms of systematic inquiry: a *rationalistic* paradigm, which embraces logical-positivistic views and deductive thinking, and a *naturalistic* paradigm, which embraces phenomenological views and inductive thinking to seek knowledge and understanding of social and organizational phenomena (Owens, 1982). Consequently, none of the methods can be considered as the best or superior to others. The best method depends on the nature of one's research objectives, attributes of the phenomena under consideration, and the constraints of the situation (Palys, 1992). What is of paramount importance, is that the research perspective matches the purpose of the research conducted (Denzin & Lincoln, 2000b; Lather, 1991; Schulman, 1988).

The purpose of this chapter is to provide a description of the specific methodological procedures for this study. In this chapter the researcher's foundation of knowledge, research methods, and research orientation selected for the study are outlined. An overview of methods selected to help answer the questions, as well as the design and the rules of rigor to which the study adhered are discussed. Next, data collection procedures and data analysis theory and techniques are presented, followed by procedures used to maintain trustworthiness and ethical considerations in this study. The chapter concludes with the description of sites and respondents.

Researcher's Foundation of Knowledge

Truth resides in the minds of individuals. People see and believe what they want to see and believe, sometimes not consciously, but because of the background brought to what is being observed. All life experiences contribute to the construction of truth as people continually deconstruct and reconstruct their personal understanding of reality. Each individual constructs his or her own reality, which is dependent on the life-world, or social world in which we live. However, as Schutz (1967) argued, this primary world or *paramount reality* is not the only world in which people live. A notion of *multiple realities,* introduced by him, refers to people's perceptions of reality in different worlds depending on situations, circumstances, contexts, and perspectives.

"Observations of the real world are greatly influenced by the knowledge about that world held by individuals and groups" (Keeves, 1999, p. 11). Schwandt (2000) stated that the lived experiences of people are, by their very nature, the lived experiences of many individuals, who are as independent in their particular thought, circumstance, and environment as their society is diverse. Shared understandings between the society members are developed through social interaction. According to this view of socially constructed realities, knowledge and understanding can be shared through the agreed upon manner, most usually language, and either oral or written texts. Co-construction of knowledge of people within the society is the subject of a *multiple realities* approach to understanding of the truth.

A methodology, according to Denzin and Lincoln (2000b), is a way people gain knowledge about the world. The methods chosen to address a research question reflect the personal belief system of the researcher. The knowledge that researchers have in their minds influences the ways in which they view the real world and the issues they address in their research activities. The researcher's foundation of knowledge, i.e., the ontological and epistemological assumptions, determines the research design and the interpretation of data obtained from the research.

As important as the researcher's knowledge are the nature of the research problem and the purpose of the research. The foundations and justification of the knowledge have dominated the debate around methods of inquiry. Keeves (1999) argued that all research in educational problems necessarily lacks foundations in the real world, as what is observed is influenced by the theories that direct the observations being made. Following the argument of Kaplan (1964), who argued that methods of educational inquiry should be prospective rather than retrospective, Keeves (1999) proposed:

> If the emphasis in educational research shifts from the foundations to the outcomes of the research, whether in terms of contributing to theory or towards social action or to both, then the choice of problems to be investigated is made in terms of the significance and consequences of the findings rather than firmness of the foundations. ... The methods employed in educational enquiry should then be influenced by the nature of the problems being considered. (p. 14)

Denzin and Lincoln (2000a) described the main aspects in epistemological theorizing that influence different modes of research, categorizing them into traditional *foundationalist* or *positivist* perspective, and new *interpretive* or *qualitative* perspective. White (1999) indicated that three modes of research, i.e., *explanatory, interpretive,* and *critical,* are influenced by a corresponding philosophical position and logic, or epistemology. Explanatory research is influenced by the positivist tradition in the philosophy of science, interpretive research is mainly concerned with discovering meaning within a social phenomenon, while critical research deals with affecting political, social, or personal change.

White (1999) continued that the explanatory approach is appropriate for the examination of a well-structured problem, in which there are "few decision makers or stakeholders, a limited number of alternatives, a well-defined problem, and agreed-on values to direct action" (p. 4). On the contrary, ill-structured problems are characterized by many decision makers or stakeholders, numerous possible alternatives, competing definitions of the problem, and conflicting values to guide decision making. The impact of societal changes on collaboration among teachers in schools, school culture, and school micropolitics are the areas that deal primarily with ill-structured problems. According to this perspective, it is appropriate to employ interpretive methods as the mode of inquiry for this study. Within this orientation, people are both the source and the object of knowledge. In the following section, I will address the research problem and purpose of this study according to such an orientation.

Interpretive Naturalist Framework

This study focused on the perceived impact of societal changes on teacher collaboration in schools. It investigated teachers' perceptions regarding the nature of broad philosophical, ideological, social, political, and economic changes in Ukraine after the end of the communist regime of Soviet Union and its impact on teacher collaboration in Ukrainian schools. According to my ontological and epistemological views, it seemed appropriate to adopt a naturalist paradigm orientation to this study.

A paradigm can be defined as an interpretive framework, or a net that contains the researcher's epistemological, ontological, and methodological premises (Denzin & Lincoln, 2000a; Guba, 1990). Paradigm is a "basic set of beliefs that guides action" (Guba, 1990, p. 17). As the researcher's ontological, epistemological, and methodological beliefs are brought together under one umbrella, they need to be interconnected, and should invariably flow constructively and philosophically. According to Denzin and Lincoln (2000a),

> The gendered, multiculturally situated researcher approaches the world with a set of ideas, a framework (theory, ontology) that specifies a set of questions (epistemology) that he or she then examines in specific ways (methodology, analysis). That is, the researcher collects empirical materials bearing on the question and then analyzes and writes about them. (p. 18)

Thus, methodology is only one aspect of a paradigm and is closely connected to ontology and epistemology. Methodology seeks to understand how one knows the world or gains knowledge of it (Lincoln & Guba, 1994). Methods depict researcher's views on what qualifies as valuable knowledge and perspective on the nature of reality, i.e., ontology. "Ontology is the concern about whether the world exists, and if so, in what form.... Because we cannot experience the world directly (unfiltered through our senses), we will never know for sure what the world really is.... It is a matter of belief ..." (Potter, 1996, p. 36). Epistemology attempts to understand the meaning of the relationship between the researcher and the known; it examines the ways of knowing. "Epistemology is the study of the nature, scope, and applicability of knowledge" (J. C. Walker & Evers, 1999).

Several terms are used to differentiate between two major paradigms. As stated before, I follow the path of the researchers (Denzin & Lincoln, 2000a; Guba & Lincoln, 1999; Keeves, 1999; Schwandt, 2000), who differentiated between *rationalistic* and *naturalistic* paradigms. As Guba and Lincoln stated, "naturalists assume that there exist multiple realities which are, in the main, constructions existing in the minds of people.... [and] naturalist assumptions are more meaningful in studying human behavior" (p. 142). Unlike rationalistic orientation, that assumes that there exists a single, tangible reality fragmentable into independent variables and processes, any of which can be studied independently of the others, multiple realities are intangible and can be studied only in a holistic and idiosyncratic fashion.

> Naturalists do not deny the reality of the objects, events, or processes with which people interact, but suggest that it is the meaning given to or interpretations made of these objects, events or processes that constitute the arena of interest to investigators of social/behavioral phenomena. (p. 142)

The notion of multiple realities and social constructions of meaning or knowledge was fundamental for this research. Social processes and interactions among participants at the school (*micro*) level as the result of societal *(macro)* level changes were of interest for this study.

Other basic assumptions or beliefs underlying naturalistic research described by researchers (Guba & Lincoln, 1994, 1999; Lincoln & Guba, 2000; Owens, 1982) included: interactive relationships between the inquirer and the object of study, each influencing the other; the investigator strives to develop an idiographic body of knowledge from which to derive a hypothesis about the individual case; entities reflect mutual simultaneous shaping; therefore, distinguishing between cause and effect is impossible; inquiries are value-bound as influenced by the inquirer, by choice of research paradigm, by the substantive theory that frames the study, by the choice of methods, and by the values inherent in the social and conceptual context; naturalistic study utilizes an inductive approach, that is, theory is "grounded" and emerges from the data; qualitative methods are the methods of choice; and research design is emergent rather than predetermined. "Naturalistic paradigm ... is essentially based upon inductive thinking and is associated with phenomenological views of 'knowing' and 'understanding' social and organizational phenomena" (Owens, 1982, p. 10).

The nature of the research problem helps to outline the methodology that is context based. There are simply no safe and non-contextual places from which the researcher can write or observe (Dimitriadis, 2001). Fine (1994) stated, in a similar way, that a researcher's goals is to avoid the objective notion that subjects of research in the behavioral and social sciences may be observed and studied in any sterile and insulated non-contextual way.

> Naturalists assert that the aim of inquiry is to develop an idiographic body of knowledge; this knowledge is best encapsulated in a series of "working hypotheses" that describe the individual case. Generalizations are not possible since human behavior is never time or context free. Nevertheless, some transferability of working hypotheses from context to context may be possible depending on the similarity of the contexts (an empirical matter). (Guba & Lincoln, 1999, p. 143)

Differences of the contexts, thus, are as inherently important, and at times, more important than the similarities.

The naturalistic orientation argues that cause-effect relationship "can never be demonstrated in the 'hard' sense; only patterns of plausible influence can be inferred" (Guba & Lincoln, 1999, p. 143). Human relationships within schools are caught up in such an interacting web of factors, events, and processes that the hope that the cause-effect chain can be sorted out is vain, and the best the enquirer can hope for is to establish these plausible patterns of influence. The enquirer can assign meaning to these relationships in order to create a coherent picture of the truth, as a product of the meaning. This orientation is peculiar to a *constructivist* framework within naturalistic interpretive paradigm.

Constructivist Perspective

Constructivism assumes the relativism of social realities, recognizes the mutual creation of knowledge by the viewer and the viewed, and aims toward interpretive understanding of subjects' meanings (Guba & Lincoln, 1994; Lincoln & Guba, 2000; Schwandt, 2000). According to Lincoln and Guba (2000), constructivism adopts a relativist ontology (relativism), a transactional epistemology, and a hermeneutic, dialectical methodology. Researchers in this paradigm are oriented to the production of reconstructed understandings of the social world. As Schwandt (2001) noted, individuals invent concepts, models, and schemes to make sense of experience, and they continually test and modify these constructions in the light of new experience. He added,

> Furthermore, there is an inevitable historical and sociocultural dimension to this construction. We do not construct our interpretations in isolation but against a backdrop of shared understandings, practices, language, and so forth. This ordinary sense of

constructivism holds that all knowledge claims and their evaluation take place within a conceptual framework through which the world is described and explained. (pp. 30-31)

Of paramount importance for the constructivist approach is the relationship between *subject* and *object* of the research, or as a more appropriate way of reference within the qualitative research, *researcher* and *participant*. Within the constructivist paradigm, researchers reflect upon their own personal history, education, and perspectives as it relates to those of the individuals observed. The enquirer and the respondent in any human enquiry inevitably interact to influence one another (Guba & Lincoln, 1999). In fact, the relationship between them is both dialectic and didactic, in which both the researcher and the participant shape and are shaped by one another. In other words, they both are the co-authors and co-constructors of the knowledge. "Our obligation [as researchers] is to come clean..., meaning that we interrogate in our writings who we are as we coproduce the narratives we presume to 'collect'" (Fine & Weis, 1998, p. 277).

The act of *coming clean*, or as Denzin and Lincoln (1994) called it *standpoint epistemology,* allows for a statement of *accountability* to a reader. Accountability is found in the researcher clear use of written language and description (Schwandt, 1994), with the special emphasis on the choice of words from a semantic and semiotic perspective (Holstein & Gubrium, 1994), so that as little linguistic interpretation as possible is necessary by the readers, who themselves will reconstruct meanings based upon their own personal history, education, and perspective (von Glasersfeld, 1998).

Another aspect of accountability is to understand the complex world of lived experience from the point of view of those who lived it.

> The world of lived reality and situation-specific meanings that constitute the general object of investigation is thought to be constructed by social actors. That is, particular actors, in particular places, at particular times, fashion meaning out of events and phenomena through prolonged, complex processes of social interaction involving history, language and action. (Schwandt, 1994, p. 118)

In order to understand the complexity of a participant's world, the researcher looks to the meaning and knowledge that can be made out of the events in which he or she have participated as actors. The researcher also looks at multiple historical, social, political, and cultural interpretations surrounding the experience. According to constructivist orientation, knowledge is not a particular kind of product that exist independent of the knower, but is an activity or process (Schwandt, 1994). In the process of storytelling (Seidman, 1998), a meaning is recreated through the dialectic nature of stories.

> When people tell stories, they select details of their experience from their stream of consciousness. ... In order to give the details of their experience a beginning, middle, and end, people must reflect on their experience. It is this process of selecting constitutive details of experience, reflecting on them, giving them order, and thereby making sense of them that makes telling stories a meaning making experience. (Seidman, 1998, p. 1)

From the constructivist point of view, the researcher, along with the participants, creates a storyline, constantly checking whether his or her construction provides a fair reflection of the stories told by the participants. The enquirer is the co-author of the construction of the meaning. However, the meaning made by the participant is of major importance for the constructivist research (Schwandt, 1994). It provides the data that lead to a better understanding of events in time. It is from this orientation that I present the methodological overview for this study.

I do not attempt to develop a hypothesis by which the perceptions and experiences of all school professionals at the school level within a context of societal changes may be explained. Rather, the purpose is to develop insights through which the meaning of perceptions of educators under such circumstances may be more fully understood. To achieve this, the study design presents these perceptions as unique, ungeneralizable, and constructed through the dialectic interpretations, constructions and reconstructions of the participants, researcher, and reader (van Manen, 1997; von Glasersfeld, 1998) as a joint construction of meaning (Mishler, 1986). In the following section, I present a standpoint from which my epistemology originates in order to *come clean* as a researcher of this study.

Personal Position

In order to understand the context of this study, it is appropriate to provide the reader with an introduction to the researcher and to clarify who the researcher is in relationship to the study. The researcher's values and beliefs influence every aspect of the research process. Denzin and Lincoln (2000a) stated, "Every researcher speaks from within a distinct interpretive community that configures, in its special way, the multicultural, gendered components of the research act" (p. 18). My background, beliefs, and values on the topic are instrumental in an attempt to identify and contain my position as the researcher and author.

My professional background and experiences with schools in Ukraine after the collapse of the USSR may be seen as influential in my decision to conduct research in this area. I originally came from Chernivtsi, Ukraine, where I completed a four-year Bachelor of Arts (Honours) Degree in English and German Linguistics and Education, followed by a Specialist (Honours) Degree in the same field from Chernivtsi National University. My professional career included teaching experiences within Chernivtsi high, private, and foreign language acquisition schools. As a student during both the Soviet and post-Soviet time, and later as a teacher in independent Ukraine, I noticed changes in the school atmosphere and relationships between people. In my studies in the field of Educational Administration, teacher collaboration, school culture and micropolitics during the times of important societal changes became of great personal interest. I believe that my background, knowledge of the historical and cultural context and language allowed me to gain better understanding of participants' perceptions of these issues through this research. Furthermore, my experience in conducting focus group and individual interviews through participation within other studies was instrumental for this study.

Epistemologically, I feel comfortable within the naturalistic paradigm. A constructivist interpretation of the origin of knowledge seems to fit my personal beliefs. Undertaking research within this orientation dictates working from the perspective of a *bricoleur* (Denzin & Lincoln, 2000a), that is, drawing upon a variety of methods and perspectives, as they are needed to adequately address the research questions. "The choice of research practices depends upon the questions that are asked, and the questions depend on their context" (Nelson, Treichler, & Grossberg, 1992, p. 2). As an interpretive *bricoleur*, I try to produce a *bricolage*, "a pieced-together set of representations that are fitted to the specifics of a complex situation" (Denzin & Lincoln, 2000a, p. 4), and is an emergent construction. In the following sections, I provide an overview of the research design and methodological techniques that are most suitable, according to my beliefs and research purposes, to this study.

Research Design

Naturalistic constructivist methodology leads to naturalistic methods of inquiry. According to Merriam (1998), "method and paradigm are inextricably linked" (p. 3). Qualitative inquiry is adequate for a naturalistic study. Although it is difficult to confine qualitative research to one definition because of its complexity, Creswell (1998) defined qualitative research as "an inquiry process of understanding based on distinct methodological traditions of inquiry that explore a social or human problem" (p. 15). Denzin and Lincoln (2000a) presented a "generic" definition of qualitative research:

> Qualitative research is a situated activity that locates the observer in the world. It consists of a set of interpretive, material practices that make the world visible. These practices transform the world. They turn the world into a series of representations, including field

notes, interviews, conversations, photographs, recordings, and memos to the self. At this level, qualitative research involves an interpretive, naturalistic approach to the world. This means that qualitative researchers study things in their natural settings, attempting to make sense of, or to interpret phenomena in terms of the meanings people bring to them. Qualitative research involves the studied use and collection of a variety of empirical materials ... that describe routine and problematic moments and meanings in individuals' lives. (p. 3)

The naturalistic approach provided the study with rich, descriptive, and generous information required for the analysis of the impact of societal changes on teacher collaboration in Ukrainian schools.

Participant Selection

My role as a qualitative researcher within the constructivist framework was to construct interpretations against a backdrop of shared understandings, practices, and language of the participants (Schwandt, 2000). McMillan (2000) explained, "The participants ... are selected because they have lived the experiences being investigated, are willing to share their thoughts about the experiences, and can articulate their conscience experiences" (p. 269). As the impact of societal changes on schools in Ukraine covered a period of approximately fourteen years, participants needed to be selected according to certain criteria. "Criterion-based sampling requires that one establish the criteria, bases, or standards necessary for units to be included in the investigation; one then finds a sample that matches these criteria" (Merriam, 1998, p. 48). Purposeful sampling is the most effective strategy to meet criteria set by the research purposes (Seidman, 1998). To gather thick and rich information from the respondents, they need to be "influential, the prominent and the well informed people ... selected ... on the basis of their expertise in areas relevant to the research" (Marshall & Rossman, 1995, p. 83).

The participants in this study were elementary and secondary school teachers in the city of Chernivtsi, Ukraine. In total, fifty-five teachers participated in the study: fifty-two female and three male respondents (the discussion of the gender representation is presented in Chapter Four). All participants were volunteers and had been in the teaching profession within the education system of Ukraine during the period of time from 1991 to 2005. Eight focus group interviews were conducted with two to eleven participants in each group. Seven of the focus group interviews were conducted with experienced teachers, while one focus group involved young or novice teachers. After the completion of focus group interviews, I invited fifteen respondents to participate in consequent individual interviews. Individual interview participants were chosen purposefully out of the focus group sample to provide a balanced representation of gender and grade levels. No further limitations were made based on age, teaching/subject area, or other individual characteristics.

Data Collection

The primary purpose of gathering data in naturalistic inquiry is to "gain the ability to construct reality in ways that are consistent and compatible with the constructions of a setting's inhabitants" (Erlandson, Harris, Skipper, & Allen, 1993, p. 81). Creswell (1998) viewed data collection as a series of interrelated activities aimed at gathering good information to answer emerging research questions. Qualitative data is a source of well-grounded, rich descriptions and explanations of processes in identifiable local contexts (Miles & Huberman, 1984). Rich descriptions and explanations emerge from qualitative methods that convey very much the web of interrelated factors associated with the situation under study (Owens, 1982).

Data collection techniques that are characteristic of qualitative research were employed in this study. Data were collected using document analysis, focus groups, and individual interviews. More detailed description of data collection techniques and the rationale for research methods for this study are provided in the following section.

Research Methods

In order to provide a better understanding of teachers' perceptions of the impact of societal changes on teacher collaboration in schools within the period of independence of Ukraine, this study utilized a variety of qualitative methods of inquiry, such as documents and material culture analysis, group interviews (focus groups), and individual interviews. I believe that a mixture of these methods produced a necessary *bricolage* to describe the issue at point. Gathering information from a variety of sources and through various methods served as *crystallization* (Richardson, 1994), both broadening my understanding and enhancing the trustworthiness of the findings. Following are the descriptions of each of the chosen methods with main characteristics, advantages, and limitations.

Documents and Material Culture Analysis

Broad macrolevel changes differently affect society and people within it. One of the impacts is the change at the governmental level. Usually, in times of wide system changes, documents and policies change accordingly. These documents form a material culture that can become of great importance for the qualitative researchers who wish to explore multiple and conflicting voices, differing and interacting interpretations (Hodder, 2000). Many areas of experience can be hidden from language, and through the use of this particular method, I planned to get a deeper insight into the nature of documents related to interactions and relationships of school members. I reviewed, analyzed, and translated into English (where necessary) a host of policies and procedures issued during the period of 1991-2005 that related to teachers' work and collaboration in schools. They included decrees, acts, and reports of the Ministry of Education, policy manuals, materials of teacher conferences, and reports of the Department of Education, and school policy manuals. The purpose of this method was to gather the necessary information about the documented influence of the societal changes on the schools. The material and information obtained from the analysis were instrumental in creating an outline of issues and questions for the next steps in research methodology – focus groups and individual interviewing.

Generally, "the interpreter of material culture works between past and present or between different examples of material culture, making analogies between them" (Hodder, 2000, p. 710). An important initial assumption that has to be made by those interpreting material culture is that belief, idea, and intention are important to action and practice. Hodder (2000) continued that at all stages, from the identification of classes and attributes to the understanding of high-level social processes, the interpreter has to deal with three areas of evaluation: identification of the context within which things had similar meanings; recognition of similarities and differences; and relevance of general and specific historical theories to the data at hand. The interpretation of the data was based on the simultaneous evaluation of similarities and differences, context and theory of the issues.

There are certain limitations and disadvantages of this method. Derrida (1978) stated that meaning does not reside in a text but in the writing and reading of it. As the text is read by different people in different contexts, it is given a new meaning, often contradictory and socially embedded. It can be concluded that there is no original or true meaning of the text without a specific historical context (Hodder, 2000). However, written texts are of great importance for qualitative research, because "in general terms, access can be easy and low cost, because the information provided may differ and may not be available in spoken form, and because texts endure and thus give historical insight" (p. 704). Historical documents and records give not a better but simply a different picture, and can be used alongside other forms of evidence so that the particular biases of each can be understood and compared. Glesne and Peshkin (1992) also noted the value of documents in that they "corroborate your observations and interviews and thus make your findings more trustworthy" (p. 52). As it was mentioned above, the document analysis partially served as a guide for the consequent focus group and individual interviews.

Qualitative Interviewing

According to an epistemological perspective in this study, qualitative interviewing and research are not based on the positivist premises of objective quantifiable data, with the prediction and control of behavior of others as the goal (Kvale, 1996). Instead, it focuses on gaining a better "understanding by means of conversations [that have a structure and a purpose] with the human beings" (Kvale, 1996, p. 11). Interview becomes "the interchange of views between ... persons conversing about a theme of mutual interest" (p. 4). The researcher's role is to be an active and creative participant by using a set of techniques that move past the mere words and sentences exchanged during the interview process (Douglas, 1985). This includes creating an appropriate climate for informational exchange and mutual disclosures. In doing so, the researcher displays his or her own feelings during the interview, as well as elicits those of the subject. According to Holstein and Gubrium (1995), the qualitative interview is dynamic, meaning-making occasion where the actual circumstance of the meaning construction is important. Seidman (1998) stated,

> As a method of inquiry, interviewing is most consistent with people's ability to make meaning through language. It affirms the individual without denigrating the possibility of community and collaboration. Finally, it is deeply satisfying to researchers who are interested in others' stories. (p. 7)

Two major types of qualitative interviewing used in this study included focus group interviews and individual interviews. The focus group may be defined as an interview style designed for small groups (Berg, 2001). Focus group interviews are either guided or unguided discussions addressing a particular topic of interest or relevance to the group and the researcher (Edmunds, 1999). Individual *face-to-face* interviews consist of verbal interaction involving "questions, asked by the interviewer and oral responses by the researcher participants" (Gall, Borg, & Gall, 2003, p. 222).

Focus group interviews. A second phase of the data collection involved focus groups, or group interviews. There are two major techniques used by researchers to collect qualitative data, participant observation and individual interviews (Madriz, 2000). Focus groups possess elements of both techniques while maintaining their own uniqueness as a distinctive research method (Morgan, 1988). The focus group is a collectivistic rather than an individualistic research method that focuses on the multivocality of participants' attitudes, experiences, and beliefs (Madriz, 2000). Within this technique, the participants interact with each other rather than with the interviewer, such that the views of the participants can emerge – the participants' rather than the researcher's agenda can predominate (Cohen, Manion, & Morrison, 2000). Thus, they are "a way of listening to people and hearing from them" (Morgan, 1988, p. 9), as they minimize the control the researcher has during the data gathering process by decreasing the power of the researcher over research participants (Madriz, 2000).

This method of data collection particularly fits into the constructivist framework chosen for this study. Morgan (1988) and Krueger (1988) stated that focus groups are useful for constructing the background knowledge and developing themes, topic, and schedules for subsequent interviews and questionnaires. Through the process of focus group interviewing, I attempted to elicit public statement from the participants of the study (a more private statement of the problem were obtained from individual interviews discussed later). With the use of focus group interviews, the general description of educators' perceptions about the influence of the macro level changes on the micro level aspects of collaboration, culture, and politics in schools was created. Some of the general issues and problems that teachers in the Ukrainian schools had to or still have to deal with as a result of societal changes were explored by this technique. As mentioned above, eight focus group interviews were conducted with two to eleven elementary and secondary school teachers in each group. With participants' permission, each session was audio-taped. Transcripts were generated from the audio recording of the focus group discussion and translated from Ukrainian into English by myself, a native Ukrainian speaker. The data obtained served as a guide for the interviews to follow.

As with every methodological technique, the use of focus groups has its limitations and disadvantages. Researchers (Cohen et al., 2000; Morgan, 1988) argued that focus groups are contrived settings that bring together a specifically chosen sector of population to discuss a particular given theme or topic, where the interaction with the group leads to data and outcomes. Their contrived nature can be seen as both their strength and their weakness. Focus groups are unnatural settings yet they are very focused on a particular issue and, therefore, will yield insights that might not otherwise have been available in a straightforward interview. Though they are economical in time, producing a large amount of data in relatively short time, they tend to produce less data than interviews with the same number of individuals on a one-to-one basis. Therefore, my plan for the study included individual, in-depth interviews as a third perspective in *crystallization* of data.

Individual interviews. The use of interviewing to acquire information is so extensive today that it has been said that we live in an *interview society* (Atkinson & Silverman, 1997). Qualitative researchers realize that interviews are no neutral tools of data gathering, but active interactions between two or more people leading to negotiated and contextually based results. Thus, the focus of interviews is moving from *whats* to *hows* of people's lives (Gubrium & Holstein, 1997). Put in other words, the purpose of in-depth interviews is to *understand* the experiences rather than to *explain*. It is from this orientation that I used the interviews as the last method in the *crystallization* of data.

No consideration of interviews would be complete without acknowledgement of major interview structures. There are two major types of interviews outlined in the literature, *structured* and *unstructured* (Fontana & Frey, 2000), or as Berg (2001) put it, *standardized* and *unstandardized*. Located somewhere between the extremes of completely standardized and completely unstandardized interviewing structures is the *semistandardized* interview (Berg, 2001). It involves the implementation of a number of predetermined questions. "These questions are typically asked of each interviewee in a systematic and consistent order, but the interviewers are allowed freedom to digress; that is, the interviewers are permitted to probe far beyond the answers to their prepared and standardized questions" (p. 70).

After the focus groups, participants were invited to participate in the individual interviews. The results of these interviews formed the majority of the data for the study. I conducted fifteen individual semi-structured or semistandardized interviews. The interviews were audio-taped and transcribed at a later date. I translated the transcripts from Ukrainian into English. The questions for the interviews were partly planned and partly prompted by the themes evident from document analysis. The questions were also prepared from the issues that emerged in the previously conducted focus group discussion. Through this technique, I attempted to contrast the public statement obtained from the focus groups and the private statement of the problem and elaboration on it from the in-depth individual interviews. Within the constructivist framework, this technique allows to co-construct the knowledge of the researcher and participants. Atkinson and Silverman (1997) noted that interviewer and respondent collaborate to create an essentially monologic view of reality.

Clearly, certain types of interviewing are better suited to particular kinds of situations, and researchers must be aware of the implications, pitfalls, and problems of the types of interviews they choose (Fontana & Frey, 2000). Human beings are complex, and their lives are ever changing; the more methods researchers use to study them, the better the chances to gain some understanding of how they construct their lives and the stories they tell about them. Thus, the *bricolage* approach, or multimethod of *crystallization* was used for the purposes of this study.

Data Analysis and Interpretation

Data analysis can be defined as a process of giving meaning to findings obtained from data collection in the study. As Berg (2001) stated, although analysis is the most difficult aspect of any qualitative research project, it is also the most creative. Because of this creative component, it is impossible to establish a complete step-by-step operational procedure that will consistently result in qualitative data analysis. "Although some of the suggestions may suit certain projects nicely, the analysis of data is primarily determined by the nature of the project and the various contingencies built in during the design stages" (Berg, 2001, p. 102). Berg continued that when qualitative analysis is undertaken, certain priorities must be established, assumptions made during the design and data collection must be clarified, and a particular research course must be set.

According to Bogdan & Biklen (1992), analysis may involve "working with data, organizing them, breaking them into manageable units, synthesizing them, searching for patterns, discovering what is important and what is to be learned, and deciding what you will tell others" (p. 153). Merriam (1988) proposed a three-level analysis of data. At the first level, the data is organized topically, to arrange the material into a narrative account or finding. At the second level, the data is systematically classified into some sort of schema consisting of categories, themes, or types. Finally, the third level involves making inferences and developing theory. Janesick (2000) explained, " the purpose of these disciplined approaches to analysis is, of course, to describe and explain the essence of experience and meaning in participants' lives" (p. 391).

In this study, qualitative data analysis was an inductive process of inferring themes and patterns from examination of data (Gall, Borg, & Gall, 1996). Merriam (2002) described data analysis as an inductive strategy: "One begins with a unit of data (any meaningful word, phrase, narrative, etc.) and compares it to another unit of data, and so on, all the while looking for common patterns across the data. These patterns are given names (codes) and are refined and adjusted as the analysis proceeds" (p. 14). Furthermore, Gall et al. (2003) added, that in qualitative research,

> analysis procedure is likely to be emergent. The same document or record can be analyzed at different points in the study, with each analysis yielding new constructs, hypotheses, and insights... Furthermore, the same document or record can be analyzed from different perspectives and for different purposes. (p. 283)

The analysis process also requires a balance of description and interpretation (Patton, 1990). The analysis process requires careful thought, reflection, examination, and time from the researcher in order to gain understanding and meaning that is respectful of and does justice to the participants who were honest and open enough to share their thoughts, feelings, and worries. Through these procedures, I tried to balance description and interpretation of the data for the analysis.

The data analysis process in this study utilized the framework outlined in the literature and discussed above. In the first stage of data analysis, I acquainted myself with the data. In the second stage, I inspected the data for patterns and themes in order to identify data categories. The data were then indexed, coded, and classified to reflect on the research questions. Coding is very important for the qualitative data analysis (Glesne, 1999). Coding is grouping the responses into categories of similar themes, concepts, or ideas. Coding requires the researcher to analyze the text in the context of categories and "forces you to look at each detail, each quote, to see what it adds to your understanding" (Rubin & Rubin, 1995, p. 251). Finally, the themes were used to explain the study clearly and meaningfully. Effective and constructive recommendations, implications, and conclusions were drawn from the analyzed, reflected, and interpreted data.

The data in this study were analyzed in three phases. First, the data collected from document analysis were reviewed and analyzed. Data were coded and emerging issues served as a supplementary guide for focus group and interview questions. Second, transcripts were generated from the audio recording of the focus group discussion. The focus group transcripts were coded, indexed, and classified in order to find patterns and themes in the data (Rubin & Rubin, 1995). The emergent themes and categories partly prompted individual interview questions. Focus group transcripts were then translated into English by the researcher. And finally, all audio-records of participant interviews were transcribed, translated, and broken into manageable pieces of data based upon themes or trends that inductively emerged through a process of repeated reading, listening, and reviewing by the researcher (Seidman, 1998). Similar or repetitive topics represented themes, which were coded. What emerged from these approaches to document and transcript analysis was a collection of important data pieces. Specialized qualitative analysis software, ATLAS.ti, was first used to code the data, and then manage and link pieces and codes to outline themes in their emergence. All data were eventually translated into English by the researcher.

Establishing Trustworthiness

When interpreting and presenting the qualitative data, the researcher needs to keep in mind that the ultimate purpose of any study is to inform the reader. The question that each qualitative researcher must ask, according to Stake (1995), is "Did I get it right?" This study dealt with ill-structured problems, characterized by many decision makers or stakeholders, numerous possible alternatives, competing definitions of the problem, and conflicting values to guide decision making. With conducting, reporting and reading studies of ill-structured problems within an atmosphere of constructivism, one may find a tolerance for ambiguity and the championing of multiple perspectives (Stake, 2000). However, researchers should be concerned with the clarity and validity of their own communications.

> Even if meanings do not transfer intact but squeeze into the conceptual space of the reader, there is no less urgency for researcher to assure that their senses of situation, observation, reporting, and reading stay within some limits of correspondence. However accuracy is construed, researchers don't want to be inaccurate, caught without confirmation. (Stake, 2000, p. 443)

Researchers need to reduce the likelihood of misinterpretation of their findings. Pivotal to this discussion are the notions of *validity* and *trustworthiness.*

Validity is the degree of confidence that can be placed upon the findings of a study. The term validity is commonly used within the quantitative paradigm and consists of such criteria as *internal validity, external validity, reliability,* and *objectivity* (Lincoln & Guba, 1985). The basic validity question might be phrased as follows: "To what degree – if at all – on the basis of evidence and rationales, should the [data results] ... be interpreted and used in the manner proposed?" (Messick, 1989a, p. 5). Validity is an integrated evaluative judgment of the degree to which empirical evidence and theoretical rationales support the *adequacy* and *appropriateness* of *inferences* and *actions* based on research data (Messick, 1989b). The term validity has become less frequently used since qualitative research has become more established within the research in education. Owens (1982) stated, "Because of the assumptions about the nature of reality and ways of understanding that reality in the naturalistic paradigm, the traditional concern for objectivity, validity, and reliability have little relevance for the design of naturalistic research" (p. 10). Validity in qualitative research deals with description and explanation, and whether or not the explanation fits the description. The term trustworthiness seems to be more applicable to qualitative research (Glesne, 1999).

Trustworthiness refers to the overall quality of the research. Lincoln and Guba (1985) argued that the basic issues of trustworthiness are:

> How can an inquirer persuade his or her audiences (including self) that the findings of an inquiry are worth paying attention to, worth making account of? What arguments can be mounted, what criteria involved, what questions asked, what would be persuasive on this issue? (p. 290)

Trustworthiness of research can be established through such naturalistic criteria as *credibility, transferability, dependability,* and *confirmability.* These criteria along with corresponding empirical procedures were used to affirm the trustworthiness of this study.

Credibility

Credibility is presented as a replacement for the paradigmatic criterion of internal validity. It entails the plausibility and "fairness" of the study. For the pragmatic purposes of this particular study, credibility was established through the use of three means: *crystallization, member checking,* and *translation audit.*

For many years, triangulation has been generally suggested as a process of establishing credibility of the study (Janesick, 1994; Lincoln & Guba, 1985; Stake, 2000). However, the idea of *crystallization* (Janesick, 2000; Richardson, 1994) was offered as a better lens through which to establish credibility of the study. Unlike a triangle, the crystal "combines symmetry and substance with an infinite variety of shapes, substances, transmutations, multidimensionalities, and angles of approach" (Richardson, 1994, p. 522). What we see when we view crystal, depends on how we view it, from which angle or perspective, and in which conditions (Janesick, 2000). Crystallization provides a deepened, complex, and thoroughly partial understanding of the topic. Postmodern and constructionist in nature, crystallization allows elaborating on the findings, not affirming them. Within this study, contextual and historical records examined in the literature review constituted one perspective on the data. Similarly, records obtained from the document analysis provided a different perspective. Focus group and interview transcripts constituted another source of data. Variety of research methods, such as document analysis, focus group and individual interviews aided in adding credibility to the study. The construction of knowledge through social means implies a use of multiple perspectives in the interpretation of questions and answers. From a constructivist view, this would constitute theoretical, investigative, and interdisciplinary crystallization.

Member checking, as described by Lincoln and Guba (1985), is the evaluation of analytic categories, interpretations, and conclusions by those participants from whom the data were originally collected. In other words, it refers to "taking data and interpretations back to the people from whom they were derived and asking them if the results are plausible" (Merriam, 2002, p. 31). Within the context of this study, member checking was accomplished through the use of focus group and interview transcript release forms. Participants were encouraged to comment upon findings and define terms as their judgment and comfort permitted.

As this study involved translation of the documents and focus group and individual interview transcripts, it was necessary to conduct the *translation audit* as an additional check between the enquirer's data and interpretations and multiple realities in the minds of informants (Guba & Lincoln, 1999, p. 147). Samples of my translations of the data from Ukrainian and Russian into English were forwarded to the colleague, a professional translator and instructor of Ukrainian and Russian in one of the Canadian universities, for a review of consistency and appropriateness of translation.

Transferability

The second naturalistic criterion of trustworthiness is transferability. Transferability is found in the "context-embeddedness" of a study. "It is the researcher's responsibility to establish whether this criterion can be met in a similar context while preserving the original findings from a study" (Leininger, 1985, p. 107). Qualitative data are not generalizable in paradigmatic terms, and the exploratory nature of this study precludes any claims of generalization or transferability to other contexts. *Thick, rich,* and *profound* descriptions of the socially-constructed meanings (Seidman, 1998) in this naturalistic study allow the readers to formulate their own interpretations and make personal judgments regarding transferability to other contexts.

Dependability

The third criterion of trustworthiness, dependability or consistency, was suggested by Lincoln and Guba (1985) as a substitute for reliability. Dependability "seeks means for taking into account both factors of instability and design induced change" (Lincoln & Guba, 1994, p. 299). They suggested that dependability can be achieved by stating the investigator's position, using multiple methods of data collection and analysis, and by describing in detail how data were collected. Merriam (1998) also suggested the use of an audit trail. Dependability for this study was sought through these means. I stated my position as a researcher, used crystallization of multiple methods of data collection and analysis, and performed an *audit trail* in the later stages of research analysis to ensure that all data were accounted for within its final presentation (Lincoln & Guba, 1985). An audit trail was conducted through the cataloguing of participant data, analysis, findings, interpretations, and conclusions in a researcher journal.

Confirmability

Confirmability assesses the accuracy of the data rather than the objectivity of the inquirer (Lincoln & Guba, 1994). Confirmability refers to "obtaining direct and often repeated affirmations of what the researcher has heard, seen, or experienced with respect to the phenomena under study" (Leininger, 1985, p. 105). One way in which a naturalistic researcher can ensure the confirmability of his or her work is by practicing reflexivity (Guba, 1981). A research journal and audit trail assisted with the recording of data and validating that my interpretation of the data was as true to the perceptions of the participants as possible. During the data collection, I conducted *walk-throughs* and *observations*, keeping the *field notes* of what I noticed in each of the participating schools. Peer reviews were also conducted with the help of an *audit group*, which consisted of three key informants with extensive experience in educational administration. One of them was an official from the Chernivtsi Region Department of Education (formerly a teacher and a principal in several schools in the city), and the other two informants were principals from the participating schools. Peer reviews refer to "discussions with colleagues regarding the process of study, the congruency of emerging findings with the raw data, and tentative interpretations" (Merriam, 1998, p. 31). As it is evident, the methods for establishing trustworthiness overlapped in some cases to meet the criteria of credibility, transferability, dependability, and confirmability in this study.

Ethical Considerations

As this study involved the acquisition of personal information, ethical principles were considered during the data collection process. Ethical guidelines were followed to ensure that all the participants of the study were treated with respect and consideration. Before proceeding with data collection and analysis, approval was sought from the University of Saskatchewan Behavioural Sciences Research Ethics Board. Application for permission to conduct the study using outlined research methods was directed to the same committee. Approval for this study was granted by the University of Saskatchewan Behavioural Sciences Research Ethics Board.

Permission was obtained from the administrative personnel of the participating schools. The participants were informed of the nature and procedures of the study. They were informed that their participation was voluntary and they had the right to withdraw from the study at any time. Every effort was made to ensure the confidentiality and anonymity of the participants, including removal of names and details from quotes and descriptions that might reveal the identity of an individual, and by using pseudonyms and numeric labels when quoting the participants' statements. Because some of the data were collected using focus groups, my ability, as a researcher, to ensure confidentiality and anonymity of data was limited. Therefore, focus group participants were informed that there were limits to which the researcher could ensure the confidentiality of the information shared in focus groups. As a condition of participation, teachers signed a consent form acknowledging responsibility and agreement to protect the integrity and confidentiality of what others in the group had said during the focus group discussion. After the completion of the focus groups and interviews, participants were given opportunity to review their responses and to make any changes to their statements in the transcripts.

Sites and Respondents

The participants in this study were elementary and/or secondary school teachers in the city of Chernivtsi, Ukraine. All participants were volunteers and had been in the teaching profession within the education system of Ukraine during the period of time from 1991 to 2005. In total, fifty-five teachers participated in this study. Fifty-two of the participants were female teachers, while only three male respondents participated in the study. Despite all the efforts on my part to get a balanced gender representation of the respondents, participation was voluntary, and the numbers above seem to indicate greater willingness on behalf of female teachers to participate in this study. However, instrumental in this case was the overall decrease of male teachers in Ukrainian schools due to the unfavorable economic and social transformations.

Having received the permission from the Director of the Department of Education to conduct the research in Chernivtsi schools, I was assisted by the Deputy Director with the purposeful selection of the school sites. The intent was to include schools of various types, sizes, and languages of instruction. Eight schools were selected, including two elite schools (a lyceum and a gymnasium school), four general secondary schools (two medium-sized and two large schools), and two general secondary schools for national minorities (a Romanian and a Jewish school). According to the Law of Ukraine on General Secondary Education, schools in Chernivtsi are classified as secondary comprehensive schools – comprehensive educational institutions of levels I - III (I level – primary or elementary school, II level – basic school, III level – senior school, as a rule including professional specialization) (Supreme Council of Ukraine, 1999). A description of each of the eight school sites follows.

Site One was a lyceum, a comprehensive educational institution of the III level with specialized and professional training. Lyceums, as a new type of general secondary schools, were introduced into the system of education of Ukraine after the collapse of the former USSR. This particular lyceum was an elite school of about 200 students and 20 teaching staff, offering programs for grades nine to eleven. There were four focus group participants, three female teachers and one male teacher, whose teaching experiences ranged from fifteen to thirty nine years. All of the participants had worked in the lyceum since its opening in 1991. Three of them had previously worked in other schools, while one of the participants had only worked in the lyceum. Two of the focus group participants agreed to take part in the follow-up individual interviews. An additional individual interview was conducted with the principal of this school, a male teacher with approximately 20 years of teaching experience and more than 10 years of administrative experience.

Site Two was a gymnasium school. A gymnasium school is a comprehensive educational institution of levels II – III with in-depth study of selected subjects pursuant to specialization. In other words, gymnasium is a general-education secondary school preparing students for university. First gymnasium schools opened in Chernivtsi at the beginning of the 19th century, but when the region was incorporated into Soviet Ukraine, the gymnasia were replaced by Soviet ten-year schools. This form of school was reestablished in the period of independence of Ukraine. This particular gymnasium was a grade five to eleven school with approximately seven hundred students and fifty teachers, offering in-depth programs of study in foreign languages. Due to scheduling conflicts, the focus group meeting was not held in this school. Nevertheless, three female teachers agreed to participate in the individual interviews. Their teaching experiences ranged from 25 to 30 years.

Site Three, was a regular general secondary school offering a comprehensive program for grades one to eleven. It was of medium size, with approximately 700 students and 50 teaching staff. Eight of the teachers participated in the study; all of them were female teachers from elementary and secondary grades. The average teaching experience of these teachers was twenty-two years.

Most of the teachers had worked in this school throughout their teaching careers. Due to problems with scheduling and teaching loads, teachers could not participate in the follow-up individual interviews.

Site Four was a medium-sized comprehensive school with grades one to eleven and an enrolment of 800 students. There were about 50 teachers in this school. The focus group interview was conducted with six female elementary school teachers, whose average teaching experience was about 20 years and ranged from 15 to 27 years. Five of the teachers had previously worked in other schools, while one of them had been working in this school since the beginning of her teaching career. Two of the respondents participated in the individual interviews as a follow-up to the focus group discussion.

Site Five was a large comprehensive school of approximately 1000 students and 90 teachers. This school offered programs for students from grade one to grade eleven. It was located in one of the highly populated areas of Chernivtsi. Due to unpredictable circumstances, only three teachers participated in the focus group. They were female teachers; two of them taught at the secondary level in the school, and one of them was a teacher-librarian. Their teaching experiences ranged from 21 to 40 years. There were no individual interviews conducted with the focus group participants. One interview was conducted with the principal, a male teacher with more than 25 years of teaching and administrative experience.

Site Six, a large school complex, offered programs for students in grades one through eleven. The student enrolment in this school was around 2000, with the staff of approximately 120 teachers, 30 in elementary and 90 in secondary grades. The school was founded in 1989 to meet the needs of the new, rapidly expanding area of the city. The backbone of the school staff came from the neighboring school that could not carry the load of the fast growing student population in the area. There were two focus groups conducted in this school: first, with eleven experienced teachers, whose teaching experiences varied from seventeen to thirty-three years; and second, with nine younger teachers, whose teaching experiences ranged from nine months to eight years. All of the participants were female teachers, representing both elementary and secondary divisions of the school. Four participants from the first focus group interview agreed to participate in the follow-up individual interviews.

Site Seven was a comprehensive educational institution with an enrolment of approximately 500 students and teaching staff of approximately 35 teachers. This school offered instruction in Romanian and Ukrainian languages in grades one through eleven. Being opened in 1991, this was one of the first Romanian schools to be opened in the city. There were no Romanian schools in the Chernivtsi during the Soviet times. Seven teachers participated in the focus group interview, all being female elementary school teachers. The number of years these teachers spent working in the school ranged from 16 to 25 years; the average was 23 years. All of them were of Romanian nationality. Two of the focus group participants agreed to take part in the follow-up individual interviews.

Site Eight, a small, comprehensive school of approximately 400 students in grades one through eleven, was established in 1991. The teaching staff consisted of 25 teachers. This school offered Judaism Immersion programs of the "TALI" system of education, which stands for "Intensified Jewish Studies Curriculum". The languages of instruction in this school were Hebrew and Ukrainian. This school was the first Jewish school opened in Ukraine during the period of Independence. Due to unforeseen circumstances, only two teachers participated in the focus group, and there were no individual interviews conducted in this school. One of the participants had worked for approximately 25 years in the school system, while the other had over 30 years of teaching experience.

Guide to the Analysis and Presentation of the Data

The findings obtained from the data analysis were grouped and presented in accordance with the research questions for the study. In order to improve readability and presentation of the data in this book, the findings were divided into five chapters. Chapter Four presents the findings related to teachers' perceptions of the nature of post-Soviet societal changes, while Chapter Five discusses the impact of those changes on schools in general. The descriptions of nature of teacher collaboration follow in Chapter Six. Chapters Seven and Eight respectively present teachers' perceptions of the external and internal factors that influence collaboration among teachers in Ukrainian schools.

Presentations of findings in the following chapters include teachers' comments from the discussions in focus groups and interviews, as well as findings from the document analysis. In each of the sections, a brief discussion of the main themes is supported by the related statements from the documents and quotations from the participants' comments. Each of the respondents' quotations, coded and elicited with the help of ATLAS.ti qualitative data analysis software, contains pseudonyms of the participants and reference paths to the focus group or interview transcripts. The reference path consists of the transcript number, quote number, and paragraph number for each of the coded quotations in ATLAS.ti. Although I interpreted and systematically analyzed the transcripts for categories, it was essential that I presented the portion that best conveyed the essence and intent of teachers' responses. The stories and long quotations presented throughout the document add depth, thick description, and credibility to the findings. Moreover, in order to depict the dynamics of the conversations and interaction between focus group participants, it was necessary to include excerpts with the respondents' interchange of ideas and thoughts.

Summary of the Chapter

The purpose of this chapter was to outline the research design employed within this study. This study examined teachers' perceptions of the impact of societal changes on teacher collaboration in schools within the period of independence of Ukraine (1991 – 2005). These areas dealt primarily with ill-structured problems, characterized by many decision makers or stakeholders, numerous possible alternatives, competing definitions of the problem, and conflicting values to guide decision making. Therefore, it was appropriate to adopt a naturalistic paradigm orientation to this study. Within this paradigm, an interpretive constructivist approach to methodology prompted the use of qualitative methods of inquiry.

The data collection techniques of document analysis, focus group interviews and individual interviews were utilized in this study. Ministry of Education, Department of Education, and school policies and procedures that pertained to teacher collaboration issued during the period of 1991-2005 were reviewed, analyzed, and translated into English. Transcripts of all focus group discussions and individual interviews were analyzed and important issues that emerge were grouped into themes. The use of these methods sought to provide the study with rich, descriptive, and generous amount of information required to the analysis of the impact of societal changes on teacher collaboration in Ukrainian schools. The data analysis was an inductive process of inferring themes and patterns from examination of data.

In order to establish trustworthiness of the study, such naturalistic criteria as credibility, transferability, dependability, and confirmability along with corresponding empirical procedures were addressed. Such techniques as crystallization of the data, member checking, translation audit, audit trail, walk-throughs, observations, journals, field notes, and peer review in the audit group were used to affirm the trustworthiness of the study. Furthermore, ethical guidelines were followed to ensure anonymity and confidentiality of the participants in this study.

Chapter 4

TEACHERS AND POST-SOVIET SOCIETAL CHANGES

The changes were very significant… (Alla, 4:1, 10)

This chapter deals with teachers' perceptions of the nature of societal changes that took place after the collapse of the Soviet Union in 1991. Respondents commented about the nature and significance of the changes that influenced their professional and personal lives. Their comments are grouped into sections describing the nature and different types of transformations in the society.

The Nature of Societal Changes

In their responses to the questions regarding the nature of societal changes, teachers indicated that their perceptions were very subjective: for some teachers, who were in euphoria about the change, everything may have seemed positive; for others, who were pessimistic about the transformations, everything may have seemed negative. However, the majority of respondents argued that it was erroneous to state that changes were absolutely positive or absolutely negative in nature. They agreed that everything was different from what it used to be as a result of the collapse of the Soviet Union, which was seen as a major catalyst for change. Moreover, several of the respondents mentioned that the country was still in the process of transition and it was hard to evaluate the nature of change and its impact on society to the fullest possible extent.

Most of the participants noted that societal changes had both positive and negative outcomes for their personal and professional lives. The most common responses to the question about the nature of societal transformations was "fifty-fifty" or "both positive and negative". Different types of societal transformations, such as economic, political, ideological, philosophical, and social, were perceived to have many advantages and disadvantages. One of the teachers depicted the nature of the societal changes in the form of a parabola:

> You know, it seems to me that changes, if shown in a diagram, could be depicted in a form of parabola, because there was recession, there was a gradual ascent of our economy, our social conditions, our social life, even our relationships with people. There was such a decline, degradation of how people talked in an illiterate, ill-educated manner, but now it's changing. As for our work, there was a period when the attitude towards teacher's work, the attitude towards a teacher himself, has changed. After some time, gradually [the attitude] began to improve, due to social changes and changes in the government that tries to raise salaries, teacher's status, etc. However, this raise is so meager that we hardly feel it. If we look at our social lives and what we received from those changes, we can see that Ukrainian people became more penny-wise and began to live economically, adjust to European principles, or those American values that you have to spend money wisely and try to save something. All those changes that happened after the collapse of the USSR led to this. It was very hard to survive. Therefore, there was a need for change. Everyone seemed to get something positive out of it; there was some kind of organizing process for our individuality, for us as teachers, and others around us. (Rimma, 8:9, 32)

Thus, as it was vividly expressed by the majority of the participants, the change had a "double-sided" nature. There were also several teachers who perceived there were more negative changes than positive. For example, one participant commented: "What I can say is that there were a lot of changes, but none of them were beneficial for common people. What was done was beneficial for somebody else, a small circle of people… As for us, these changes went in a different [negative]

57

direction" (Vaselyna, 4:2, 18). However, none of the participants indicated that the nature of societal changes was solely positive or solely negative.

Types of Societal Transformations

Along with their perceptions regarding the nature of societal changes, teachers discussed changes in the various areas that had significant impact on their professional and personal lives. Their responses were grouped according to the following categories of changes outlined in the purpose of the study: *economic, ideological, philosophical, political*, and *social*. Economic change comments referred to the state of economy and transformations that affected the economic conditions of Ukrainian society after the collapse of the USSR. Ideological change referred to the societal transformations connected with the collapse of the Communist Party ideology of the Soviet Union. Discussing philosophical change, respondents related to the transition to different philosophies, perspectives, and systems of values and beliefs in the society. Political change presented the discussion about the shift in the civil, national, and public policies, as well as structure, order, and behavior at the government and local levels. Social change referred to change in the nature, the social institutions, the social behavior or relations of Ukrainian society, communities of people, or other social structures. These categories are mainly heuristic and there is a great degree of overlap between them.

Economic Change

The most frequently discussed area of societal changes was related to the economic situation in the country during the period of independence of Ukraine. Within their responses, teachers compared the state of economy in the Soviet times and the economic conditions of independent Ukraine, reflecting upon both positive and negative characteristics of economic change. The general feel of their responses was that, depending on categories of people, economic changes had their advantages and disadvantages. While transition to market economy and capitalist system allowed certain categories of population to increase their income and establish their own businesses, teachers remained disadvantaged due to inability to adapt to changing economic realities. One of the teachers noted:

> The changes were very significant. First of all, transition to market economy relations: we were used to work [in school], but now there is an opportunity to earn money somewhere else... We were brought up in one style, so to say – work. We weren't conscious of a possibility to earn money at the market... within that transition. It seems to me that this is most significant change. But it all depends on different categories of people: there were people who remained at work and were valuing this position as the apple of their eye; there were also others, less loyal to their position, who went and tried different things, earned some money and feel secure now. However, if you look at it from a certain perspectives, there are pros and cons. As it turned out, those people who were intellectually prepared [educated] by our Soviet higher education institutions, appeared to be in the lowest strata of the society, because they remained at their jobs, they had no opportunity to fulfill themselves in business, due to the fact that there's no possibility to do that if you are working [in school]. There was another drawback: in our higher institutions the issue of business as such was not studied, it was considered amoral, something from a capitalist society... and we were brought up differently, there were different ways to earn money... As it seems to me, that was the most significant change. (Alla, 4:1, 10)

There were several other respondents who discussed transition to a different system of economy. However, the above comment captured the life of teachers and choices they had to make in the beginning of the independence period.

Several respondents believed that transition to different economic relationships were instrumental in changing the social status of teachers. Such factors as economic change and ability of others to earn more than teachers influenced the societal attitudes towards schools and teachers. Other factors that influenced teachers' economic conditions were inflation, the need to work at two or three jobs to provide for their families, and finally, resigning as teachers to pursue more lucrative careers. One respondent, for example, noted:

> The social status of teachers changed, due to the fact that most people involved in schooling made money in other ways, which were not always honest. However, in comparison with teacher's salary, their income was 3 or 5 times higher. Sometimes, they earned 10 or 100 times more, depending on the nature of their activity. Certainly, societal attitudes towards teachers were changing as a result of these things. During this period, many left their teaching jobs. Besides, 1993, 1994, and 1995 were the years of high inflation, when amounts were changing considerably in the span of several months. In addition, teachers' salary payments were withheld. All of that influenced the conditions of teachers' lives, their consciousness, and somewhat collaboration with other teachers. Many teachers left their jobs in that time, they started working at the market, started businesses; in other words, tried to survive in those circumstances. Those who remained in school, searched for additional means of earning money. In order to survive in that situation and earn extra money, teachers relied on after-school or home tutoring or worked at several jobs, sometimes in several schools at the same time. This is one of the factors that influenced teachers' work. (Arkadiy, 14:2, 12)

Unlike the above comments that described the general picture of the influence of economic factors on teachers' lives with their advantages and disadvantages, the other comments were more specific about their positive and negative factors.

Positive factors. The factors that were seen as positive changes in the economy included development of entrepreneurship, permission to open private businesses, ability to earn extra money, permission to go abroad, and relative economic stability. One of the respondents noted that development of entrepreneurship and small businesses were some of the advantages of economic changes.

> For people, it has become possible to carry on business without obstacles... It was impossible before, but now people can carry on business.... But nevertheless, a lot of people managed to get up, and now feel more or less free and independent in terms of material welfare due to the development of entrepreneurship. A lot of small businesses were opened... I have more opportunities to compare things than others... they don't have [opportunities]. I can compare things because we moved to Russia in 1985 and moved back here from Russia in 1998. And what was here before, and what was here in 1998, it was such a big contrast... Those who stewed in their own juice did not notice anything, but it was very notable for us... What I left, and what I found here after thirteen and a half years... it was visible... It was developing... for example, in Russia there wasn't anything similar, no freedom or liberty... For a long time, everything was held in the hands of the state. When we used to come for a visit [to Ukraine], there was everything you needed in the stores here... the commerce was developing... They didn't have that there [in Russia].... I see those small businesses and firms develop and produce goods... and especially in the last couple years I notice a lot of people rise on their feet... We can sense that... (Lyudmyla, 1:10, 53-61)

Several teachers were confident that societal changes were positive, rather than negative, and their material welfare had improved as a result. One respondent believed that the economic situation gradually became more stabilized during the years of independence of Ukraine. Despite the fact that for many of her colleagues that was not the case, as they left their jobs, she believed that her situation was stable:

As Ukraine became independent 14 years ago, during each year life becomes more and more stabilized... even at work, during the last 14 years of a transition, a lot of teachers left their jobs, which is sad because they were good teachers, but their social status and their salary didn't allow them to work in their profession. For me personally, due to my family and their support I still managed to work [as a teacher], and I am very happy that I didn't leave this job. It is much better now, there is more stability. If you look at my family, my parents are pensioners and have a decent pension; I think my salary is at least within the limits of an average standard of living. However, with the changes that are happening right now, I don't feel very confident in the future. Maybe, this will change eventually. Everything that happens is for the better - that's my opinion. (Tonya, 17:1, 10)

Some of the teachers indicated that freedom to cross the borders of Ukraine and go abroad for trading purposes had positive economic outcomes for many people, who were involved in the process of buying goods abroad and selling them at the markets in Ukraine. In this respect, Lyuba observed:

For me personally, these changes related to material welfare. Salaries were increased; there were more opportunities to earn money. However, these opportunities to earn more money came up in other areas, not as a teacher. My husband went abroad, bought and sold cars, just like others who started doing business at that time. Therefore, there were more opportunities to earn money. I think these changes allowed everyone to work, even if they earned just a minimum wage. There is such an opportunity, it depends on person's desire to work or walk around as a beggar. (Lyuba, 9:1, 10)

Moreover, a possibility to go abroad in a search of employment was perceived as a positive change that allowed people to improve the financial conditions of their families:

The only change that was beneficial to me is that people were allowed to go abroad for work. Because, if they didn't allow people to find employment in other countries, I wouldn't be able to survive and provide a good living for my son. He had a trade certificate, but all factories and plants were closed in Chernivtsi at the beginning of these 14 years. All enterprises were closed; none of them functioned at the time when he obtained a technician's degree. He graduated from the mechanical-technological technical school, and there were absolutely no jobs in his specialty. Therefore, he went abroad to earn money and there he tries to survive. I haven't seen him for 7 years. This is the only change: they gave a possibility to find a job somewhere to survive. (Lyubomyra, 12:1, 10)

Another positive outcome was the ability of teachers to get credits from the banks to help with their financial situation.

What is unbelievable is that with our low salaries banks started credit programs for teachers. It is really good, because we can feel as normal people again: have an automatic washer, just like all normal people; have a better fridge, and not a small one, I would say, a very-very small one; buy furniture of better quality than before. Another thing is our salary. What has become better is that they finally started to pay it regularly; though it is scanty, it is paid on time, and we know that there will be advance payment on the 16th day of the month, and you can plan ahead; you know that there will be a full pay-day on the 30th. It is better, because you know what you can count on. (Lyubomyra, 12:5, 22)

However, along with the positive aspects of the credit program for teachers, there were drawbacks in terms of low teacher salaries:

I *did* notice that they allowed teachers to register for a waiting list for an apartment [provided by the government] ... and take a credit. But they didn't let teacher pay that credit off, because even if there is such a possibility to get the credit, there is no possibilities to pay that credit off, even in 30 years, just by means of the teacher's salary. Teachers will not be able to pay it off from their salaries. (Valentyna, 5:3, 32)

Teachers also added that in reality their salaries increased in the previous years. However, this was not a significant benefit for them, as the prices and cost of living increased too. Therefore, despite all the positive economic changes, teachers believed that negative factors were more prevalent.

Negative factors. Many teachers attributed the negative economic condition in the country to the fact that everything went upside down and the whole system of economy had to be rebuilt. Instability, unemployment, industrial decline, government corruption, poor financial situations and delays in salary payments were mentioned as the negative characteristics of economic transformations in Ukrainian society. Some of the respondents' comments indicated that the economic situation became worse, as industrial giants that functioned in Chernivtsi during the Soviet times were closed:

It seems to me that over the last years economy became even worse.... In our city, during the times of the Soviet Union, there were plants and factories functioning, but now there is nothing in Chernivtsi... Decline!!!... Why? Because everything was ... dispersed across the whole Soviet Union. For instance, some parts were produced across the Soviet Union, and at that time they wanted to open a lamp plant, but now it's impossible to do. That's why a lot of businesses are closed. It seems to me that it became even worse than it used to be in the Soviet Union. (Oksana, 1:8, 43-47)

Several respondents discussed the poor economic conditions and unemployment as shortcomings of the changing economic relationships, which resulted in poverty and appearance of homeless people on the streets.

There are many drawbacks, and a very big drawback is *unemployment* that we have now... which we didn't have... When I tell my son now about what it used to be like in the past, that if a young man came from the military service, after 2 or 3 months, he had to go to work... it was possible to choose where he wanted to work. And now? That's a huge shortcoming. Look how many people are unemployed, homeless... It was unheard of before that someone would rummage in the waste... Now you sometimes get sick from seeing how they stand and take something out of every waste container. That's terrible for us. Unemployment is a huge shortcoming that we see. (Emilia, 4:4, 18)

The following exchange between Oksana (O) and Lyudmyla (L) expressed the perceptions of the greater difference between the wealthy and the poor in society, which was not so obvious during the Soviet times:

O: I'd add that one can see now a greater difference between the wealthy and the poor. If it was veiled somehow before...

L: [interrupting] No, everyone was equal then...

O: Yes, everyone was equal then... But now [the difference] is very noticeable... There are people now who are beyond the poverty line, and there are people who are above the line...

L: The line of wealth...

O: Of course. If you consider those who started business going to Yugoslavia... Well, if you can call that a business, all they did was "buy and sell",

L: It was a kind of commerce...

O: Yes, you can call that commerce... So those people are better off now, they rent good offices, open their own firms... those people... But teaching profession... as it was poor, so it remained [poor] today... But in front of our school you can see people who even today rummage in garbage, collect food waste and eat... This year, my friend from [abroad] visited me, and she was shocked to see a man having breakfast... may God forgive me... over the garbage container, getting food waste from there and eating it... It was very scary... And at the same time, there are people who spend all their time, from morning till night, in casinos... So, we didn't feel such a difference before... Now, it is visible... (1:12, 63-75)

Moreover, these respondents connected negative developments in the country's economy to corruption at government and local levels. Lyudmyla and Oksana described corruption in the government in terms of avoiding tax payments and seizure of state property:

> L: ... when Verkhovna Rada [Supreme Council [Parliament] of Ukraine] passes normal laws... limits should be set to close the loophole that they used in order to take possession of the state enterprises... but others earned by their own hands, or as they say here in Ukraine, by their own hump [or hard toil]... and there are those who just grabbed it.
>
> O: If they say that there are members of parliament in Verkhovna Rada who have 350 million dollars in their accounts, and they pay the same taxes as a poor teacher pays from her 400 hryvnyas [national currency, UAH]...then you can understand what it is... And... before the Orange Revolution they probably paid even less...or kept in the shade.
>
> L: They haven't paid anything, they had fringe benefits... (1:15, 81-85)

Another respondent was confident that corruption at the governmental level negatively influenced the country's economy, as she believed that top officials were involved in gaining wealth by illegal actions:

> You know any event has both positive and negative sides. The positive side: we gained democracy! However, how do we use it? What does it mean? Does it mean an impunity, disrespect of the laws? It all starts with the top level of the government. This is due to the lack of skills. Maybe we should have been taught to use it, and then... I read yesterday that [Minister of Economy of Ukraine] bought out the shares of 'Inter' TV channel having paid for them 200 million dollars. Tell me please. He is a relatively young, smart person...I consider him a very highly intellectual person, I thought that economy will rise to the unknown levels. What happened? Where is our economy? Dragging behind! However, [the minister] managed to pay such a sum. Tell me, I have been working for over 40 years. What have I earned? Yes, maybe I am not a business lady; I have worked as a school principal for 15 years and haven't earned anything for myself... Even if you think of a sum 100 times less, I didn't earn that. Where do they take that money? (Lena, 7:17, 49)

Corruption at the macro (government) level was seen as the cause of bribery and corruption at the micro level, including the system of education:

> [In the USSR] those who entered higher education institutions - usually they were the smartest ones, it was rare that someone could bribe someone. What happens now? Only those who have money study now. But those who are smart - seldom do smart and talented study in higher institutions. That's how it is. However, we will see the consequences of this in 10-20 years in what kind of doctors, specialists we will have... because there are instances when students of higher institutions do not even prepare [for classes], do not even take textbooks in their hands – they know that it costs 25 EURO to pass the examination, so they relax and hang out... And that's the majority. (Emilia, 4:4, 18)

Teachers believed that the above-mentioned phenomena of bribery and corruption were prevalent in society and had significant implications for their work. Teachers felt these negative aspects greatly decreased students' willingness to study in schools, as students saw that their future success would depend more on financial prosperity than on their knowledge.

Negative aspects of the economic situation were seen to directly influence schools and teachers' work. Schools were forced into the survival mode due to the lack of funding from the government for programs and resources. As a result, teachers had to work without appropriate textbooks and other instructional resources:

> As for the economic situation in the first few years, it was difficult to buy textbooks, as there was no funding or support from the government. Even now, they provided us with the textbooks for elementary grades 1 to 3, but, unfortunately, their level is not adequate for our school, as we have an intensive study program, and traditionally our standards are very high. Unfortunately, the level of textbooks is inadequate, and we have to make our own lesson plans to add to the textbook recommended by the Ministry of Education or use other textbooks to keep the high level of learning in our school....
>
> It used to be very difficult. And it is still difficult, because you have to find different ways to survive when you haven't received salary for 3 years. Also, it influenced our work, as we could not create our own teaching and methodological resource base.
>
> By the way, I forgot to mention that now we have good methodological resource books, and we often receive them from abroad as humanitarian aid. We did not have anything like that in the first years of independence; there was no access to advanced technology and resources. We had to make everything up somehow, and then it turned out that what we made up had already existed and had a certain name. (Sophia, 22:2, 12-16)

The issue of teacher wages and salary seemed to be the most widely mentioned negative factors of economic changes. Some of the most frequently discussed aspects were low teacher salaries, delay in salary payments, and increase in the cost of living. Comparing their salaries in the Soviet Union and independent Ukraine, many teachers indicated that under the Soviet regime, they could afford to do more with the amounts they received as school teachers; moreover, they had enough to help their relatives:

> For 90 rubles I could really live for a month, save some for summer vacation, and help my mother.... And [my apartment expenses were] paid by the state. As a young specialist, in the village, they paid for the coal, firewood, apartment.... At that time my rate of wages was 1.5, and I earned 170 rubles, whereas, my mother, as a medical worker, received 80. Thus, I had enough to help my mother and go on vacation... (Oksana, 1:30, 442-469)
>
> I will tell you that I used to go to two resorts [in the summer].... I used to get vacation pays and together with my husband, we had more than 2000 [rubles], and during the summer we could afford to go to two resorts – to the seaside and to the spa. That's how we used to live. ...We dressed up really well... and never starved... (Ilona, 3:13, 214-228)

A few other teachers also commented along these lines. In the following excerpt, several focus group participants, Anna (A1), Lena (L1) and Antonina (A2), discussed so-called "savings-bank books" or saving accounts, where teachers were able to set aside money from what they had been paid. After the collapse of the Soviet Union, all of those books were annulled and teachers lost all their savings:

> A1: What is the most important in regard to the economic situation is that as a young specialist in 1981 when I started working, from my salary of 110 rubles I could set aside 50 rubles for the savings-bank book...
>
> L1: Which have disappeared eventually...
>
> A1: ...and for the rest, 60 rubles, I could live for a month, buy clothes... but as for my salary now, not to mention that I can't set anything aside, it is impossible to exist even in regard to the subsistence minimum wage.

A2: I would like to continue along these lines. As a mathematician, I like numbers. Even if we disregard the money [on the savings-bank books] that has disappeared... Think of this: Those who had seniority [length of service] over 15 years received almost 200 rubles. I could add 40 more and I could buy a fridge for 240. I do not set anything aside, but imagine if I set some amount aside for three months, I could buy this, and this, and that. Nowadays, we can't buy anything. I bought a fridge for a credit, but I have been paying it off for two years already. I am praying at it ... and I think that it's good that they gave me this credit on one hand, but on the other hand, what if it starts to break and I haven't paid it off yet? (5:10, 63-69)

In addition, several respondents commented that teachers' salaries remained at the same low level due to the overall poverty and inability to pay taxes in the society.

Several respondents stated that the most difficult period of time for them was right after the proclamation of Independence of Ukraine, when prices were changing every day and the level of inflation was immense. Often teachers were not paid at all or there were considerable delays with salary payments. As Tonya noted, the most difficult period was:

I would say...1990-1994, those four years when they didn't pay salaries, when we weren't sure about 'the ground where we stood'... I don't want to say that material welfare is at the forefront of my life, but a lot of things depend on it. I think that this period was very hard in the life of all Ukrainians: for 70 years we were brought up within a certain society and system of values, and it all has suddenly changed. Beginning of 1990's was the hardest period. Right now we are used to a different life.

Interviewer: What was the longest time they didn't pay salaries [to teachers]?

During this very period of time, beginning of 1990's... till mid 1990's.

Interviewer: How long? Half a year?

No, it was more than half a year. Two or three years. It's not that we weren't paid at all, but there was a huge delay in payments. For example, we would receive vacation pay in October or November, or salary payments would be delayed, but it never happened that we weren't paid at all; at least I know that was the case in our city, Chernivtsi. It happened in other cities, though. There are many criteria that influence our salary, such as experience, degrees, and teacher categories. None of these were paid at that time, just the rate... though it was paid with delay too. They are talking about returning those debts now, with all of the additional payments for those years. [They weren't returned yet]. (Tonya, 17:3, 18-30)

One of the teachers, however, stated that salaries weren't paid for even longer time than two or three years. She also added that the arrears of wages have not been returned in full:

Interviewer: What was the longest period when teachers didn't receive salary?

I think it started in 1995. Yes, from 1995 to 2003. Only for the last two years we started to feel a little bit better, as normal people.

Interviewer: Did they pay off the arrears of wages?

No, they weren't paid off, and I am afraid that they will not be returned completely. I would have to be paid a lot more for prolonged meritorious service. Nobody even talks about paying for having worked a certain quantity of years, because there is no funding. Unfortunately, those savings that I managed to put aside during the Soviet times were annulled when Ukraine became independent. In those times teachers were able to save some money, and I, too, put 2000 rubles aside. Nevertheless, I lost them; though I could have spent them on something. Unfortunately, they will not be returned at all. (Lyubomyra, 12:5, 24-30)

Additional data were also found in the analysis of the documents. In July 2005, Cabinet of Ministers of Ukraine enacted a decree about the order of paying off arrears of wages to the workers of system of education of Ukraine. This referred to payments for long service increments and vacation pays during the period from January, 1997 to August, 2002. Furthermore, official minimal monthly salary of a teacher, as of September 1, 2005, was 332 UAH [approximately 70 CAD] (Chepil', 2005).

Respondents believed that school teachers were more preoccupied with how to survive in such circumstances than with how to teach and grow professionally. One of the teachers expressed the view that poor salaries and delays in payments made teachers think more about material welfare than spiritual development:

> Another thing is that we have a lot of trouble now because we are not materially capable. We can't afford those things that could fill our souls. We think more about how to fill our stomachs. We had a one-month delay in the salary and you had to scrape off all money in reserves to make that pancake, cook potatoes, because you have no money to buy other things. What if you ran out of those things? In a couple of weeks you would not even be able to have that in your house. It's very depressing when a person is concerned with material encumbrance. This influences almost everything: children, us, teachers, our students. Maybe, if these problems were solved, our ideals would change. For example, I dream to see the world. I would like to go abroad, not for business; I am not interested in clothes, fashionable things, etc. I would like to see cultural monuments of the world art. I teach foreign literature and 'my mouth waters' when I talk about Dresden Gallery, Louvre, something else. You look at those illustrations, those photos, and think, 'God, I will pass away, half of my life is gone, and I haven't been a part of that'. Why? Just because of money. If I had money, I would spend it on that. It seems to me that people of my generation feel the same. In the West, where the system is put right, pensioners can afford the rejuvenation: they travel; they participate in some organizations, charities, etc. They have means for that. That's why I think that our life is much worse compared to that of our colleagues abroad. (Stella, 7:14, 77)

She concluded that it is very depressing to always be concerned with material encumbrance rather than professional duties.

As a result of various negative aspects of economic change, many educators left their teaching careers in search of better-paid and more prestigious jobs. As some participants observed, this trend was especially evident among male teachers, who moved out of their teacher positions due to low salaries, delays in salary payments, and loss of teacher status. As main breadwinners, male teachers found themselves under immense pressure to provide for their families and believed that as teachers they could not fulfill that responsibility. This trend started in the first years of Independence and continued to grow in the recent years. One of the participants, Sonya, shared about a 24-year old male teacher who had worked for 2 years in their school and traded teaching for a better-paid job at the market:

> I don't know about his plans; maybe he wants to continue his education, wants to get married, or has some other dreams. Can this young man afford all of this being a teacher? By the way, he belongs to the category of teachers who work very well, students liked him very much, and he blended very well with the school collective. He was offered a job outside of his specialty, but the pay is two or three times higher than that of a school teacher. He said that he did not even hesitate to accept that offer. (13:2, 74)

Document analysis also revealed that many male educators resigned as teachers and either worked outside of their profession in Ukraine or went abroad to Spain, Portugal, Norway, or Russia to provide for their families (Myts', 2004). In addition, statistical data from the UNESCO Global Monitoring Report indicated that male teachers in the 2002/2003 school year constituted only 1% in primary education and 22% in secondary education institutions (UNESCO Institute for Statistics,

2005).

Summary. This section described the respondents' perceptions regarding the economic transformations in the society after the collapse of the Soviet Union. In general, teachers reflected upon both positive and negative aspects of economic change. The factors that led to positive changes in the economy included development of entrepreneurship, permission to open private businesses, ability to earn extra money, permission to go abroad, and relative economic stability. Rebuilding of the system of economy, transition to the new economic relationships, inflation, instability, unemployment, industrial decline, government corruption, inadequate financial remuneration, and delays in salary payments were mentioned as the negative characteristics of economic transformations in Ukrainian society. As a result of these changes, schools had to survive without appropriate funding, support, and resources from the government. Moreover, comments of the participants indicated that the societal attitudes toward schools and teachers changed due to the fact that teachers' job lost its prestige and financial profitability. Therefore, many educators (especially male teachers) left their teaching jobs in search of more lucrative careers. The topic of societal attitudes toward schools and teachers will be elaborated on in greater detail in the later sections of this chapter.

Ideological Change

The teachers' responses indicated that most of the ideological transformations were connected with the collapse of the Communist Party ideology of the Soviet Union. The issues discussed by the respondents included ideological pressure, ideological training for teachers and principals, ideologically-laden system of youth organizations in schools, and change in the perceptions of moral values and ideals.

Several respondents reminisced about the ideological pressure they had to withstand in the Soviet times. One of the respondents described the number of hours she had to spend as a university student on the subjects that inculcated students in the ideologies of the Soviet Union. Furthermore, as a school teacher she had been required to use aspects of ideological training in the process of instruction:

> We studied a lot of redundant stuff in the Soviet times. When I checked my addendum to the diploma and counted the hours, it turned out that we spent 30 hours on Methodology of Teaching, while we spent 200 hours on Political Economy, a lot of time on Scientific Communism, different types of history, like history of Communist Party of Soviet Union. These subjects are not necessary now according to the present lifestyle. ... When I was a young specialist, I had never gone to bed before two o'clock in the morning, only after I went over all the lesson plans and made sure it related to the program of study. I saved all those lesson plans and one can vividly see the ideology that was offered to us. In fact, when a principal visited classes, he always wanted to hear where Brezhnev was at that time... I remember, when I had an open lesson, and a deputy secretary of the Regional Committee of the Communist Party was supposed to come... but somehow he didn't come to class, so the principal came alone. At that time, I was teaching from the biography of Leo Tolstoy in Grade 9 (we used to have 10-year schools then)... And the latest news at that time was that Brezhnev visited 'Yasnaya Polyana' reserve... When I told him that he almost covered me with kisses, because I managed to connect such a story with Brezhnev. (Stella, 7:3, 16)

Another focus group participant, Lena, had a similar story to tell. However, unlike the previous respondent, she did not conform to the rules and decided not to connect the topic of her lesson to the Communist Party resolutions:

> I once had a topic about Artiodactyla, and I had to connect it to the materials of the Communist Party Congress... I was overwhelmed! I thought of many ways how to do that... No, it was about Perissodactyla. All I could talk about was equestrian sports. I told them that

they will have their Party resolutions later, and taught a lesson according to my plan. What else could I do? (Lena, 7:3, 18)

The same respondent reminisced about the fact that in order to become a principal, one had to occupy several positions to gain experience and go through all the stages of professional and ideological training:

We should not blame everything to the old system. You know, we all were so glad to see the new system. We were very happy. We have survived through a lot within the [old] system. You see, people came into the new system without the experience; cadres used to be connected with politics before. The secretary of the City Committee of the Communist Party told me once, 'One more year and we wouldn't be able to make you a principal', because I would have been 45 years old. I was 44 years old at that time. 'We wouldn't take you as a principal'. I had to go through re-training courses... A person had to go through all the levels of occupation, all fields of work. I did that: I worked as a secretary of Komsomol [Комсомол (an abbreviation of Коммуністичний Союз Молоді or the Young Communist League) - the third echelon of Soviet Youth organizations] organization, a member of Party Bureau, a supernumerary secretary of district committee of Komsomol, a member of regional committee of Komsomol, then I was sent to professional courses three times, all-Ukrainian conferences... I continued to study. Another thing is that I knew all the tricks of the trade of school life, from all sides. That was a sure thing that it was hard to fool me when I became the school principal. (Lena, 7:10, 53-55)

During the Soviet era, the ideological education in the schools relied on the system of youth organizations that was prevalent in the system of education. One of the respondents described them as ideology-laden organizations that disciplined students. She also believed that existence of such organizations, despite their ideological bias, had positive outcomes for organizing students:

It was both positive and negative. There was the Zhovtenyata organization [Жовтенята - Ukrainian for *Oktyabryata* or *Children of October*, the first echelon of Soviet Youth organizations)], Pionery organization [Піонери - the *Pioneers*, the second echelon of Soviet Youth organizations], Komsomol organization [Комсомол (an abbreviation of Коммуністичний Союз Молоді or the Young Communist League) - the third echelon of Soviet Youth organizations] that disciplined children more. From the very beginning, in 1990s, everything was collapsing, so for the first 2 or 3 years there were no organizations at all. Children were between the society, school and parents in some kind of space... Now there are difference organizations, like Kozachata [Козачата - little Cossacks], Strumochky [Струмочки - Brooklets], Barvinchata [Барвінчата - little Periwinkles], that unite students. We hope that sometime there will be one organization; it will be more convenient, stable, and better. (Nina, 2:5, 30)

The collapse of the system of youth organizations, which was aimed at upbringing youth and students in the spirit of Communist ideology, resulted in the weakened ideological pressure in the schools. Teachers did not feel as much ideological pressure in the times of independent Ukraine as they did in the Soviet times. As a result, moral values and ideals in the society and schools have changed:

First of all, our field of work has changed substantially due to the fact that there was less ideological pressure on us and there were fewer problems that were solved by the Communist Party Regional Committee or Komsomol Regional Committees. There is greater freedom in the direction of work and in decision-making. On the one hand, it is really good, but on the other hand, it is hard to reorganize after having always worked according to one schedule, and now you have complete freedom. It affected the society too. The moral values have changed. We used to consider Pavlik Morozov a hero; he was a role model for children. Nowadays, we, older generation, try to keep silent about this issue, because younger generation considers him as a family traitor. According to the moral assumptions of present time, his actions are considered negative. The moral values have been revised according to the actions of heroes. Olexandr Matrosov, who used to be an ideal of boldness, courage, and patriotism, is spoken of as a person who drank a lot and covered the loophole. They started to talk about Zoya Kosmodem'yanska – that her great heroic deed was fictitious. For us, older generation teachers, it is really hard to orient ourselves in this, because since our childhood we were brought up that these were real heroes and we honestly considered that true and sincerely believed that those people had the exemplary traits of character. (Stella, 7:1, 10)

Former ideals of the Soviet times and their significance have been revised in times of Independence. The following exchange between Stella (S) and Lena (L) vividly described the shift in the perceptions of ideals:

S: It used to be different before: if someone was a patriot, then he did some heroic feats; if someone was good, like Vladislav Titov from 'Against all the Deaths' - a story about a coal miner who lost arms and legs saving his friends, when he threw his body over the burning cable to prevent the explosion in the mine…

L: Or Matrosov who threw himself onto the embrasure…

S: Yes, now they say that Matrosov was a drunkard, and [Titov] was a fool because he did something like that. Children are inclined more to the latter point of view, but not to what the people from older generations tell them. (7:16, 143-147)

Such shift in the system of ideals was observed not only in schools, but in the society in general.

Summary. This section described the respondents' perceptions regarding the ideological transformations after the collapse of the Communist Party ideology, which was dominant in the Soviet society. The respondents discussed the issues of ideological pressure of the Soviet regime, ideological training for educators, and ideologically-laden youth organizations in the Soviet system of education. They observed that the weakened ideological pressure in the independent times led to changes in the system of moral values and ideals.

Philosophical Change

Teachers reflected upon events and phenomena related to the transition to different philosophies, perspectives, and systems of norms, values, and beliefs in the society. Although the experiences and backgrounds of the respondents were diverse, common perceptions of philosophical change emerged. In the discussion of philosophical transformations in the Ukrainian society during the period of Independence, the following aspects were mentioned by the respondents: perceptions of national identity, development of Ukrainian language instruction, establishing of national schools, freedom of conscience, freedom of speech, freedom of religion, and change in the system of norms and values.

National identity issues. The fact that Ukraine became independent from the Soviet Union was very important in the lives of teachers as it brought change in their self-perception as citizens of the new country. Though it required time for teachers to realize it, they continued to support this event in the life of Ukraine. For some, it was a long-awaited change, and because of hope they were ready to overcome all difficulties of the transition period. Others expressed doubts and disbelief and compared things to the Soviet times.

First of all, the most important change was that Ukraine became independent from the Soviet Union. For teachers, it was a transition in their self-perception as teachers. It was a societal change that occurred at the level of consciousness, as teachers identified themselves as citizens of independent state, Ukraine. As a result, they had to include this perception into their subjects, instruction, education, etc. This transition momentum was observed for some time, as people still identified themselves as citizens of the Soviet Union. This transition was noticeable until 1993 or 1995. It was very obvious in the society: people continued to speak Russian; transition from instruction in the Russian language to Ukrainian language instruction was very difficult. People doubted whether transition was the right thing to do; periodically, doubts would come up in conversations about whether life was better or worse in the Soviet Union, etc. Teachers, as society members, always compared what used to be with what was happening at that time. This societal change was very noticeable. (Arkadiy, 14:1, 10)

One of the factors that contributed to the development of awareness of the national identity was the language. Article 10 of the Constitution of Ukraine (1996) guaranteed free development, use, and protection of Ukrainian language, as well as languages of national minorities. Gradually, Ukrainian language became more widely used in the society for everyday communication and instruction in schools:

The most important thing was that we started speaking Ukrainian language, and people learned that there is such a country as Ukraine. In addition, 20 years ago when my children were born, my husband said then, "Even if I have to drive for 20 kilometers, I will still drive them to the Ukrainian school [where language of instruction is Ukrainian]", because our school was Russian, and Ukrainian was taught as a Second Language. When he saw me marking students' exercise books, he was shocked that children do not know their native Ukrainian language. He said, "I will take them anywhere to have Ukrainian language taught in that school." Nowadays, though they speak Russian when they call home, within the school setting they communicate in Ukrainian. This is already a big advantage. They know they are Ukrainians, they grow up knowing this. (Lina, 18:1, 10)

However, not only people of Ukrainian nationality experienced change in the development of their national identity. In general, awareness of other nationalities in the society increased. According to the Constitution, citizens of Ukraine that belong to national minorities have a right, guaranteed by Constitution and educational legislation, to receive education in their native languages (Ministry of Education of Ukraine, 2004). One of the recommendations from the local educational authorities was to consider multiethnic specifics of national education in multinational Chernivtsi region (Department of Education and Science of Chernivtsi Regional State Administration, 2003). Such national minorities as Romanian and Jewish people became able to practice their traditions, speak their native languages, and provide education to their children. Many respondents indicated that national schools became places for nurturing their cultures:

Also, development of national schools… something, that wasn't allowed in the Soviet Union times. Our school was founded in 1991, and we received the Charter of Honour from our President at that time, Kravchuk, who greeted us with the opening of the first Jewish school in Ukraine. This can be considered a change too. (Oksana, 1:4, 18)

As for my family, opening of this school was very important for us, because my husband was a principal and he opened this school. This was the first school in the center of the city, as there were no Romanian schools in the city during the Soviet Times. There were a few in the rural areas of our region; in the city, they were in the outskirts. This school was opened in 1991. (Lyuba, 9:2, 12)

Most of the participants believed that the opening of national schools after the collapse of the Soviet Union contributed greatly to the development of identities of national minorities.

The stories of the events significant to the participants were often profound and extraordinary. The following story depicts how difficult it was to identify with the national minorities in the Soviet times, and how it changed with the collapse of the USSR:

We used to have a Jewish school in Chernivtsi before, it was closed ..., there was a Jewish theater and a school, they were closed... When we opened our school in 1991, we used to have a very small building, a former kindergarten with windows that grew into the ground, just like a country hut... That was our first building. We had 80 people... we didn't have our dining hall, and when we used to walk with children to a different school for lunch, our kids were walking on the streets and singing songs in Hebrew. You should have seen those people on the streets... who haven't heard Hebrew language in Chernivtsi for a long time! Some speak Yiddish, but here are children, Grade 1 students... they were born without any complexes, they were conscious [of their origin] at the age of 7, they turned 7 years old in 1991. These grade-one students were walking on the street, not afraid to wear kippah on their heads, a little skull cap... so they were walking and freely singing songs about Jerusalem in Hebrew as people stopped on the streets, turned around and could not understand what was going on... our children didn't have any complexes... It was so wonderful... We used to walk sometimes and turn around, afraid of what would happen... you know what could happen to Jewish people and other minorities... In 1991 it was very interesting to observe all that...when children would freely walk on the streets and say, "I am *Jewish*, I'm not afraid of this, I *am* Jewish!" When he was asked who he was, he would say "I am Jewish." (Oksana, 1:19, 213)

An event like this was deemed unimaginable and impossible during the Soviet regime. As a contrast to the above story, this respondent recollected about a little girl who was afraid to say she was Jewish in the Soviet times:

I used to work in a different school - and we had a teacher who was Jewish and had a little girl at home, Renata... when we came [to their house], she said to us, "Ring the bell and ask her name", we asked and she said her name was Marusia... Her name was Renata, and she was taught to say that her name was Marusia so that people wouldn't know that she was Jewish... and then she ate matzah [Jewish bread]... and when asked, "What do you eat, Renata?" she would say, "Chips". That little 4-year old kid could not say that her name was Renata and her last name was Korenburg, for example; could not say that she ate matzah, because it was prohibited at that time. So, 1991 came and we were able to open this school, speak freely... Nowadays, when children sit on the other end of a trolleybus and a teacher enters through the front doors, they can shout across the trolleybus, "Shalom". Thus, children are not afraid now. It means a lot! Praise God we have this! (Oksana, 1:19, 217)

The respondents in this focus group believed that the above events were indicative of a greater freedom of conscience than was observed during the Soviet era.

Freedom of religion. Several participants shared their experiences with a greater freedom of religion in comparison with the Soviet times. They reminisced that expressing religious beliefs and attending the church in the Soviet times were prohibited. One of the respondents mentioned how she was afraid to express her Christian beliefs due to the fear of losing her job in the school:

When the Soviet Union collapsed, even in the last years of the Soviet Union, people obtained liberty – churches were opening, we could take our children to church, and people turned to God – things that were absolutely forbidden in the Soviet Union. In the Soviet times, whenever there was a religious holiday, there were different activities planned in the school, such as staff meetings, associations meetings, etc., which were obligatory to attend. In the times of independent Ukraine, all of this disappeared, and people experienced religious liberty. During the Soviet times, we could not even christen our children. I remember an instance when one of my colleagues christened her child and immediately lost her job. I christened my children in the times of independent Ukraine, because, to be honest with you, I was afraid... afraid to lose my job... (Roksolana, 10:3, 18)

Evidences of freedom of religion were also observed in the analysis of Ministry of Education of Ukraine decrees and acts. These documents and statistical data revealed that course of Christian Ethics had been officially taught in Chernivtsi schools since 1999 with the purpose of surmounting moral and spiritual crisis in the country and promoting moral and ethical education of youth (Religious Information Service of Ukraine, 2006).

Closely connected with the religious freedom was the notion of changing loyalties in the society. Respondents believed that people's ideological and philosophical views changed according with the times. When it was forbidden to attend churches, they were loyal to the Communist Party; nowadays, people are loyal to churches:

> I can't miss the opportunity to say that all those who punished common teachers for attending the church, baptizing their child, or being godparents for their friends, now have put such crucifixes on their necks that the world hasn't seen. The same people! Tell me how that is possible! ...
>
> When I first came to work, I got my first reproof... For what!? The secretary of the school [Communist] Party committee comes to my class and says, "Kids, who has at home... (It was Grade 1, I was teaching in elementary school at that time) ...Kids who has those nice, colorful eggs at home?" Of course, if they are nice and colorful, then grade one students all raise their hands. "And who has those big kalaches [kalach - kind of dough roll], baked in a clay stove, at home, that you brought to the [Orthodox] church?" Of course, all grade one students raise their hands. So, my first reproof was because my students went to church to hallow paskha [Easter cake]. When they came to my colleague's classroom and asked the same questions ... in general, my colleague had students of Jewish nationality, because the teacher was Jewish... but no one knew that they were Jewish at that time... and all children of Jewish nationality started to raise their hands, until the teacher told them, "Why do you raise your hands? Church?! Easter eggs?! So, the kids of that age were bribed... if that's the right word... by the fact it was nice, to get a record of how many children were in that church... And now these secretaries of [Communist] Party committees put crosses on their necks and stand in church... Maybe, they pray for their sins or put on a show...or because it's fashionable now? (Oksana, 1:21, 225-229)

This respondent also believed that ideological loyalties may change again with time:

> Who are in power now? The same Komsomol workers, Party members, who hid their Party-membership cards on the shelves....And then they'll retrieve them again, when the time comes, and take their crosses off [their necks]... and will be [in power] again ... (Oksana, 1:23, 236-240)

Thus, the change in loyalties was seen as a temporary phenomenon, prone to change along with the shift of perspectives in society. Through their responses, teachers expressed the uncertainty that change was permanent and believed that the society was still in the period of transition.

Freedom of expression and speech. Another freedom mentioned by teachers was freedom of expression or speech. The respondents believed that it was closely connected with the national identity that established after the declaration of Independence and hopes for a better future:

> The most significant changes? People realized that they are Ukrainians, that they have their own country, the country of Ukraine. People can speak freely, freely express themselves... about what we read in the history, what we strived for, and dream that it will come true... sooner or later... and we will become a really independent country. (Lina, 2:1, 10)

> People became more liberated, can express their views freely, both negative and positive, and dream about better future. We hope that it will come true one day and we'll see it, not just our children, or grandchildren. (Nina, 2:2, 14)

Teachers claimed that society became more liberated and people were no longer afraid to express their opinion, even if it was a criticism of the government or school officials:

> I wanted to say about the freedom of speech. There is definitely change in that. You can freely express your point of view, you are not afraid to say something... unlike it used to be when we were afraid to say something about those Ministers, there wasn't anything like this before. That is an advantage. (Emilia, 4:3, 18)

> On the one hand, it is more open, we became more liberated, and we can express our points of view. We are not afraid of anyone. When I was a student myself, there was this feeling of awe, and I was always afraid of the principal. Nowadays, we communicate at all levels, at the same time respecting older people and following the subordination in school. (Antonina, 11:3, 14)

Access to published works that were forbidden in the Soviet times was seen as a great contribution to the freedom of expression: "Access to published work... If before we had to read, say, Sakharov, on the sly, then now we can freely find his work in stores or get it from the library... There is no prohibition on literature now..." (Oksana, 1:7, 35). Her colleague also mentioned the access to information without any censorship, which was observed in the Soviet times: "[There is] no censorship... Something that we couldn't do before... We have a lot of information ... about the country, people... It became easier to work in the school..." (Lyudmyla, 1:7, 37). Teachers indicated that their worldview became broader, as a result of access to information and knowledge that was unavailable to them before the collapse of the Soviet regime. Teachers were able to have access to information that was no longer single-sided, but was expressed from different perspectives:

> Also, the history. We didn't have literature before. I remember when in times of Gorbachev, there appeared first books and textbooks; we loaded our library with them, because there was no Ukrainian literature at that time... There were no books by Hrushevsky or other famous [Ukrainian historians]; we only taught from the Soviet textbook, we only knew what was conveniently described from one perspective, but we didn't know the other perspective on the history, about Mazepa and others. It was one sided, we knew about them, but from a different perspective. Nowadays, our children have opportunities to learn [from a different perspective], and it's readily available. They say that people seek something that's not easily available, but when it is available, they don't want to use it. When everything is allowed, it's not used very often. (Lina, 18:4, 12)

Though freedom of speech was mostly seen as a positive change, some pessimistic attitudes were also expressed by the participants. One teacher explained: "Freedom of speech - we have the right to say whatever we want. However, we do not see any changes as a result of this freedom" (Lyubomyra, 12:4, 18). This teacher felt that despite the fact that people were given the right to freely express their opinions, they did not really have a say in what was happening in the society.

Change in norms and values. Respondents discussed that as a result of philosophical transformations in the society, the existent system of values, norms, and beliefs was deprecated. However, the new system of norms and values has not been fully established yet. A number of respondents believed that monetary values prevailed in the society because respect depended on one's wealth. One of them explained that society strove for money and material welfare:

> It seems to me that a lot of old [norms] were deprecated, but the new [norms] have not established yet....
>
> I mentioned some of the examples before about the reviewed patriotism. They bring some kind of psychological discomfort in perceptions of what is good and what is bad. Our society is sharply divided according to their points of view. It is really hard for a young person to find out where truth is and who is right. Our country is still in the condition when

everything is boiling and 'the i's aren't dotted and the t's aren't crossed'.

Therefore, it is very difficult to define an ideal of what they used to call before, 'a moral look of the communism builder', which you had to strive for and according to which you had to construct your stereotype. It does not exist now; everything is deprecated, everything from the past is bad. What does 'good' have to be like now?

As [my colleague] mentioned, somehow a rich person is [more respected]. At least they consider themselves as such. But in those foreign cheap movies that come to us, you will never see how someone earns those millions. Never. On the contrary, you see how they spend the whole day in the restaurants, bars, different love affairs, etc., but no one knows where the money comes from. Therefore, our youth think that it like that abroad and we have to look like them and wait for the money to fall on your head from above. (Stella, 7:15, 127-141)

The subsequent conversation between the focus group participants conveyed the shift from collectivistic to individualistic philosophical views in the society:

The only thing here is that we used to say, 'Think first about your Motherland, and then about yourself'. Now, it's, 'Think first about yourself and then about others'. This might be the reason. God's commandments say, 'Don't kill. Don't steal'. What do we have? A completely opposite situation. Why do we have that? (Lena, 7:9, 49)

Many of the respondents, especially the teachers in the focus group conducted with the young teachers, indicated a greater emphasis on individuality in the society as compared to the Soviet times, when collectivistic perspectives prevailed.

Summary. This section described the teachers' perceptions regarding different aspects of the philosophical change. In their comments, respondents dwelt upon the issues of national identity, development of Ukrainian language instruction, and establishing of national schools. These aspects were regarded as contributors to the increased freedoms, such as freedom of conscience, freedom of speech, and freedom of religion. Respondents also indicated a shift from collectivistic to individualistic views in the society. Similar to ideological changes, discussed in the previous section, the philosophical transformations resulted in the change in the societal system of norms and values.

Political Change

Teachers regarded political change as the shift in the national, civil, and public policies, as well as structure, order, and behavior at the government and local levels. In their responses, teachers discussed the issues of gaining independence, building democracy, establishing language policies, open borders, changes in the government structure, and relatively recent events of the Orange Revolution.

Most of the participants named the Declaration of Independence and the process of establishing of the independent state of Ukraine as the most significant political events in the post-Soviet period. Other important events related to the Independence were the first Presidential elections, the establishment of national symbols, and complete change in the government structure and system of elections. One of the respondents, a history teacher, viewed the Declaration of Independence as the starting point for all the other societal changes. She noted:

I am a history teacher. The question you just asked is the whole course of Grade 11 [history]. In order to talk without any proofs, and for a short period of time, I can't even think of what to start with... Societal changes were colossal: the State machinery has changed, the socialist Soviet Union collapsed, and independent Ukraine was established. Everything else follows from this. (Sonya, 3:5, 14)

The same respondent continued, noting that Independence was unexpected and Ukraine was not ready for it; therefore, Sonya believed, it was not used to the fullest extent:

> As for the historical point of view, it was obvious that what happened after August events of 1991 has changed the status of our country. It also became obvious that - as a history teacher, I am very happy about this - that our country became independent at last. In the history course, we could only talk about how Ukrainian people fought for independence. Independence fell from the moon on us, that's my opinion, but we can't state that we are independent right now, because of the government changes, that's the 13th now, and what is happening in our country now... As a history teacher, I analyze all of this, and I don't understand what is happening... in spite of the reports on TV and articles in newspapers that everything is all right. I disagree with many of those conclusions. (Sonya, 3:8, 14)

Mixed feelings about independence were expressed by another respondent. On the one hand, she was happy to see Ukraine become independent; on the other hand, sovereignty of Ukraine meant that she was separated from her family and relatives in Russia:

> Another change that affected me was that Ukraine became independent. On the one hand, I am happy that this happened, because I realize that each country develops in its own direction, it has to develop, and this is a natural process, and we should be happy about this... there were many examples like these in the history. But because I have Russian roots, it affected me as I had to worry about crossing borders, passports, money. It also affected my late parents, because they could not visit us and see their grandchildren very often. We could see all of this affecting our everyday life; it affected us very much. (Lyuda, 23:1, 10)

For several of the respondents, the issue of independence and sovereignty was closely tied with the development of democracy. They believed people started to realize that they have power to change things in the country. Some of the respondents' comments about democratic development reflected this point:

> Well, in 1991 Ukraine was declared an independent and sovereign state, and we are slowly moving towards this. In my opinion, we realized during this time, 13... 14 years, and even last year events showed that people can make decisions in what happens in the country... (Tonya, 2:4, 22)

> At first, there was a little confusion in our society about what to do and how, but then people assumed the responsibility of doing it. They started to realize that everything depends solely on them and that, only due to their hard work, they can achieve something in the society. (Sofia, 2:3, 18)

Many respondents viewed freedom of speech as one of the most significant aspects of democratic development. Answering the question about the particular political changes, Lyudmyla noted: "Political changes? Big changes! A big change, first of all, is freedom of speech: people started to express their opinion more freely, their perspective of what is happening in this world..., mostly in this country, and in the world as well" (1:5, 26). She was also convinced that a possibility to speak Ukrainian language freely was a consequence of policies and political decisions that indicated a shift towards a democratic society. However, several participants expressed mixed feelings about freedom of speech. For example, Iryna believed that "the only positive change is freedom of speech, where one can talk openly and express personal views. However, it is sometimes limited" (21:1, 14). Another respondent added, "as for the freedom of speech, I start thinking that it would be good if it did not exist - it would be easier for me to sleep" (Antonina, 5:5, 43).

The possibility to go abroad and cross the national borders was perceived as a political transformation. In the following exchange, Lyudmyla and Olena discussed their thoughts on this matter:

> L: What else political? A possibility to freely cross the border of our country in any direction, and that's without any future consequences.

O: Also, there aren't any limitations.

L: Yes, no limitations…

O: Before, this right was given only to the Komsomol [Комсомол (All-Union Leninist Young Communist League)] workers or workers of the [Communist] Party, but now, anybody can use this [right], and without any problems cross [the border] with visa and passport. (1:5, 26-32)

Open borders and opportunity to go abroad had a significant positive impact on the schools in terms of learning exchange and professional development. Teachers believed it was a benefit that children from their schools could study abroad. The respondents in one particular school, both in focus group and individual interview discussions, indicated that after 1991 their students were able to study in Belgium, Romania, France, and Canada. One respondent shared the following:

For my friends, there was an opportunity to travel and see the world, not just with the purpose to earn, but to see, learn, and borrow from others' experiences. We went to different schools [abroad] for professional experience exchanges. We saw and took a lot of interesting and useful material for our work. Such changes helped in terms of general development. (Lyuba, 9:3, 14)

The overall perception of the ability to cross the country's borders due to the political freedoms was mainly positive among the respondents.

Most widely discussed political issues related to the change in the government structure and system of elections. Respondents mentioned such transformations as the collapse of the former political order, the establishment of multiple political parties, reforms, government efficiencies and inefficiencies, and more recent developments, such as the Orange Revolution and subsequent events. Teachers concluded that the gist of political changes in the previous 14 years lay in the change of political structure, the change of governing body, the change in priorities, and redistribution of the state property. The phrase that several of the teachers used to characterize the change was "everything was upside down". For one of the respondents, the most significant societal changes were those that related to the area of politics. Describing political changes that affected her most, she noted:

First of all, the change of order. We used to have the Communist Party, now we have totally different people who come to power, they start to govern the country seemingly in a different manner, but as a result, those changes led to the fact that living become more and more difficult for people. I can't understand that. On the one hand - they are different people; they say that they fight for truth, improvement of people's well being. On the other hand, everything is slipping and life becomes worse and worse. All of this affects the status of a teacher, his/her material, psychological, and other aspects. (Iryna, 21:1, 14)

Comparing the Soviet and Ukrainian systems of elections and government bodies, teachers reflected upon the shift from a single-party to a multi-party system. One teacher also mentioned the possibility to advance one's professional career without a party membership or affiliation, which had been impossible in the Soviet times. She stated:

It is also possible to push one's career without any political associations or party membership… it is possible. Of course, some people seek loopholes into some parties, regardless of whether their principles suit them or not… But in most cases, a person that has no party memberships can nevertheless achieve something… get education… It is present, and is … notable. How many parties we have… Before we had one party, and now… (Lyudmyla, 1:6, 33)

Despite the change in the government and parliament structures, as teachers noted, the government officials did not have knowledge or expertise to carry out their professional responsibilities. As Mariya put it, "it seemed that leaders didn't know what they were doing. I realize that as a common teacher I don't fully understand functions of the top governmental positions, but, their dysfunctions were visible to the naked eye, even for a common person" (20:3, 18). As a result, government did not function effectively and reforms did not get implemented. Analyzing the causes of slow reforms and government inefficiencies, Olena and Lyudmyla expressed the opinion that the same bureaucrats remained in power; they changed political loyalties and affiliations in order to continue in government. These participants shared the following thoughts:

> L: That's why everything moves very slowly in Ukraine, all the reforms... The same people remained [in power]... Maybe at the top, some of them were fired...

> O: Mostly, those are the same Komsomol workers...

> L: If they assigned a new region governor, the rest of subordinates remained the same...and the do the same things...

> O: So what if they resign? Just like in that fable where they threw the pike back into the river... They resign from one position, and get assigned to better position, a "warmer" one... (1:23, 230-236)

Another perceived cause of government inefficiency was a disorder in the institutions of national governance and disrespect in communication with people. The following excerpt of a focus group discussion between Lena and Stella conveys the point how government officials set a poor example by poor conduct and communication practices:

> L: The manner of communication...

> S: We see how people in our government communicate... even our President takes liberties with such phrases as 'a journalist's ugly face', etc. [The former prime minister] was accused of calling somebody names. Therefore, our government officials take liberties with this, and it goes down the ladder. Children are the ones who suffer from this the most, because they look at the reputable men and women who call each other names...

> L: Or fight in Verkhovna Rada [Supreme Council, Parliament]...

> S: So they [children] think it is possible in other relationships. We have a saying that 'The fish decays from the head'. I wish we had order in the upper strata, a certain system, and, foremost, the respect for the working people... (7:12, 65-71)

The phrase used by Stella, "the fish decays from the head" described the significance of the impact of changes at the governmental level for the whole nation.

Some respondents discussed the fact that government officials do not help or care about the nation. They believed that they are more worried about their own welfare than the welfare of the country. However, despite the prevalent negative perceptions about the government effectiveness, there were those who believed that "the government started to think a little bit about common people, especially teachers" (Roksolana, 5:1, 10). At the same time, it was emphasized that this is connected with the latest political developments following the Orange Revolution.

The topics of the Orange Revolution and Presidential Elections of 2004 were common in the focus group and interview discussions. Reflecting upon those events, several of the respondents shared that they were not interested in political developments in the country before; however, as a result of the events of the Orange Revolution, they became more aware of the politics. Mariya, one of the teachers, described the emotions teachers experienced:

> All of the latest events and development in Ukraine, especially after the Orange Revolution, have great impact on us: we relive those events, we still discuss them... I, personally, as well as my closest colleagues, perceive the events that happen in the country as our personal wins or losses and are looking forward to stability in the country. (Mariya, 20:9, 62)

Another participant reflected upon the fact that staff were free to vote for whomever they wished in the last Presidential Elections. "For instance, when we had Presidential Elections, people voted for whomever they wanted. It was completely free; some wore orange ribbons, some didn't, some were against everything - because they wanted so. We couldn't do anything like this before" (Lina, 18:8, 32). For Lina, it was an indication of greater freedom of expression.

Despite the prevalent positive comments about the political transformations following the Orange Revolution, several teachers were disappointed that the new government did not address teacher issues and teacher status in the society did not change. One of the respondents, Arkadiy, commented:

> Let's look at the latest period: events of this year, either calendar year or school year, starting from September, 2005 to September, 2006. Significant change in the society during this period did not influence the status of the teacher at all. What I mean is that teachers feel that they are not quite deceived, but forgotten for sure. The social status of teachers didn't change, while most of the teachers fully supported the ideals proclaimed at the Independence Square. They expected that government change will lead to the change in societal attitudes, including attitudes towards teachers. Teachers want to stop being a puppet in the society - a person, fully dependent, materially and morally, on commands of the government. They want to feel real subjects not only of the schooling process, but of societal activities as well. These hopes haven't come true for them yet. I don't know what it will be like in the future, but nowadays, they are disappointed. (14:3, 14)

As indicated above, teachers felt like puppets in society, fully dependent on government policies. Though they put much faith in the new government, they believed that their needs were not fully met.

Summary. In their responses regarding the political change after the collapse of the Soviet Union, teachers indicated that the issue of gaining Independence was one of the most significant changes in their lives. Teachers perceived it to be instrumental in developing democracy, freedom of speech, establishing of the national language policies, and opening country borders. Political transformations at the government level led to a change in the political order, government structure, multi-party system, and reforms. The respondents addressed the issues of the government inefficiencies, lack of support and care for common people, and disorder at the governmental level. Also discussed were the impacts of relatively recent political developments related to the Orange Revolution and Presidential Elections of 2004.

Social Change

Teachers viewed social change as transformations in the nature, institutions, and relations of society, communities of people, or other social structures. For many of the respondents, changes in the social sphere were the worst, because people lost the former way of life to which they were accustomed and had to adapt to the new social realities. Among the most important social issues discussed by the participating teachers were the changing relationships in such social institutions as family and community; decline in the nation's health, both physical and spiritual; destruction of the system of social guarantees; and, greater differentiation among socio-economic levels in society.

Most commonly discussed were the issues related to the changing nature of social relationships in families and communities. The participants indicated that relationships became hard-hearted and colder than they used to be, and people are more isolated and withdrawn. One of the respondents observed:

> And we get the same things that exist abroad: you have to visit your mom by invitation (but we [used to] have different, friendly relationships); it seems to me that people become hard-hearted; in regards to a spirituality, people used to be softer, but now everyone becomes unsociable, withdraws into oneself or own circle, thinks of how to earn more, how to get

something, how to settle the children. Material welfare means a lot for every family. Really, there are many homeless, many poor... many children who do not attend school, because their parents are abroad earning money... children are left on their own, because if they are left with a grandpa or grandma, they don't want to listen to them... This is also a problem. (Lyuba, 4:8, 24)

Many of the responding teachers supported this view and mentioned how children are affected by the fact that their parents went abroad in search of employment and left them to be brought up by grandparents, relatives, or, sometimes, even close friends. Lyuba's colleague, Emilia, was very emotional when she discussed this issue in more depth:

As for the children's upbringing - I would say there are more drawbacks. Upbringing of children is lacking in many things now. One of them is the fact that many parents are abroad. This is a big drawback. I pity those children who don't have mothers beside them. For example, in my class last year a girl suddenly started crying. It was Grade 1. I asked her what happened, and she said, 'I miss my mom, my mom is not with me, others have their mom with them...' She started [crying], and I see tears in the eyes of another student. Another example happened recently when mother of two of my students went abroad in search for a job. Children suffer. They are brought up by others who they stay with, but it's not a proper upbringing. They are more prone to a bad behavior. They are brought up by the streets.

Another thing: there is a children playground beside the building where I live. Oh, my God! I am shocked! There are children that spend the whole day there, from dawn until dusk, without any supervision [by their parents]. This is a reflection of that drawback that parents have to leave their children and go abroad. ... Because there are no jobs and they need to feed and clothe their children. Also, if you want your children to go to any higher education institution, the only way is to leave everything and go abroad to earn money. How many families [are destroyed?]... I think more than half of the families of those who go abroad are ruined. This is horrible. Thus, upbringing is not proper. Who takes care of those children? On numerous occasions, children came to school dirty, not washed; some friends of their mother take care of them. Unemployment is the biggest [problem] that causes all of those other drawbacks. (Emilia, 16:1, 10-18)

Results of the monitoring research of psychological problems in student environments revealed that 20% of students in Chernivtsi region had a mother working abroad, and 12% have a father working abroad. Moreover, this research indicated that 11% of them experienced rejection in their student collectives (Botyuk, 2007). Another study found that, as of January, 2006, there were more than 1600 students of migrant workers in the schools in the city of Chernivtsi ("Mother of every fifth pupil is working abroad," 2007).

Therefore, according to Chernivtsi educational authorities, pedagogues needed to take into consideration the fact that significant percentage of parents were away from their homes, and children did not receive appropriate upbringing from them (Department of Education and Science of Chernivtsi Regional State Administration, 2002). Moreover, unfavorable socio-cultural conditions in society contributed to the increasing tendency towards the signs of negative behavior among children and youth: "Against the background of societal disorders and devaluation of moral and common human values, environment generates criminal customs and traditions among youth" (Department of Education and Science of Chernivtsi Regional State Administration, 2003, p. 16)

These changes could not help but affect the schools and teachers. Several participants recognized the significant consequences these developments had on teachers and schools in general. After reflecting, this respondent described the following:

I would like to add that the attitude of the state, parents, and children towards teachers has drastically changed. I don't blame children for that, I think, it's the state's fault, first of all, because a lot of parents went abroad and left their children... Children are brought up by themselves or relatives... but, most of them... many of them are not brought up well enough. Therefore, their attitude towards studying is not the same as it used to be. It seems to me that before, the majority of students were more in earnest about studying than now. (Hanna, 3:9, 20)

Several other teachers were concerned that improper upbringing by parents negatively influenced children's academic abilities and achievements. One respondent, Lena, believed that this process began before 1991, in the last years of the Soviet government when educational responsibilities were not performed properly, but merely to check points off the list of assigned activities. She commented:

There is no mutual connection between parents and children; parents either have no time to communicate with their children or cannot physically do that. You know, if I feel dishonored or my family feels dishonored... how can it be so that [a child] from our family was poorly brought up or did poorly in school? A child has to study according to her abilities. What do we see now? It is lost, it was lost... and it didn't depend on any political regime... We haven't started to lose it in 1991; we have started to lose it long time before that. It seems to me that we've received the product that was lost in the last years of the Soviet government. (Lena, 7:6, 41)

The lack of communication between parents and children was perceived as a significant factor that affected students' achievements in school. Lena and her colleague, Stella, stated that parents try to compensate their lack of communication with money, or in other words, they "fill the moral deficit with the material one" (Lena, 7:18, 141). As a result, teachers faced the extremely difficult task of being both teachers and parents to their students. Stella noted that parents expect teachers to bring their children up in the school and do not make efforts at home:

It is very hard to work in schools, especially nowadays when parents isolated themselves. They send their kids to school and we have to take care of them. They say 'That's your problem, I sent the kid to you'. But our school does not cover 100 percent of their time: they don't sleep here, they don't eat here, they communicate at home. Therefore, when they only see the conversations about money and how to earn them at home, what high ideals, what patriotism can we talk about? If they see that it doesn't 'smell' like money there, it is not of interest to them anymore. I can judge by my daughter: I tried to pass my ideals to her, but the influence of her environment is too great. (7:13, 71)

Drawing from other respondents' comments, it seemed that school was seen as the only place that educated children. Teachers expressed the point that as a result of social transformation at the family and community levels, the cultural development of society degraded. One of the respondents noted:

You know, it seems to me that after all those big changes the culture is hurt the most. People are chasing money because of all the possibilities to earn money. Some become rich, others become poor. Therefore, it turns out that those who have money are omnipotent and can do anything, but those who have no money, even if they are smart, they can't fulfill themselves because they have no material capacity. (Lyuba, 4:8, 24)

While many of participants discussed the material side of change, Lyuda was more concerned about the spiritual condition of youth:

What we learnt and tried to achieve remained in us, and somehow we try to instill greater spirituality and greater culture in students. Culture is inculcated by culture; but there the level of culture in the society is very low. Due to the fact that everything collapsed, the foundation beneath our feet was removed. In our city I noticed there are less cultural developments - there is no decent theater in the city that would work for youth, because young people need to be brought up on theatrical art and examples; there is no decent cinema sector that would help young people develop. Thus, no one else educates children except schools. Parents are put in such economic situation that they do not have time to bring their children up. The life has turned more towards the material side - how to get food and sustain living, in other words, how to 'support your 'pants from falling' - maybe such words sound rude. Our spirituality is gradually disappearing. (Lyuda, 23:2, 14)

Lyuda continued that the general spiritual degradation of society was the most important change that affected her personally and her family. She viewed spiritual degradation not only as the degradation of the high moral values, but as "a spiritual degradation in the applied or practical sense. For some reason, people value professionalism less in some areas and more in other areas... there is more irresponsibility" (23:6, 10). She also believed that there were material and economic reasons for such social transformations.

Several other teachers expressed similar concerns about the degradation of moral and spiritual health of the nation. This respondent maintained that teachers are caught in the middle, between the society and students, teaching spiritual and moral values:

A teacher in our society falls within a position between what is outside of school and what is in school. We are like that buffer that keeps that society back and tries to teach *something*. However, this *something* does not coincide in any form with what is there outside the school gates. (Larysa, 5:9, 61)

The respondents stressed the negative influence of mass media on children's mentality. Some teachers were indignant about the low-grade commercials and movies on television that oppose such "elementary things, like ethics and esthetics" (Stella, 7:11, 63). Her colleague, Lena, was more eloquent about this matter:

Another thing is the moral and spiritual health of the nation. Nobody cares about this yet. It seems to me that it should be taken care of first of all. There is no moral health; there is no spiritual health... What do we see on television every day? Personally, I can't stand it when I switch the channels and see either murders, or something else....

Either we want it or not, the human psyche, especially the child's one, is such that it absorbs everything. Then we think why kids are so cruel, why a kid thoughtlessly throws a bottle out of the window, why a kid thoughtlessly abused his peer, why... It happens very often. (Lena, 7:5, 33-39)

In her comment, Lena referred to an incident that happened in their school two days prior to the interview, when one of the students, a 12-year old girl, suffered severe head injuries from the glass bottle thrown by another student from the eighth floor of an apartment building near the school. This respondent further continued that the deterioration of spiritual and moral upbringing influences students' mental health:

We talked about television, but look at the compact discs, how many of them rent them... few go to the library, but many go there to rent movies, watch them on the computers and video players. All of this willy-nilly influences child's mentality; their mental health deteriorates, and they get addicted to all of that. (Lena, 7:7, 45)

Lena concluded that as a result of degrading mental health, students' attitudes towards schooling have changed and their interests in learning have plunged.

Along with the topic of moral and spiritual health, the respondents mentioned physical health of the nation. Several teachers discussed the loss of free medical care and general inability of the population to pay for costly medications and services. They explained that despite the fact that formally medical care remained free, in reality people had to pay for rendered medical services. This participant shared her concerns about this matter stating that deterioration of nation's health was the first negative aspect of the social change:

First, it's the nation's health… in a true sense of the word. We lost free medical care. I know people who underwent serious surgeries… I know many women for whom it was problematic to give birth to a child… I was born in 1949, and all of this in my times was free! Do you understand? Everything, including medication, like aspirin… Everything! Now, it seems to me… how would I phrase it, there is an unannounced genocide. The nation, that is, all of those people who require social care, are doomed for extinction. That's my point of view. That is why, all that is positive in society is crossed out by the fact that many people are doomed for extinction…a large stratum of population… And whatever we say, whatever humane, nice, or bright we sow in schools, if [a student] comes home and sees that his grandma is dying and his mother cannot afford to buy medication, and his grandpa cannot undergo a surgery because they don't have money, or his uncle doesn't have money for a [heart surgery], then… However, we all have the right for free education and medical care… (Ilona, 3:12, 46)

Several respondents indicated that the notion of *social care for teachers* as such had disappeared: "Teachers used to be paid to go to different places to improve their health; they do not do that anymore. Nobody will give us a resort pass and nobody will give us a kopeck [penny] to improve our health. As a rule, government does not have money for that" (Lesya, 6:2, 38). For these teachers, loss of free medical care was part of the bigger issue of decreased social guarantees for population in the period of independence. This respondent reminisced about social guarantees provided in the Soviet times:

[W]ithin socialism of the Soviet Union, we had guarantees, firm guarantees, we definitely knew what to expect, and now we don't know anything. We live by today. We have no social guarantees, we are in a whirl, everyone is a part of a crowd… (Lyuba, 4:8, 24)

Teachers regarded pensioners as one of the strata of population that were most affected by the withdrawal and decrease in social guarantees. This respondent noted: "Retired teachers are very offended: their pension is lower than the subsistence wage or the minimal cost of living. Is it fair?" (Stella, 7:13, 71).

Social change was perceived to be closely connected to the economic transformations in the society. Transition to a different system of economy and decreased social guarantees were perceived to be instrumental in changing of the socio-economic status of Ukrainian population. Describing the social relationships after the collapse of the USSR, one of the respondents indicated a greater differentiation in the socio-economic status of various levels of society:

In general, society has changed immensely. During the Soviet Union times, there was only one stratum of society – one solid mass. Officials never descended to the lower layers of society; they never collaborated or communicated with them; they had their own cars, etc. In general, all people were at the same level of prosperity and used public transportation. People could not stand out against a background of 'one gray mass'. Nowadays, there is a great differentiation in society. There are very rich people, people of moderate means, and simply poor people; and this is very vividly evident in the society. (Roksolana, 10:8, 156)

Greater differentiation in socio-economic status was seen as having a significant impact on relationships between people in different societal groups.

Summary. This section revealed the participants' perceptions regarding the social change in Ukrainian society after the collapse of the Soviet Union. The respondents felt that relationships in communities and families became hard-hearted and colder than they used to be, and people were more isolated and withdrawn. They recognized the lack of connection and communication between parents and children that influenced students' upbringing, attitudes towards others, and achievements in schools. Teachers were concerned that many students were being brought up by grandparents, relatives, or parents friends due to the fact that their parents went to work abroad. The respondents also recognized the deteriorated moral and spiritual wellness, as well as physical health of the nation. Decrease in social guarantees for population and changing economic relationships led to greater differentiation in the socio-economic levels in the society.

Chapter 5

IMPACT OF SOCIETAL CHANGES ON EDUCATION

School is a reflection of the country; it is a micro-country. It has opposition, extremists, different political allegiances, etc. School reflects absolutely all events in Ukraine. (Viktor, 15:3, 64)

Most of the participants in this study indicated that it was impossible for them to separate their professional experiences from their personal lives in their responses. Therefore, the majority of their answers were directly or indirectly connected to schools. Respondents described a school as a mini-system, a mini-model, or a barometer that reflected all events in the society. These views were summarized by the comment of a school principal, who believed that "school is a reflection of the country; it is a micro-country. It has opposition, extremists, different political allegiances, etc. School reflects absolutely all events in Ukraine" (Viktor, 15:3, 64). Teachers observed the direct impact of societal changes on schools, and this explains why many of the discussions in the previous section were related to the school setting. Similarly, stemming from the analysis of the relevant educational documents was the evidence of direct impact of societal transformations on the system of education:

> The situation in Ukraine is characterized by socio-economic instability, significant recession of production, decrease in the level of life of the majority of people, deepened stratification of population according to the income level, devaluation of societal moral norms and values, and criminalization. All of these factors intensify educational problems... (Department of Education and Science of Chernivtsi Regional State Administration, 2002, p. 10)

In this chapter, I present the discussions about the societal influence on schools and teachers that were not identified in the previous chapter, such as transformations in the system of education; transition from the Soviet model of education; educational reforms in the new, Ukrainian, school system; and change in societal attitudes toward education.

Transformations in the System of Education

In their responses, teachers indicated that the system of education changed as a result of societal changes. The shift in societal views and perspectives and transformations in economic, political, and social spheres in the years of Independence were instrumental in bringing change to Ukrainian schools. All of the respondents believed that the changes were oriented toward Western (European and North American) educational systems. In several focus groups, teachers discussed such changes as natural consequences of the events in society. One of the participants noted: "It's not the government that sets such tasks; time requires [change].... Time and life require change. And we have to keep pace with it" (Nina, 2:11, 194-198). Among other significant factors that initiated transformations in education were changes in students' needs and intellectual capacity. Teachers stated that children became more educated, informed, and intellectually capable, possessed creative skills, and had no inferiority complex. As one principal put it, "Students are changing quicker than teachers. Teachers are the products of their epoch, and their transformation is slower than that of students. Therefore, many efforts are made to help teachers understand today's students and find pedagogical methods and approaches to individual students" (Arkadiy, 14:5, 70). Changes in the education system helped schools and teachers to adapt to the new realities.

Transition from the Soviet System of Education

The majority of respondents agreed that the transition from the Soviet system of education has not yet been completed. Several teachers commented that despite the numerous changes, many characteristics of the Ukrainian system of education were the same as in the Soviet system. They continued that they could not fully evaluate the results of such transformations, as the new system was still in the process of development:

> In general, there were dreams that everything will be different! However, it didn't lead to a total change in views and perspectives and a difference in our work. We still have a command system: we must fill out all the documents and do everything as commanded. (Lina, 18:5, 24)

> The Soviet system still remains. We have the same plans. Even if we write different headings, almost everything is still the same. (Lina, 18:19, 74)

> If I said that there is a drastic difference, it would not be true. Programs have changed, and that is a great advantage, because after the Independence I didn't feel like praising [Communist] Party... I have done that for too long, as that was the nature of our work. Nowadays, it seems to me that the reform period hasn't been completed yet; it is still at the developmental stage. (Mariya, 20:5, 83)

The respondents believed it was difficult to move away from the system of education in which they had been inculcated for more than seventy years. They also agreed that schools needed more time to implement innovations offered by reforms in the educational sphere. Major characteristics of this transition period are presented below.

Instability. The initial period of transition was marked by instability and characterized by the lack of direction and goals. Many of the participants perceived reforms as the attempt to destroy everything that existed as unnecessary and old without any idea of how to create something new. They believed the initial endeavors lacked the unity of direction and foundation to build upon. One of the most experienced teachers, Iryna, stated that they crossed out what they used to have and moved in some direction without any goals, not seeing or knowing what it was toward which they were moving:

> It seems to me that there *was* a system in the Soviet Union, a very clear-cut and efficient system, but we are gradually destroying it...completely. Yes, I understand that there were many things that needed to be changed, but they had to create some kind of theory of how to do that, and only then, start working according to that theory. What did *we* do? We completely destroyed what was done before: today - we work according to one program, tomorrow - according to another program. Every year we have a different textbook; a textbook is far from being adequate for instruction.... Children, most often, do not understand what is written in those textbooks - they are very hard to understand, especially recently published ones. (Iryna, 21:16, 62-64)

Similar concerns were expressed by other respondents. One of Iryna's colleagues, Sophia, described the difficulty of working in the school at the beginning of the transition period:

> It was very difficult at the beginning, as there was no clear-cut program of studies, no directions as for what to do and how to do it. Every year, the requirements for the exams were changing: one year, they wanted written exams, the next year - oral exams; examination questions didn't correspond to the material taught in the school program. It was difficult in this regards, as we had to catch up with those requirements at the end of the year. (Sophia, 22:1, 10)

Furthermore, she continued that teachers hoped for greater stability after the initial period, but unfortunately, stability was not achieved: "Programs keep changing; they can't come to an agreement on them. Requirements for the exams and tests constantly change; they require different documentation each year" (Sophia, 22:4, 24).

School democratization. In the first three to five years in the early 1990's, teachers observed a period of 'school democratization', characterized by rejection of the ideological aspects of the Soviet education and shift in the focus and goals of education. One of the participants, Volodymyr, posited that at that time "the ideological base of the old school was totally destroyed. Actually, it was thrown away as garbage... all ideas, as well as all visual aids" (19:6, 30). This allowed the schools to shift the focus from Soviet to Ukrainian perspectives:

> First of all, everything in the Soviet system was connected to Lenin, Communist Party, whether you solved math problems with children or taught Ukrainian language (which was scarce, because everything was instructed in Russian, and I taught in Russian for the first 15 years of my teaching career). Nowadays, we have textbooks, with good material. Everything is dedicated to Ukraine, nature and environment, which is very important for children, as they need to learn how to love and see what is around them, and preserve it. At that time, everything was tied to the main goal 'Forward to communism'. Nowadays, there is more humaneness and spirituality in textbooks and upbringing itself. We pay more attention to spiritual and moral development of children and have many resources that can be used for these purposes, be it a math or language assignment. Right now, I am teaching a series called 'Oral folk art' - we teach children to love the achievements of our Ukrainian people in the past. Hopefully, this will allow us to bring up a generation of Ukrainian who will love their own Ukraine. (Lyubomyra, 12:16, 74)

The majority of ideologically-laden activities from the Soviet system were discarded. However, some of them remained in schools, albeit under new names:

> We used to have a game called "Orlyonok" [Little Eagle], now we have "Kozatski Zabavy" [Cossack Games]. We used to have 'Molodaya Gvardiya' [Young Guards] organization, meetings of local Party organizations' secretaries. All of this is absent now: that's what has changed in the system. There are fewer marches... Remember Pioneer Day march in the city? It's obvious: no Pioneers, no marches. (Lyuba, 9:6, 50)

In order to substitute the Soviet youth formations, such as Komsomol, Pioneers, and Zhovtenyata, a number of formal student organizations were introduced: Kozachata [Little Cossacks], Strumochky [Brooklets], Barvinchata [Little Periwinkles], and Ukrainian Scouting Organization "PLAST". Also, religious education was introduced in the school program. The main objectives of these changes were to provide moral and spiritual education and to unite students in schools.

Instructional freedom. The period of 'school democratization' resulted in greater freedom in the choice of instructional materials, freedom of conscience, and freedom to implement certain instructional methodologies. Some of the subjects were removed, and some new ones were introduced into the system. Most respondents observed a significant change in the direction and activities in schools, as teachers received greater choices and freedom in the use of methods and materials in the process of teaching. One respondent stated:

> We received greater freedom in teaching: we were allowed to bring our own changes into the program of studies, choose the textbook for the class that we thought was necessary, effective, and expedient for [instruction] in our school. This was a very positive side of the changes in our lives. (Sophia, 22:1, 10)

Another participant, a school principal, described the freedom that teachers had in regard to instructional methods, personal points of view and interpretation of instructional material, and curriculum planning:

> There is greater freedom in selection of instructional methodologies and methods; greater freedom in the teacher's rights to interpret different views and express personal opinions; and greater freedom in terms of independence from political concepts, views. There isn't a single directing political force, and teachers can express themselves as they see fit in regards to their political views. Personal views can be freely expressed, but the main point is not to impose them on other people. In Ukraine, there is more freedom in curriculum than in other countries. I had an opportunity to work with colleagues from different countries, and their curricula were more rigid. Our curriculums allows up to 10 percent of curriculum time to be dedicated to the profile or course selection of a certain school. I think even 10 percent is not enough, but we don't know how the increase of this percentage will impact the schools. (Arkadiy, 14:5, 68-72)

Several of the participants also mentioned that it became easier to teach due to a variety of authentic methodological literature and instructional materials available for teachers.

Many of the respondents indicated that, as a result of greater freedom and flexibility in instruction, their work became more interesting and creative. One participant, with extensive experience of being a teacher and a principal, posited:

> I have been working in the system of education since 1978; therefore, I have had an opportunity to compare education in the Soviet times and after the collapse of the Soviet Union, in the times of independent Ukraine. The work became more interesting. There is more freedom, more possibilities for creative approach to work. (Viktor, 15:2, 10)

Another participant compared the work of a teacher in two systems, Soviet and Ukrainian, and believed that encouragement and development of creativity became an integral part of the new system:

> Changes were significant, because 14 years ago a person had to act as a steel mechanism, as a robot - they said, you did, no thoughts, nothing - but now we can use our creativity, and it seems to me that school administration and Department of Education strove toward the development of creativity in the schools. One example is the introduction of classes with advanced learning of subjects that functioned the way I wanted to teach and imagined my work as a teacher. (Roksolana, 10:1, 10)

Roksolana concluded that creative approaches to teaching resulted in greater effectiveness of her own and her colleagues' instruction.

The move towards creativity in instructional approaches was given considerable attention in the focus group with the beginning teachers. One of the participants, Tasya, indicated such a shift came as a result of understanding that students' needs have changed. She stated that unlike the older generation of teachers, younger teachers understand the fact that students are interested in learning and want to work in certain directions. Younger teachers supported the idea that students can choose to learn what they want. Tasya continued:

> Older generations do not understand this: 'There is a standard rule and it has to be like that'. We are trying to adjust to [students' demands]. Look at such subject as drawing: it is a common subject, but they used to say that it's 'useless'. It was always like that; somehow we thought that way. Now that I have been a teacher of fine arts for 3 years, I noticed a big difference. When I first came to school, there was a standard rule to be present in the class; nothing else mattered. Now, there is more interest in it. First of all, because we try to combine it with other possible subjects, and also students like when I bring music... and we work with music. (Tasya, 8:5, 28)

Other participants acknowledged that students set new demands and teachers tried to adjust to them in their teaching methods.

Increased administrative control and supervision. Interestingly enough, many of the respondents observed a tendency toward a more rigid control of teachers' work in the recent years. One of the respondents presented an overview of the period of transition in the system of education, indicating the causes that led to a stricter supervision of teachers:

> [During the period of 'school democratization'], the school administration, just like the government of Ukraine, was busy with survival (as well as every teacher at that time). Thus, the school administration - at all levels, from the Ministry [of Education] to the city [Department] officials - had no ability or knowledge to manage teachers. Therefore, teachers, on one hand, were left in the lurch, and on the other hand, depending on their vision, level of development, willingness to work, or abilities, could actualize themselves as teachers; that is, teach the way they thought was right, according to their standpoints. The prevalent principles were the common humanistic values, and at that time teachers were controlled less; there was less reporting to the above levels... After a time of total control and supervision of the Soviet school, there was a period when teachers could actualize themselves as personalities. That is, a teacher could not only prove his or her points of view, but also share them with students. After 1995 or 1997, the government 'came to its senses', and bureaucratic machinery started working full swing.... This caused non-stop requirements and commands to grow in frequency with every year. (Volodymyr, 19:6, 30)

Teachers sensed that too much was demanded from them and they were controlled and supervised more than necessary. Several respondents believed that there was even more paperwork in the recent years than in the Soviet Union times. At the time of the interviews, they stated that they had only been working for two weeks in the 2005 school year, but still had not settled their accounts with all paperwork and reporting.

> We became overloaded with different reporting; we sank in paperwork. It turned out that for one hour of pure work we had to spend about five more hours of writing something: reports, creative work, plans, analyses, other things... It became harder for kids to study due to constant cross-checks and examinations with different forms and names... and different directions, i.e. attestations, monitoring, and so forth. But the essence remains the same - to check. (Antonina, 5:6, 47)

Other teachers indicated that paperwork impeded creativity, as they did not have time to "look up" due to the constant flow of papers: "Teacher's job became a paper mania. It changed from creative work and became a paper mania. A teacher needs to fill out so many different papers that he doesn't have time for creativity" (Zinaida, 6:3, 40). Participants were convinced that increased paperwork did not allow them to reach their full teaching potential.

Reforms in the School System

Analysis of the documents revealed that during the years of independence of Ukraine, schools underwent significant changes. The most crucial documents of this period were the State Program "Education (Ukraine in 21 century)", Laws of Ukraine "About Education" and "About General Secondary Education", Decree of the President of Ukraine "About the Improvement of Functionality and Development of General Secondary Education", Decrees of the Cabinet of Ministers "About the transition of general secondary education institutions to the new content, structure, and 12-year school program", and the "National Doctrine of the Development of Education" (Bauer, 2001; Department of Education and Science of Chernivtsi Regional State Administration, 2003).

As for the respondents, discussing the period of transition and changes in the system of education they mentioned a number of reforms: the establishment of Ukrainian language as the main language of instruction; the emergence of elite schools and schools with specific instructional profiles; the switch to a 12-year school system; reviewing of the grading scale and marking procedures; and the introduction of new school curricula and programs of studies.

Many of the respondents believed that the establishment of Ukrainian language as the main language of instruction was the biggest reform in the school system. Ukrainian language became widely used for instruction and everyday communication in schools. Besides, schools were also able to offer instruction and programs in Russian, Romanian, and Hebrew.

Development of new types of schools was seen as another significant reform. Several respondents mentioned that the establishment of elite schools, such as lyceum or gymnasium, was of great benefit to the Ukrainian system of education. The purpose of such institutions was to provide high quality instruction and to educate the nation's elite. They added that it had been impossible to establish elite schools in the Soviet times. Schools with profile instruction – an intensive study program of specific subjects, such as mathematics, biology, chemistry, foreign languages, etc., were also introduced.

When asked about the reforms, most of the participants connected the question with the change in the length of time students were required to attend the school. A 12-year school system was introduced in 2000 to substitute the 10-year one that functioned in the Soviet Union and first ten years of independence. Teachers expressed mixed feelings about this transformation. On one hand, teachers believed it relieved the pressure on teachers and students due to the fact the curriculum was extended for two more years. On the other hand, teachers believed it was difficult for students, as they had to start attending school at the age of 6 and study for 12 years. Moreover, teachers felt it had a negative influence on student retention and required more effort on their part to keep students interested in studying. One teacher added that the 12-year school system had been introduced without proper preparation: "In order to switch to a system where students go to school at the age of 6, they needed to create a necessary foundation, a good program, good textbooks at first, and then do the switch... but not bring children to school and then start changing it" (Sofia, 2:12, 218).

The change from a 5-point to a 12-point grading scale was perceived with a more positive attitude by teachers. They believed it allowed them to be more objective in marking students' knowledge, provided greater flexibility, and shifted the emphasis from the mark to the level of student achievement. Unlike the previous one, the new grading scale allowed teachers to fail the students if they were not performing well in school. One teacher reminisced at length about the 'hoops' she had to go through in order to fail a student in the Soviet times:

> We didn't have the right to put "2" [fail, on a 5-grade scale]. As a math teacher, in order to fail a student, I had to not just go through all pedagogic councils [staff advisory meetings], but have an exercise book with all extra hours that I spent tutoring this student....I had to visit child's parents at home, and advise parents about that. There was a special exercise book where it was marked that I was at their home and told parents that their child is not studying well. I had to write a letter to the [parents'] employer... I used to go to 'Electronmash' plant and notify a special committee on plant – school cooperation.... I went there and the chair of the committee had to put his signature that I was there and told them that the child is not studying well.... It was a shame for the family that I, as a teacher, came to the plant and complained that their child was a bad student... They had to [approve] the marks for the quarter. And after that I could fail the student... Moreover, I had to go through a number of requirements, and then give student a mark of "2". (Lyudmyla, 1:37, 363-371)

Lyudmyla concluded that the new grading scale simplified the marking procedures and allowed teachers to mark students' achievements according to their knowledge.

Reforms in education resulted in the introduction of various new school curricula. Most of these types of curricula emphasized the development of learning skills of individual students.

Summarizing the main differences between the Soviet and Ukrainian systems of education, this respondent stated:

> The Soviet education model was based on the so-called 'collective education for societal needs' with the certain number of engineers, teachers, doctors, etc... in which whoever was able to achieve success could go up the ladder. Nowadays, the system is based on the search for the most gifted children and assistance in their development. That's it. It seems to me that this is the main difference: that [Soviet] system was based on the collective learning and this [Ukrainian] system is based on individual learning. (Volodymyr, 19:3, 50)

The focus on individual learning was also mentioned by the participating teachers in other schools. In one particular school, all participants in the focus group and individual interviews mentioned such curricula as "Developmental Instruction" and "Personality Oriented Approach to a Student", which focus on individuality. The latter was seen to be "observed in the process of learning, where personal skills of every child are taken into consideration, and in the process of upbringing, because every child is an individuality and requires special approaches" (Tonya, 17:27, 134-136). Tonya added that this approach gained significance in the work of their school during independence. Moreover, teachers in this school observed a greater emphasis on this approach on the part of the government and education officials. The tendency towards individualization of education was especially evident in the guidelines of the State Program "Teacher":

> Transition from industrial to informational-technological society is impossible without the establishment of individually-oriented methods in education, maximal individualization of educational process, conditions for self-development and self-education of students, and thoughtful consideration of personal abilities and life values. (Cabinet of Ministers of Ukraine, 2002, n. p.)

Similar to the national guidelines, local educational authorities indicated that "the priority task of modern Ukrainian schools is provision of favorable conditions in the educational institution for the development of individuality" (Department of Education and Science of Chernivtsi Regional State Administration, 2002, p. 11).

Societal Attitudes toward Education

The majority of the participants acknowledged that the events that happened outside school had immense influence on their work. Discussing the reflection of societal events on their schoolwork, two respondents stated:

> Due to the nature of our profession, we can't express our feelings in class. Generally speaking, when a teacher steps into the class, he has to leave everything that bothers him behind that class door. He has to come to the class to support students, teach them something. We have to follow the above principle. (Tonya, 17:5, 148)

> As a matter of principle, [societal events] should not have any impact. My family and social life should not have any influence on my work in school. This is a general teachers' principle that always remains true. In reality, it does influence our work, because we are people with emotions, thoughts, and views - regarding the elections, meetings, events - which will always have impact on our work. (Volodymyr, 19:4, 106)

In their responses about the impact on their work, participants frequently referred to the changes in societal attitudes toward education.

Being active members in societal development, teachers felt that attitudes towards school and teachers had deteriorated and exerted negative influence on their ability to provide high quality instruction to students. They discussed the observed differences in perceptions of schools and status of teachers in present day Ukraine, as compared to the Soviet times, on the part of the government, parents, and students. Summarizing such differences, one teacher commented: "The school lost its prestige, the authority of the teacher was undermined, and the eagerness to study decreased both in children and parents" (Lyubomyra, 5:2, 22).

Most of the respondents indicated that teachers' work became more difficult because the authority, prestige, and reputation of the school, in general, were lost. Stemming from this was the lack of trust of teachers' work. In one of the focus groups, participants shared a story about the Department of Education officials who doubted the validity of final examination marks for honor students from graduating classes in all schools in the city; therefore, they ordered the establishment of a group consisting of the university scholars and other officials to reevaluate the results. It turned out that all students but one proved their results. Teachers believed that this was a demonstration to children, parents, and the whole society that teachers were not trusted anymore.

Participants believed that teachers used to have more authority and respect, and their views were taken into consideration by other people. Several of the respondents posited that teachers used to be held in such respect in society that others took their hats off and bowed when encountering them on the street:

> My grandma, who was illiterate, often said, 'There were times when a teacher used to be called Pan [Mister] Teacher, and people used to take their hats off in front of him. And now, he is a Pan [Mister] Broom, who is used to stop up every gap' [Ukrainian proverb, "to do everything you are told; run errands"]. (Sofia, 2:7, 251)

Another teacher even reminisced that when she became a teacher at the age of nineteen, older people took their hats off and bowed down to her in respect.

Many of the respondents observed a complete absence of respect toward them and their work by society, parents, and students. One respondent maintained that "a teacher possessed almost the last place in the society" (Olena, 1:26, 299). Described was also the general feeling of abjection among school teachers:

> Societal attitudes toward teachers changed immensely. We feel *abjection*! Not in regards to our salary. We feel abjection from parents, government, mass media... I have to admit that there are still many people who acknowledge teachers' importance, remember their teachers from the past. Nevertheless, there is this feeling of *abjection*. Before, I could proudly say that I was a teacher, and there was nothing negative about it. Nowadays, I see that everyone has something negative to say about school, be it from their past experiences in school or present experiences of their children or grandchildren. In reality, I think upbringing of children became very expensive and, I would say, *inconvenient* in our society. Therefore, who is the easiest blamed for all that? Of course, the school and teachers! This is the easiest. (Lyuda, 23:3, 140)

Another respondent also believed that teachers are blamed for everything negative that happens in society:

> However, it's not always the inspiration that we bring to school. Sometimes, when we take trolleybus to school or talk to others, we hear that teachers and doctors are blamed for everything. Everything that happens in the society is blamed on teachers and doctors.... Sometimes we feel like proving them wrong and arguing, but I think we are past that stage now. We simply ignore such comments, provide them with examples, and don't want to argue with others about that... However, if we brought all of that negativity to school, then we would not be able to work, because there is enough of it in school. We try to bring positive things to school, and leave negative behind. (Lina, 18:30, 154)

As a matter of fact, several focus group participants stated that they used to be proud of being teachers and that, hitherto, the word 'teacher' had a prestigious connotation. Nowadays, they are sometimes ashamed to say who they are. Larysa provided an excellent picture of teacher feelings: "It used to be an honor and respect before; now it is a shame and humiliation!" (Larysa, 5:11, 77).

Very often, teachers experienced humiliation and disrespect from the parents of their students. Some of the teachers shared their stories about parents who treated them or their colleagues in an impudent and derogatory manner, blaming teachers for poor performance of their children in school. Also, several respondents reflected about being treated in an offensive way by their own students:

> A teacher, an honored teacher, stands before a student and explains the lesson, while a student views the teacher not as a person who has a certain baggage of knowledge, certain intellect, certain morale, certain spiritual experience, but simply as some kind of garbage. (Lena, 7:7, 45)

For some of the participants, student disrespect of teachers was one of the worst feelings, as teachers felt they had devoted all of their energy to educate students not only academically but also based on proper moral and spiritual principles.

Several other teachers indicated that the culture of education excellence among students had disappeared and that students lost interest and motivation to perform well in the school. They believed that in general students became lazy, irresponsible, unaccountable to parents and teachers, and valued money more than knowledge. In addition, teachers observed a weakening of school discipline that led to permissiveness and undue familiarity in many of the children:

> Right now we're reaping the fruits of period, when children were allowed to do anything they wanted. This permissiveness led to the point when it is impossible to gather children together, have a normal lesson. Students do not know what 'no' means; they can come forward and take anything they want from the teacher's desk. As an older teacher, I am simply shocked with this. Teacher's desk always used to be a 'sacred place' for a kid, and now they take anything they want without asking for permission. They are not brought up in a proper manner. (Roksolana, 10:6, 62)

Khrystyna supported this by saying: "A student sits and doesn't give a damn about anything.... And you have to be happy that he sits in your class; and be glad that he hasn't *sat on your head* yet" [Ukrainian proverb, "to walk all over, to push somebody around"] (6:7, 157-163). Several other respondents also maintained that students assumed an attitude of defiance towards all authority, including school administration, teachers, and their parents.

Similar attitudes towards education were observed by teachers among students' parents. They noted that parents became indifferent to their children's achievements in the school. One of the participants believed that the roots of such lack of concern were very deep:

> I think that during these 14 years the society came to the conclusion that absolutely everything can be bought: a diploma, a school certificate, anything. I recollect the instance: last year I had to teach 6-year olds, because I teach foreign language in elementary grades from time to time. I know from previous years that as soon as we finished the lessons in kindergarten, parents met their children after the last lesson and usually asked a teacher, 'How is my kid doing?', 'Does she know anything?', 'What can we work on?' However, I was shocked last year: I am coming out of the classroom, there are a couple parents by the cloakroom waiting for their kids, and none of them asked, 'How is my kid doing?' I was so surprised; it was like a shock for me. They are absolutely uninterested – a kid could go to school for a year without a textbook and an exercise book, and that was absolutely normal to them. Why?! Because parents, especially young ones, are confident that even if their child doesn't study well in school, they will be able to buy her anything she needs. (Roksolana, 5:14, 382)

Roksolana added that parents become busier and spend less and less time on raising their children. As a result, teachers have to deal with students who are "raw" – they do not know the basics of knowledge acquisition or behavior in the school.

Discussing teachers' status in the Ukrainian society, several participants mentioned that teachers are deprived of their rights. Teachers were viewed as puppets and service people in society. One teacher described the following:

> Unfortunately, the attitudes toward teachers are not the same as they used to be in the Soviet times. A teacher is more like an attendant or service person now. They bring children to school and tell us that we *must* take care of them; they always say that the child has the right and we must teach that child. Nobody is concerned about the teacher's rights! Especially younger parents that who bring their children to school, now have a negative attitude. Not a negative attitude, but rather a consumer-like attitude. We are more like a maintenance staff. Of course, there are people who treat teachers differently. I am not saying that such an attitude is widespread, but unfortunately it is present and money decides more than professionalism and skills of the teacher. (Sophia, 22:7, 84)

Besides being deprived of their rights, teachers complained about immense pressure put on them to provide high quality education and be responsible for students' achievements:

> You have to understand what is going on that this stage - a teacher is completely deprived of any rights. A teacher can be very easily thrown out of the job - parents just need to collect enough signatures and a teacher can be easily fired from school. On the other hand, there is an immense pressure on a teacher that has to 'charge' all of the students with his or her energy, no matter what they are like; disregard offensive parents; and teach those students at least something. (Iryna, 21:6, 171)

Iryna perceived the pressure on teachers to be considerable higher than in the Soviet times.

The respondents believed that, as a result of post-Soviet transformations, society became indifferent and lost interest in education. Thus, the quality of education has gradually decreased. Volodymyr argued:

> During these 14 years, to be honest, 'true' education has disappeared [in Ukraine].... Most of all it was caused by the societal disuse and lack of demand in education, the lack of interest in education on the part of government and [leadership] elite ... Right now, society is not interested in education at all. That's one. This is the first reason why there is no education. Secondly, that peculiar, elaborated, even totalitarian, system of education of the Soviet Union, let's say, even in two-thirds, gave knowledge. (Volodymyr, 3:17, 190)

At this point in the focus group discussion, a colleague of Volodymyr started arguing with him and stated that "totalitarian Soviet system gave absolute knowledge" (Ilona, 3:17, 194). They came to agreement that in the Soviet times education had a greater value in society because of a greater demand for knowledge and opportunity to move up the social ladder. Volodymyr continued that it was the shift in societal values and perceptions of knowledge that led to the degradation in the system of education:

> Students are not interested in their marks at all, because half of them are without parents to control them now. Besides, it doesn't matter to them how well they do in school. The majority of them say, 'Why should I be an excellent student? Why do I need those marks if I can't enter any [higher education institution] without money?'
>
> That is why students are not interested in good knowledge. So far, knowledge is worth nothing in their opinion. During these 15 years, this led to a complete loss of value and depreciation of education. Knowledge is not considered a societal value anymore. Natural sciences, as well as arts, are completely destroyed and devastated, and we will not be able to present our society or compete on a worldwide level anymore. Even our city competitions will be canceled soon, just like with other disciplines. With the reforms we turn back to the average American or average European system [of education] - 'Pray to God so that a student could at least read' - because a significant part of graduates in the

West cannot even read. We are moving towards this too, and that is our near future. (Volodymyr, 3:17, 204-208)

Furthermore, teachers were concerned about the tendency in society that everything could be purchased. One of them, Stella, posited: "It's not new that there are ads in the newspapers like 'Will write term papers for money'. It means that some young people or students get their education by means of somebody else's work" (Stella, 7:3, 16). They believed the quality of education was negatively impacted by this fact.

Discussing other possible reasons of changing societal attitudes toward teachers, several of the participants mentioned the shift in teacher's role in the society. They believed that teachers became a less significant source of information for students in the world of multiple sources like press, television, and internet. Volodymyr posited:

A more information-based society cannot afford to have a teacher as a main source of knowledge for students as it used to be 100 years ago. Therefore, a teacher is not a source of knowledge anymore, and as a result, to a certain extent, a teacher is not an appropriate authority in passing the knowledge. Next, because of all this, the main teacher's task now is not to pass the information, but to develop a student's personality, find out about his abilities, help develop those abilities, teach how to learn, develop research skills at the basic level, and ideally, become a coach in exploring the world for a student. (Volodymyr, 19:5, 26)

Others supported this point of view by stating that teachers' role was to know how to direct students, make them interested in searching for knowledge, and show them how to work properly on achieving individual goals.

Despite the prevalent negative attitudes toward schools and teachers on the part of society, many of the teachers expressed the feeling of hope that attitudes would change for the better. Moreover, several of the participants already noticed gradual improvement in the attempts to raise teachers' salaries, value teachers' work, and foster teachers' status in society:

As we were informed during the Soviet times, the Soviet Union occupied one of the first places in the world for the levels of education, erudition, etc. Nowadays, the interest of children and attitude of parents towards education has been lost. It was lost because people found themselves in such conditions when they just tried to survive, not to say anything about other areas of life. I think now it's coming back to its place, people realized that education is necessary for everyone. I hope that with every year people will be more appreciative of the school, the knowledge that children receive here. (Tonya, 17:4, 68)

She concluded with the hope that the priority will not be given to material welfare, but to spiritual and educational values in society. Other teachers also had an optimistic outlook that societal attitudes toward school and teachers would improve in the future.

From Context to Professional Collaboration

In this chapter, I reviewed the participants' perceptions of the impact of broader societal change on schools and teachers. Summing up teachers' responses, one may state that fourteen years of independence were seen as a period of multiple transformations in all spheres of life. Education was not an exception in this matter, and teachers observed direct relation between the events that happened at the macro, societal, level and changes at the micro, school, level. The following chapters will present a more detailed discussion of the perceived impact of such transformations on teacher collaboration in Ukrainian schools.

Chapter 6

THE NATURE OF TEACHER COLLABORATION

Just like in any society, collaboration in our school ranges from competition and unacceptability to family-like cooperation. (Volodymyr, 19:9, 42)

In this chapter, I discuss the participants' perceptions of the nature and state of teacher collaboration in Ukrainian schools. Teachers' responses are grouped into two broader categories: the role of collaboration in schools and the description of collaborative activities involving teachers in schools.

The Role of Collaboration in Schools

When asked to dwell upon the role that collaboration played in their schools, teachers discussed different facets of collaboration, its importance and benefits for their schools, characteristics and mindsets of joint work, and challenges to the process of effective collaboration. Their responses are presented in the following sections along with information from the document analysis.

Facets of Teacher Collaboration

The notion of *teacher collaboration* was understood variously by the participants. They viewed it as joint work among teachers within the same school and collective work of professionals from different schools in the city. Discussing the nature of teacher collaboration *within* the schools, the participants differentiated between the professional and personal sides of joint school work. One participant stated: "Within the school there are collaborative, friendly relationships and mutual support regarding many questions, not just those that pertain to teaching, but also many other life situations when we need to support each other" (Ivanna, 6:11, 62). *Professional* collaboration seemed to deal with academic issues such as curriculum and lesson planning, organizing and attending meetings, creating and sharing of instructional materials, to name a few. All teachers viewed this as a formal part of school life. *Personal*, or informal collaboration, on the other hand, was perceived to be related to everyday situations in schools that involved warm, family-like atmosphere, mutual help, friendly advice, emotional support in difficult situations, common celebrations of birthdays, dealing with student issues, etc. Though participants distinguished between professional and personal collaboration, most of them believed that both of these aspects were interdependent and closely interwoven, and needed to be looked upon as parts of the same phenomenon.

Importance and Benefits of Collaboration for Teachers

Most participants viewed collaboration among teachers as an integral part of collaboration among all stakeholders in the school. Several teachers commented that a school simply cannot exist without all the "links", such as administrators, teachers, parents, support staff, and students, being tightly intertwined and working together. One of the participants explained the importance of collaboration in the form of interpersonal interaction and support:

I think it is very important. We can't work without …. collaboration between all links of a school: starting with the janitor (the way she cleans, what the halls are like, whether it's well aired and clean, whether the floor is washed - it all influences the mood of all people in the school), and finishing with collaboration with our students. It's impossible to live without it in the collective. It's all about mutual support! How nice it is when you are sick or something happened to you, and some of your colleagues visited you and said a good word. You know, it's better than any medicine. (Lena, 7:26, 81)

Lena concluded that collaboration was one of the necessary components of everyday life in schools. Many teachers supported this point of view by stating that collaboration is essential for existence of a school, because all the "links" work for the same cause: educating new generations. "We have one goal: to educate a person. Only if we work cohesively, can we reach this goal" (Sasha, 5:18, 91), posited one of the participants. Another participant, Lyudmyla, believed that a teacher cannot exist in some kind of vacuum, but will always be with children or other teachers. Furthermore, she added that school, as such, cannot exist without collaboration. Her colleague, Oksana, supported her point: "Just like one can't build communism in a separate house, a home-room teacher in his one class can't do anything without help from the whole collective. Or, without help from parents" (1:44, 157).

Similarly, collaboration among teachers was deemed by *all* of the participants to be vital and extremely valuable for schools. Several teachers argued that one cannot be called a teacher if he or she does not collaborate with colleagues. Many of the respondents compared teacher collaboration to a *lubricant* that keeps the school "machine" or "mechanism" working smoothly. Lyudmyla commented:

It's impossible to work without the support of each other. Sometimes I need to be backed up; sometimes somebody needs help, piece of advice, counseling - it's all interconnected. It's a single mechanism. Just like a clock: if the clock is tuned up and without breakage, it works fine. However, if there's a little breakage somewhere, it starts to slip. (1:44, 173)

Within this "mechanism", teachers were seen as the wheels that make all the parts of the school move.

It was perceived that the improvement in the quality of the teachers' collective or staff came as a result of collaboration among pedagogues. For some of the participants, the level of collaboration was the indicator of a staff's quality that affected the image of their school in the city:

Collaboration means that we, thank God, are not the last school in the city, and that people think well about our school, students come to us, and we do not worry about not having sufficient enrollment for Grade 1. If we didn't have collaboration, there wouldn't be a common opinion about our school and we wouldn't be here. (Nina, 2:16, 72)

For Nina and her colleagues, a good image of the school in the city was like a "balm for the soul". Teachers from other schools also added that cooperative work among teachers contributed to their positive image among students. One participant commented that "[teacher] collaboration definitely has positive characteristics … in regard to teaching and upbringing. Children notice the relationships among teachers, and a good atmosphere in pedagogical collective influences the student collective as well" (Sonya, 3:20, 62). Another respondent believed that teachers need to be role models in collaborative relationships, because children sense whether their teachers work separately or together and follow their example.

Characteristics of Teacher Collaboration

In their responses about the nature of collaboration in schools, teachers provided a wide range of descriptors. These characteristics, as summarized by Volodymyr, ranged "from competition and unacceptability to family-like cooperation" (19:9, 42). On one hand, the majority of participants described the nature of teacher collaboration in their schools in a positive light as family-like, close-knit, friendly, and kind. Many of the comments emphasized the fruitfulness and effectiveness of teacher collaboration. Lyuba described it as: "Fruitful, efficacious, positive, friendly, and mutual. In one word, it can be characterized as 'normal'. It brings results, because we are together; therefore, we learn from each others' experiences" (9:11, 118). Some teachers believed that good results depended on the level of *harmony* among teachers - the more harmonious the collaboration; the better teachers did their job. Other respondents perceived collaboration of teachers to be benevolent, inspiring, amicable, well-wishing, fair, tolerant, warm, cooperative, compassionate, strong, hard working, respectful, and trusting.

On the other hand, some teachers' views of collaboration indicated the presence of competition, conflict, and argument in the process. It was due to the fact that teachers "can't always agree with each other" (Lina, 18:2, 44). One teacher also commented about so-called "diseases" in the school staff that affected collaboration among teachers:

> If it weren't for some elements, some 'diseases' in our collective, I would describe collaboration as friendly. We treat each other with respect and understanding. However, we do have some 'thorns' [in our collective]. Overall, there is mutual understanding, good attitudes, and mutual support. (Emilia, 16:6, 44)

Thus, despite the overall positive descriptors, collaboration possessed characteristics that influenced joint work among school teachers in a perceived negative manner. Several teachers added that it was easier to collaborate with some teachers than with others.

Mindsets of Teacher Collaboration

Besides the characteristics of teacher collaboration, the participants outlined, directly or indirectly, several principles that guide joint work among professionals in their schools. The analysis of focus group and individual interview discussions revealed that participants' responses related to four major mindsets: *mutual help, lifelong learning, communication,* and *leadership.* Some of these were indicative of almost all focus group and interview discussions, while others were mentioned by fewer participants. Their perceptions regarding each of the mindsets are presented in order of frequency of mention in this section.

The first and by far the most frequently mentioned was the *mutual help* mindset. Mutual help was viewed by the teachers as a building block of teacher collaboration, both in professional and personal contexts. In their professional matters, teachers observed collaboration in the form of mutual advice, the primary purpose of which was to prompt colleagues about being wrong in certain situations in order to avoid similar mistakes in the future. Another important aspect was sharing of experience and instructional materials. As Vaselyna phrased it,

> We always shared our experience, always helped each other.... It is obvious that not everybody has everything he needs, that's why we share information and materials, help each other, give advice. In regard to this, I am really comfortable in this school. When I used to work in a different school, it was more of an 'everyone for himself' approach. Here, we are all together, almost always. (4:18, 58-60)

Her colleague, Maryna, added that teachers live and work in harmony with each other: "...we always share; worry for each other, when we have open lessons or other activities; help each other; think of each other; provide each other with advice, ideas. It *is* present here, and *nobody* can take it away from us!" (4:18, 62).

Similarly, mutual help and support were observed in collaboration in regard to personal and non-professional issues:

> [Collaboration] is hard to express in words! There was a very difficult period of time in my life - I came to school and I felt better. Each teacher would encourage me in different ways. This humane treatment is excellent among us. We always have guests, open public activities, and we *help* each other. We ask what each of us needs. We help each other with advice or even lesson plans. Everything is done together. If I have something that may be helpful to others, I share it. Though we are few in the elementary school, we do have good relationships. We all have a significant teaching experience, and our relationships are very

good. It concerns different aspects: if there is a personal problem, there is always somebody with whom you can share and talk. (Emilia, 16:7, 48)

Some responses indicated that it was customary for teachers to provide material or financial support for their colleagues in difficult situations. As Masha put it, "if any distress happens to somebody, God forbid, we put money together, visit, sympathize, and help with whatever we can" (6:9, 197).

The respondents perceived that the degree of mutual help among teachers depended on such factors as proximity in a subject area or affiliation with a grade level; for example, elementary, secondary, or high school classes. Tonya posited:

First of all, in our school we help each other, starting with subject parallels and ending with grade levels from 1 to 4 of elementary school. During my 15-year teaching career, I worked in a different school for 12 years and 3 years in this school. If I could compare these two, I would say that elementary schools are more closely bound than secondary or high school collectives. We have common interests… we try to live as one family, help each other with different problems… at work and even after work when people get together according to their interests. We don't have teachers being separate from others or trying to show off in front of others. On the contrary, if someone learnt something new, heard about new forms of teaching, does something better, we always share with others. (17:8, 46)

In several schools, teachers indicated that greater collaboration is possible among teachers in similar or identical subject areas or within the same departments. Sonya reasoned that many subjects had common points of contact, and that such collaboration among teachers positively affected the whole process of schooling.

Comments relating to the second mindset, *lifelong learning*, were also frequent (though not as frequent as the comments about mutual help). Lifelong learning emerged as one of the most important constituents of collaboration. Lyubomyra stated: "If I stop learning, I will stop being a teacher. The best teacher is your colleague at work" (12:11, 54). According to the respondents, every teacher is capable of providing colleagues with valuable insights into teaching, upbringing, or approaching students:

I learn from others; I learn all my life and think that people need to learn from each other and draw on experiences of others, because a person learns as long as he or she lives. Everyone has something interesting. Having visited other schools and colleagues' classes, you see some interesting elements and adopt those elements from others [in your teaching]. (Lyuba, 9:14, 30)

Several teachers believed that despite the age, experience, or career length, all teachers have the capacity to teach their colleagues:

You know, there are young, but very talented teachers. As for us, older teachers, no matter how hard we try, we have an established model of instruction. Every teacher has his or her own methodology of instruction, creative strategies, and communication with other teachers. I learn something new, even from the younger teachers. I borrow something good from them; they borrow something from me that they like and can implement in their lessons. Communication is very important. (Lyubomyra, 12:11, 52-54)

Teachers indicated that common planning and common problem solving contributed both to personal and professional learning. Moreover, learning from mistakes was considered an effective way to avoid problems in schools.

A third mindset, *communication*, also received considerable attention in discussions. Communication and discussion were viewed as the best means to collaborate with colleagues in the schools. Several respondents mentioned that they communicate to share experiences, problems, successes, and achievements within the school collective. Furthermore, in some schools teachers indicated that they meet together to discuss strategies to improve their instruction and make lessons more interesting for students. According to Mariya, collaboration, in the form of communication with other teachers, results in a continuous progress in work and allows teachers to avoid isolation:

> Frankly speaking, isolation or loneliness is very bad. Our work is communication - communication not only with students, but also with other teachers. In order to have a constant progress in our work, we communicate not only in regard to certain personal issues, but also professional issues. We ask each other for assistance, we consult each other, and receive help. This is first. The other aspect of this is that those are the people who are close to you in spirit. It's sometimes easier to share some personal matters with your colleagues. A human being lives by communicating with others; a person cannot be separated from everything else. (20:13, 46)

Mariya concluded that sometimes people in the school collective are closer than some family members and relatives. Thus, communication was viewed not only as a professional tool of collaboration, but also as a form of psychological and moral support for teachers. Such aspects as integrity, honesty, trust, and tolerance were seen to play a very important role in the communication process, contributing to effective and open communication among teachers.

Despite the fact that comments regarding the fourth mindset, *leadership*, were the least frequent, it was still considered an important notion associated with the dynamics of collaboration. The mindset of leadership in teacher responses consisted of two aspects: *teacher leadership* and *administrative leadership*. Teacher leadership seemed to be an important aspect of collaborative work. Lina explained how this type of leadership was expressed in their school:

> There are those teachers who come to school, work, and do their job bona fide. However, there are those who do their job, but want their work to be noticed; they want to be first in everything. It is not bad: a human being works to be noticed. This is *leadership*! When psychologist comes to school and distributes surveys, one of the questions is this: Who do you turn to [for help] the most? In other words: Who do teachers address most in their work? There are different situations described there, and that's how they identify the leader of the collective. (Lina, 18:16, 60)

This teacher emphasized that such a leader doesn't have to be in an administrative position; it is the "natural leader", the teacher to whom others turn most, who is respected, and who is tacitly recognized by others to be the leader. An integral part of being a leader among teachers was the willingness to collaborate. As Sonya put it, "If there is a will, there is a way. There should be a willingness to communicate, achieve something new, show initiative, and encourage others to do the same" (13:7, 40-42).

Another aspect of leadership discussed by the participants was *school administrative leadership*, or administrative involvement in establishing collaborative relationships and activities among teachers. In one school, both interviewed teachers considered the principal's role as key in building collaborative relationships among teachers:

> I think [collaboration] goes down from our head - administration and principal - who manage to unite such a collective and make sure everyone is comfortable in it. Thanks God, all factions and dissensions pass us by. This happens among teachers in other schools, while it is absent from our school. Therefore, it is nice to work in such a collective. (Sonya, 13:5, 32)

Her colleague, Volodymyr, provided an interesting analogy adding that the principal, as a leader, "attempts to form a family-like collective, in which there is a father and family members. Those who are older, take care of younger ones, help them, and supervise them, of course" (19:9, 40). Sonya provided an example of their principal's leadership in action:

> This year we moved to a new building, and our principal spent the whole summer in this building working along with teachers. We assembled the desks, moved them into

classrooms, painted the walls, and so on. This work brought the pedagogical collective together. We saw each other in a slightly different perspective; as well as our principal, who didn't hide from work, but worked along with us. (13:10, 58)

Thus, personal involvement of the principal was seen as an indicator of collaborative leadership.

A respondent from another school stated that "principal and vice-principals always encourage collaboration and sharing of new knowledge among teachers" (Antonina, 11:13, 68-70). Another respondent described the administrative leadership in the school where she worked as the process of *organization*: "[Administration] organize everything. Most of the time, collaboration is mandated by administration, not by teachers. All events that involve collaboration are organized by administration!" (Iryna, 21:18, 72-74). She continued that despite its mandated nature, teachers support such collaboration: "Why wouldn't they? All of the organized events are interesting. For example, psychological games where we act as students. These games are very interesting, because you see and learn many new things and strategies that can be used in classes" (21:18, 76-78).

Challenges to Effective Collaboration

When asked about the aspects that impeded the process of teacher collaboration, some of the respondents believed that there were no significant limitations or challenges in their schools. They stated that all necessary conditions for joint work among teachers were present in their schools, such as stability of tenure and cohesion of the staff. In their opinion, if there were any minor limitations, they were based on the personal characteristics and work preferences of individual teachers. However, there were other participants who indicated the existence of major constraints that limited the extent to which they could work together and hindered the development of effective collaboration among teachers. Discussions in focus groups and interviews related to such issues as lack of time, differential difficulties related to communication and cooperation between teachers of different age groups, "forced" or "mandated" collaboration, lack of resources, and lack of formal system of collaboration.

First of all, the most frequently mentioned limitation was the *lack of time* to participate in collaborative activities. Sonya asserted that time was the only limitation she could think of: "Time! There is not enough time, because we are overloaded. Our schedule is intense: we have eight lessons a day, and we teach till four o'clock every day. In this regard, time is a scarce resource" (Sonya, 13:7, 42). Other respondents observed that communication between teachers was limited only to short periods of time early in the morning, before classes, or late at night, after teaching and preparation time, or during holidays. The breaks were spent on supervision, helping students, or preparing for the upcoming classes. Moreover, teachers indicated that much of the after-school time had to be spent meeting the needs of their families.

Also discussed was the issue of limited time for classroom visitations. As Tonya said, "Due to the program of studies and scheduling we have few spares when we can visit others' classes.... The only challenge is that we can't go to our colleagues' classrooms to observe as often as we would like" (17:10, 54). Another factor that contributed to insufficient time for collaboration was increased paperwork. Arkadiy asserted that instead of working with other teachers on bringing about positive changes into the school, he was caught up in an endless trail of paperwork that needed to be submitted to the administration. He concluded: "Teachers are overloaded with tasks, reports, paperwork that hinder their creativity. All of this influences relationships, collaboration, etc.... Frankly speaking, we are turning into statisticians and clerks that deal more with regulatory documents than teaching" (14:8, 24-26). For Arkadiy, increased paperwork and teacher overload influenced the moral aspect of collaboration – *creativity*.

Differential difficulties related to age and experience came up second in the frequency of mention by the participants. The difference in age and teaching experience was perceived as a significant limitation for collaboration among teachers in several schools. This was especially visible in the conversations with younger teachers' focus group. Almost all of the participants in this group believed that working together with older and more experienced teachers was a challenge. They stated that younger teachers collaborate well among themselves and help each other in difficult situations, while there is limited collaboration between younger and older colleagues. Moreover, several respondents stressed the fact that older teachers in their school tried to put the pressure on the younger ones or sometimes, even put them down. On this point a teacher with three years of experience commented:

> Not all older colleagues are like that, there are those who really try to support you.... But unfortunately, a lot of them do not understand us; they think we come to school, start introducing everything new, and want to change them. We don't want to change them; we want them to help us to achieve new levels, because nobody can become a teacher in a year. It comes with time.... Therefore, in regard to your question, older teachers do not want to understand us, don't want to accept us into their collective. (Nelya, 8:27, 43)

Nelya and her colleagues asserted that as a result of lack of understanding and support, collaboration between younger and older teachers becomes difficult and sometimes even impossible.

On the other hand, several older respondents stated that different generations of teachers have different systems of beliefs and ideals and differently perceive the impact of surrounding events based on their upbringing and common interests. That is why teachers seem to collaborate more frequently with colleagues who belong to the same age group. Lena explained that she would rather collaborate with an older colleague,

> [Because] if I share anything with a person closer to my age, she will understand me and share my views. Young teachers have totally different views. Maybe we used to be like them before, because the problem of young and old generations in an eternal problem. (7:26, 99)

Lena's colleague, Stella, was concerned that younger teachers in their school did not value the fact that both professional and personal matters could be shared with school colleagues in order to receive necessary support or advice. Thus, joint work suffered because of challenges related to differences in age and teaching experience.

So-called *mandated collaboration* ranked high in the list of limitations and challenges to effective collaboration. In their focus group and interview responses about limiting factors of collaborative work among teachers, some of the participants stated that *voluntary* collaboration could not be limited in any way. However, if these teachers felt they were forced to work together, such efforts were perceived to be of little benefit (sometimes, even in vain) and not capable of producing any significant results. Other teachers discussed the presence of both voluntary and compulsory collaboration in the schools. Furthermore, Rimma specified that teacher participation was voluntary, but many of the collaborative activities in the school were mandated by administration: "it's not that teachers are forced [to collaborate], we agree to participate voluntarily. It's more like planned or mandated collaborative activities [on behalf of school administration]" (8:17, 165). So-called "*prescribed collaboration*" was also discussed by a number of other participants. Lena commented:

> The problem is that collaboration is planned. I wish it were done in an arbitrary way: whoever wants to present at the pedagogic council meeting or conference may present; whoever wants to say something may do so. Sometimes, it is prescribed: everything is preplanned, so that it will go smoothly. Everything should be said according to the plan: who says what and to whom. (7:27, 93)

Lena's colleague attributed such collaboration to the previous system of education, "where everything was done just to check it off the list. Not from the heart, but to check it off. Now we see the remnants of that" (Stella, 7:27, 95). Many other respondents also felt pressure and authoritarianism in the organization of collaborative activities on the part of administration in their school.

Judging from the frequency of mention, the respondents considered the *lack of resources* as yet another significant limitation to their cooperative work. In two of the schools, almost all teachers indicated that in order to conduct lessons they have to borrow instructional material from each other. Though such sharing of the materials may seem as a collaborative activity for some, for those teachers it was a challenge. In some cases there was only one book on a certain topic to be used by all teachers in the school. In other cases, several teachers discussed the lack of visual aids and display materials for their classrooms. They stated that schools used to provide teachers with methodological and display materials in the Soviet times, but during the independent Ukraine times (and even at the time of study), due to the insufficient funding, teachers were forced to get everything at their own expense. One of them shared the following example: "We even had to buy one set of wall charts for three teachers from our own money! Three of us chipped in and bought a set of charts for the Ukrainian lessons for three classes" (Lyubomyra, 5:22, 163). Lack of printed materials and resources was also acknowledged in one of the analyzed documents: "Since 1998, because of inflation and abrupt decrease in the purchasing capacity of educators, published resources became limited and only produced if there was a request" (Department of Education and Science of Chernivtsi Regional State Administration, 2002, p. 7). Thus, publication of resources decreased with the limited purchasing capacity of educators and schools.

Finally, *lack of formal system of collaboration* was named by two participants as one of the challenges for effective joint work. Some of the participants believed that there was no formal system for teachers to collaborate, share their experiences, and increase the level of professional growth. Iryna asserted that despite her and her colleagues' efforts, there was no high-quality system of collaboration: "Yes, collaboration exists, we try to do something, but it is like a common interests club, we can get together, discuss something. However, it is not done with the [systematic] approach" (21:13, 46). She also believed that schools did not have a solid theory that would coordinate teachers' collective work in the instructional process. Throughout her interview, Iryna repeated over and over again that collaboration hadn't become systematic in their school and was *random* in nature; it only occurred when there was an urgent need to get something done. She described teachers who systematically shared their experiences as "fanatics". Another respondent, Roksolana, expressed a similar point about barriers in working together, stating that "there is no broad-range collaboration. But if there is a need, then everyone gets down to business" (10:25, 46). These two teachers believed that a lack of formal system or theory of collaboration impeded teachers' potential for collaboration.

Collaboration in Action

In their discussions, participants mentioned a number of ways in which teachers worked together in the same schools and described examples of joint work among colleagues from different schools in the city. According to the respondents' comments, some of these activities were representative of collective work in all schools, while others occurred only in several of the schools in the study. They also differed in the degree of occurrence in individual schools: in some schools they became common practices, while in others they were less frequent. These practices are grouped in the following categories according to the frequency with which they were mentioned by the participants:

- common planning of school activities;
- common sharing of instructional materials;
- methodological associations (professional associations of teachers of the same subject);
- interdisciplinary integration;
- cooperation among subject and homeroom teachers;
- classroom intervisitations and observations;
- mentoring;

- pedagogical council (collegial body of school administration, consisting of all teachers and administrators of the school) and staff meetings; and
- external collaboration with teachers from other schools in the city.

All of these categories are discussed in a more detailed manner in the following sections.

Common Planning of School Activities

The majority of respondents asserted that practically all of the activities during the school year were collaborative in nature. General educational functions received top priority in schools. For example, common planning and participation were observed in organization of holidays, celebrations, and ceremonies, preparation of seminars, research and practice conferences, assemblies, parent-teacher interviews, and interdepartmental projects. Moreover, all teachers were expected to be involved in the organization of those activities. Roksolana explained:

> If there is a seminar organized in the school, then everyone is involved, sometimes one department, sometimes several departments together. Of course, we always try to show the best side of our school; therefore, one person in unable to do everything. If there is no help, there will be nothing organized. (10:25, 46)

Another respondent stated that planning for school activities is "not an individual work, it is a collective effort. Just like the saying goes: 'It is the individual that accomplishes something, but it is a group that participates in discussion that leads to action'. Two heads are better than one" (Mariya, 20:27, 111). This respondent stated that teachers relied heavily on collective involvement.

In several schools, respondents viewed extracurricular activities that joined teachers of different subjects as an example of collaboration. Mentioned were such activities as sports tournaments, educational trips, camps, and academic competitions. Tonya commented:

> In our school we have a well-organized extracurricular program. During the school year (beginning of the fall - end of spring), we go on the road trips to famous sights in our Bukovyna region. Not just with one class, but with three or four classes together in order to have a closer group of students. Students learn how to work together with others, grow closer to each other. We find 'common language' with kids through these activities, too. We can also communicate with other teachers during that time. (17:11, 58)

The participants from the Judaism Immersion school also described how teachers worked together in so-called "school camps". In these camps, organized and funded by charitable organizations from Israel, teachers from their school worked as counselors alongside colleagues from the USA, Canada, Israel, and other countries. The respondents from an elite school noted that teachers collaborate in the process of preparing students for academic competitions, such as school, citywide, or national *Subject Olympics*. "There is a very close collaboration there, because, as a rule, students are trained by several subject teachers" (14:7, 32), posited Arkadiy.

Common Sharing of Instructional Materials

Most of the respondents indicated that teachers share their lesson plans and other instructional materials with colleagues. That in itself was perceived by many participants as a fundamental concept for collaboration, as Roksolana maintained:

> If we have anything good, we share. Every five years a teacher goes through attestation, where we share our materials. Very often, we have seminars or open lessons, where we show our best practices that we would like to share with others. It is up to those who attend presentations to adopt any of those materials or not. (Roksolana, 10:31, 142-144)

In addition, several teachers indicated the existence of both informal and formal sharing of materials.

While conducting a focus group interview in the school where Roksolana taught, I visited the vice-principal's office and noticed binders with such labels as "Summary of Teachers' Work Experience" and "Dissemination of Experience". In the individual interviews, I asked teachers to dwell upon the meaning behind those binders. Lyubomyra explained:

> It is a continuous process. The binders are there all the time, and from attestation to attestation, which is conducted once every 5 years, all teacher experiences are collected there. At the end of the 5th year, experiences are summarized and teachers participate in attestation with development and improvement of professional experiences. Our experiences are studied and summarized by the vice-principal: we describe all our accomplishments in 5 years in regard to professional development, and report at the end of 5-year period. (12:26, 139)

All four interviewed teachers in that school seemed to be very pleased with the way this process of sharing of work experience was organized. One teacher observed:

> Personally, I don't like systematization, and it is a great drawback for me. However, I like how our vice-principal does it. For example, she is in charge of several departments with a certain amount of teachers. She has a separate binder for each teacher. When a teacher conducts an open lesson, she is present at the lesson and immediately asks him to provide lesson materials, which she inserts into the binder with his name. Or there is an interesting class activity - it goes into the binder. Teacher may forget about those things, but the vice-principal has everything in the binder, and when there is teacher attestation, she includes those materials in the process. This is a very positive thing. (Roksolana, 10:32, 146-148)

It was strongly emphasized in the participants' responses that those materials were an open source and could be easily accessed by any of the teachers. Lyubomyra provided an example of how summaries of teacher experiences were used:

> For example, I work on the development of coherent speech; others work on the development of logical thinking. Therefore, I can come there and borrow something about the development of logical thinking or creative abilities of students. Some of my colleagues went to a seminar dedicated to differentiation; I wasn't there, but they brought back some great material and approbated it in their classrooms. Why wouldn't I take the binder, read about their accomplishments, and learn from them if it works well, and I really need that for my classes? Another example is interactive learning - I take the binder, read, and borrow something for my instruction. This is an obligatory process, otherwise, it would sit there as a dead stock. (12:26, 141-143)

Alternatively, some teachers published their methodological works in professional journals, seminar collections, conference proceedings, and book series. Sonya noted: "I published a collection of seminars for Grade 10, and it was distributed among teachers from other schools. I think it is very beneficial to them, because they can see, learn, or borrow something from those materials that I have compiled and used in my instruction" (13:8, 46). For teachers this was a form of collaboration and an opportunity to let their knowledge and experiences be used by colleagues not only from their school, but from other schools in the city and Ukraine, too. Teachers were also expected to share materials and information with colleagues, in both formal and informal settings, after attending conferences, seminars, or teacher competitions. However, the analysis of document data revealed that despite the fact that many teachers attended different seminars organized by the regional department of education, only one-third of those teachers initiated sharing of acquired knowledge and materials with their colleagues (Department of Education and Science of Chernivtsi Regional State Administration, 2003).

Methodological Associations

The majority of the participants associated teacher collaboration with *methodological associations*. Teachers defined methodological association as a group of teachers of a specific subject, for example, mathematics or history, that meets to discuss professional issues, review programs, plan curricula, exchange experiences, schedule mutual class visitations, implement new Ministry of Education policies and regulations, mentor novice teachers, present achievements in their subject area, etc. Viktor, a school principal, described the process of the formation of methodological associations and their cooperation with the school administration:

> Principal's order or bylaw #1 in the beginning of the year deals with the formation of methodological or profile associations from the best teachers in each subject. They suggest and advance ideas about how to improve methodological work of a certain subject, pass their information to the administration, and together with them, we coordinate our actions to make methodological work the 'lighthouse', which will guide our actions in today's education. (15:11, 46)

The responses from different schools revealed that methodological associations were present in all schools and met five or six times a year. Antonina clarified: "Usually we have six meetings during the school year: once every two months; plus, a special meeting at the beginning of the year, where we decide on the programs; and a final meeting at the end of the year, where we discuss the results of the year" (11:11, 60). If it were necessary, teachers initiated extra meetings of their methodological association:

> Sometimes, we initiate methodological association meetings to discuss the appropriateness of using certain methodologies or techniques and share certain instructional novelties that we learnt about. We regularly hold these methodological association meetings and discuss, for example, something new that we read in our professional journal or newspaper on mathematics. Alternatively, we can discuss and plan the activities for 'Mathematics Week', which is held once a year for the whole week: official opening, closing ceremony, publishing of announcements, timetable of open mathematics lessons, or intellectual competitions for grade parallels [all classes of the same grade], such as 'Brain Ring', etc. We discuss, take counsel with each other to avoid blunders in order to make it more interesting and to unite the students in those activities…. Thus, our methodological association benefits children and teachers. (11:10, 52)

Meetings could also be initiated by school administration, depending on the need of teachers of a certain subject area: "If, after a month of work, administration sees that certain subject areas need improvement in regard to methodological development, then we organize a special meeting of a certain association. Then, we analyze the achievements and discuss the areas of improvement" (Viktor, 15:11, 50).

For many of the participants, methodological associations played a very important role in their schools. First of all, they allowed establishing greater integration among teachers across subject areas. Antonina posited:

> We have meetings of just mathematics methodological association or sometimes, we get together with physics and computer science teachers, because we depend on each other in instruction. For example, physics teachers cannot start teaching certain assignments until their students learn about derivatives in math. I have my plan to teach derivatives in the middle of semester, while they have to start at the beginning of the year. Therefore, we discuss this issue at the joint methodological associations meeting and either decide to move the topic for a later time in physics, or adjust the math program according to the needs of physics teachers. The same is with the computer science teachers, when they introduce a

program with formulas, but they can't move forward because students do not know those formulas. (11:12, 64)

Working together in methodological associations also helped teachers to provide better education to groups of students with various needs:

> We have classes with various academic levels of students. We used to have 'correction classes' [modified classes], but then students felt offended by being put into those classes for academically challenged or disabled students, and they were cancelled.... Therefore, they decided to establish profile classes in math, economics, science, physics and math, languages, as well as regular classes called "general". Of course, these classes have different curriculum. The seminar will take place only in December, but we already gathered twice at our methodological association meetings. We initiated meetings ourselves, because every teacher has some ideas and we all want to present our best practices.... Right now we are working on how the same topic can be presented in classes with different profiles, be it a general or math profile class. However, to make everything look nice, we discuss different ideas and give advice to the teacher who is responsible for that topic. (11:12, 66)

Thus, by providing teachers with the time and opportunity to meet and discuss their field-related issues, methodological associations served as facilitators of collaboration among teachers of the same or similar subjects.

Interdisciplinary Integration

Many of the respondents perceived interdisciplinary integration to be a primary foundation of the schooling process. Ilona termed it as *the foundation of foundations of schoolwork*:

> In a school, a physics lesson, foreign language lesson, or the like, cannot exist separately. Nowadays, the information flow is so expansive, so strong, that it is impossible to teach just 'pure' science. It's impossible to teach language without history, literature, geography, nature studies. As well, as history is impossible without the foreign language. Integration is first and foremost... This integration is further developing with the span of time, and you can't find a so-called 'pure' subject in the school now. (3:22, 87)

Interdisciplinary integration promoted the development of professional collaboration in the school: teachers were involved in organizing interdisciplinary lessons, such as binary, combined, and integrated lessons. Sonya made mention of the following examples of integrated lessons:

> Personally, I organized lessons together with teachers from the department of Ukrainian literature, such as Ukrainian literature and history of Ukraine in Grades 9 and 10. Also, there were integrated lessons about the world history and geography, history and foreign literature. These are not mere words, but students are really interested in those lessons, as they see two teachers in a class teaching a completely different lesson. These are the activities that I am involved in. As far as I know, other teachers work in the same direction: the department of English language collaborates with foreign literature; English language with physics; history with English language. (13:5, 30)

A biology teacher, Lena, discussed her involvement in the integrated lessons on ecological problems related to Chornobyl tragedy organized together with a teacher of physics. Her colleague, Stella, described the use of binary lessons in their school:

> For example, we practice binary classes in foreign literature and English. There can be a complete change in the structure of the lesson, or it can be built on various episodes. For instance, if we study the works of Goethe, the German poet, I invite a German language teacher to read the verse in German. We studied Robinson Crusoe last year, and it was a very nice lesson by our young teacher and a vice-principal who teach English; they combined English lesson with the content that we study in foreign literature. (7:29, 115)

These teachers concluded that the use of integrated methodologies was supported and promoted by the new 12-year school program in Ukraine.

Cooperation among Subject and Homeroom Teachers

A number of the respondents indicated that there was a very close cooperation between subject and homeroom teachers. One respondent commented:

> Practically all who are sitting here are homeroom teachers. A work of home room teacher is impossible without communication with subject teachers. We simply won't have information and will lose the thread of communication with students. (Lesya, 6:12, 74)

Homeroom teachers believed that constant exchange of information with subject teachers helped them address students' needs and deal with issues in more effective ways.

Besides working together with subject teachers, homeroom teachers collaborated in everyday work among themselves. Some respondents indicated that they have formal meetings five times a year, work closely together, because all issues are similar in different classes, and very often they help each other with teaching or substituting for one another. Arkadiy added that teacher substitutions were another form of joint work among homeroom and subject teachers:

> Look at teacher substitutions, when one of the colleagues is sick, goes away on a school trip, or attends a meeting: it is another form of collaboration, because teachers pass materials to each other, share lesson plans, help teach lessons, provide instructional support. (14:7, 36)

He continued that there were formal substitutions, as well as so-called "friendly substitutions", when teachers had urgent things to do outside of school, and colleagues volunteered to teach their classes.

Classroom Intervisitations and Observations

Classroom intervisitations and observations that frequently occurred in schools were considered by participating teachers as highly collaborative in nature. They discussed formal observations in the form of an *open lesson*, mandated by the school program or administration and open for administrators, teachers, or even parents to attend; and informal visitations initiated by teachers themselves. According to the responses, open lessons and mutual classroom visitations were common phenomena in all schools. They served a two-fold purpose: to observe colleagues' instruction, learn new techniques, and adopt new elements in teaching; or, to provide advice, support, and assistance to colleagues. Antonina explained:

> All teachers have agreed that we can visit each other's lesson anytime, because we are colleagues. I can simply come to my colleague and ask if she does not object to my presence in her classroom. I take a place in the back, students have no problems with that, and I simply observe her lesson. The goal of such observation can be either to learn something or give advice to that teacher about her instruction. Sometimes, colleagues ask others to observe lessons in order to improve their instruction. After the lesson, I will point to her mistakes, if any. It is still better than having a supervisor in the classroom. Or we observe lessons to learn from each other, because each teacher has his or her 'zest' in teaching. Even young teachers teach us different things they have learnt somewhere else that we don't know. (11:11, 56)

Some schools had also established an "open door" policy to classroom visitations:

> If there is an open lesson organized by a teacher, everyone who wants can visit it. If someone has a lesson at that time, administration always tries to assist them in any way to make it possible for them to observe that lesson. For example, we encourage young teacher to visit lessons organized by more experienced teachers. We encourage an 'open door' policy: please, come in, learn, ask for advice. (Sophia, 22:11, 36)

Very important for teachers were post-observation discussions of open lessons as opportunities to evaluate lessons and provide feedback to colleagues.

Mentorship

Mentoring, as a type of collaboration between experienced and novice teachers, was frequently discussed by the participants. More experienced teachers mentored novice teachers (often called as "young specialists") in formal and informal ways. Informally, they offered advice and assistance in regard to teaching techniques, methodological matters, and extracurricular activities. As Stella put it,

> We, older teachers, can offer a lot of help to the younger teachers about extra-curricular activities. Also, [we can offer advice] to school administration who are younger than we are, so that they would take our opinions into consideration and we would feel needed here. It means a lot too. They say that a person is happy when he or she is needed by somebody... How many young [teachers] ask me about a class-book or a plan, and I can't say no. You feel that you teach them, you feel like an experienced teacher. Therefore, collaboration is present everywhere. (7:29, 117)

On the other hand, several of the participants observed younger teachers offering suggestions to their older colleagues, which was also a form of mentoring. A few respondents also mentioned formal mentorship program, "The School of a Young Teacher", which provides support services for novice teachers to help them join the pace of school work.

Pedagogical Council and Staff Meetings

Also common to all schools were *pedagogical councils* and staff meetings. Unlike methodological association meetings mentioned earlier, pedagogical councils gathered *all* teachers in the school. Document analysis revealed that pedagogical council is a continuing collegial administrative body that consisted of all teachers and was headed by the principal. It is a professional council that deals with issues directly related to the organization and improvement of education. The number of meetings of the pedagogical council during a school year depends on the necessity and expediency for the school collective, but cannot be fewer than four times a year (Cabinet of Ministers of Ukraine, 2000).

Participating teachers indicated that in their schools, pedagogical council meetings occurred before the beginning of the school year and several times during the year. These councils were organized in the form of seminars on the problems or issues of instruction of various subjects and involved joint work of teachers who exchanged information, outlined discussion topics, and presented on selected issues. Lina commented: "We have very interesting pedagogic councils: there are no lectures; we divide into small groups, and every group has its issue, which is prepared and discussed during the pedagogic council" (18:15, 56).

Teachers also discussed collaboration during the formal or informal staff meetings. "Every Monday, our principal gathers all teachers for a meeting, where we discuss current school issues for that period of time", stated Mariya (20:16, 58). Besides regular staff meetings, teachers got together for so-called "five-minutes", short staff meetings to discuss issues or problems that needed urgent attention.

Inter-School Teacher Collaboration

Many of the respondents believed that the nature of teacher collaboration could not be fully understood without looking at the *external* collaboration among teachers from different schools. Roksolana explained:

> There is a very close collaboration with colleagues from our school, as well as other schools in the city, because we teach one subject, and we would like to learn something new from

other teachers. Very often we observe open lessons in other schools, attend their seminars, or invite teachers from other schools to our open lessons or seminars. This way we learn many new things, because you won't go far in your professional development if you 'stew in your own juice'. (10:22, 34)

Moreover, some participants mentioned that colleagues from their schools conducted master-class instruction for teachers from other schools and professional development activities at the Institute of Post-Diploma Teacher Development [formal regional teacher education organization established by the Ministry of Education]. A number of teachers also described their involvement in the work of citywide methodological associations, organized by the methodological office of the municipal Department of Education. For instance, Antonina commented:

There is also a citywide methodological association, in which I participate as a representative from our school. The school representative attends citywide methodological association meeting once a month or once every 2 months, and later reports to the school association and facilitates discussion of citywide issues at the school association meetings. In fact, we deal with all issues of mathematics instruction, from curriculum to extracurricular activities. (11:11, 56)

Besides citywide level cooperation, several teachers mentioned working together with colleagues at the national level:

…Our citywide methodological association of history teachers is very active. We receive support from the all-Ukrainian teacher organization 'New Age', which organizes various trainings and seminars for teachers from all regions in Ukraine. Coaches and trainers from Lviv and Kyiv come to Chernivtsi; they also invite us to attend seminars in Kyiv, Lviv, and other cities on Ukraine. At those conferences, we communicate with history teachers not only from our city, but from all regions in Ukraine. They provide funding for teachers, including travel and accommodation expenses. Those seminars organized by 'New Age' are very interesting, and they promote collaboration among teachers. Our school is very active in this organization; I am the executive board member. Many students' and teachers' competitions are sponsored by 'New Age', and I think that existence of such teachers' organization is very positive. (Sonya, 13:8, 50)

These participants praised the existence of such types of teacher organizations as "New Age", because they allowed them to be involved in collaboration with their colleagues from other regions of Ukraine.

Summary: The Essence of Teacher Collaboration

This chapter contained the description of the respondents' perceptions regarding the nature and state of teacher collaboration in Ukrainian schools, which varied significantly according to contexts of individual schools. Teachers' responses indicated that collaboration was very important and beneficial for teachers, both in professional and personal matters. The nature of teacher collaboration was characterized by a variety of descriptors, ranging from the family-like cooperation to competition and unacceptability. Several principles were seen to guide joint work among teachers in schools, such as mutual help, lifelong learning, communication, and leadership. The extent to which teachers were able to work together was perceived to be limited by lack of time, age and experience related issues between teachers of different age groups, mandated collaboration, lack of resources, and lack of a formal system of collaboration. In their discussions of various ways of working together with their colleagues, teachers emphasized common planning of activities; common sharing of instructional materials; methodological associations; interdisciplinary integration; cooperation among subject and homeroom teachers; classroom visitations and observations; mentoring; pedagogical council and staff meetings; and, external collaboration with teachers from other schools in the city.

Chapter 7

SOCIETAL CHANGES AND TEACHER COLLABORATION

One can't live in society and be outside of society. (Lyuba, 4:18, 44)

In this chapter, I present the participants' perceptions of the impact of external post-Soviet societal changes on collaboration among teachers. Teachers' responses included, but were not limited to, the discussion of the following issues: the nature of teacher collaboration in the Soviet times; changes in the content and format of collaboration as a result of various societal transformations; and, the perceived future direction of teacher collaboration in the light of current societal developments.

The Nature of Collaboration in the Soviet Era

Those of the participants who had worked in schools under the Soviet regime presented an overview of what teacher collaboration was like in those times. Their comments addressed collective nature of teachers' work, the political and ideological context of collaborative activities, and well established system of mentorship and support for novice teachers.

Collective Nature of Work

Many of the participants believed that the work of teachers during the Soviet Union era to be highly collective in nature. They viewed Makarenko's collectivism as the guiding principle of teacher collaboration at that time. The essence of the notion of the *collective* was that teachers' individual interests had to be subdued to the interests of the school collective. Lyudmyla commented: "That's how it was in the Soviet Union: a collective was above all, while family or personal views were moved to the background" (1:28, 301). For many teachers in that time that meant that their school collective was of the highest priority: they had to "go all out in school", putting everything else aside as secondary. One teacher stated, "The 'Soviet school' taught and encouraged teachers to devote themselves fully to their work in school" (Sonya, 13:6, 36). Also mentioned was collective responsibility of teachers for everything that happened in the school. Treating everything with full responsibility developed "communist endurance or toughness in teachers to haul everything on their shoulders and do everything with conscience" (Lyubomyra, 12:15, 70).

Political and Ideological Context

The majority of the school collaborative activities in the Soviet times were seen to be politically and ideologically-laden. Many of the respondents reminisced that the Communist Party directed teacher collaboration through Party assemblies, Komsomol [the Young Communist League] assemblies, professional union meetings, Political Information hours and Political Studies for teachers, Pioneer organization, Pioneer bonfires, and subbotniks [*subbotnik* - a day of voluntary work for beautifying the school, city, etc.]. Volodymyr commented:

> The Communist Party was our leader and it influenced relationships in every collective, including pedagogical collective. There was a Party center in our school, which controlled, influenced (sometimes positively, sometimes negatively) our school collective. It functioned parallel to the schoolwork and struck the keynote of schools' policy. (15:5, 18)

Organized collaboration was seen as a mechanism for uniting the school collective and for bringing teachers together. However, some teachers indicated that there had been little voluntary collaboration, as most of the activities were obligatory for all teachers. A few respondents also reminisced about a very rigid supervision and control over teacher participation in all activities.

Support System

Many of the respondents believed there had been very strong collaboration between novice and experienced teachers in the Soviet times. Schools provided beginning teachers with a "strong" system of support through mentorship. Many teachers noted that in the Soviet times, a young teacher had always been provided with the mentor who attended the lessons, offered methodological help, and assisted with advice on how to deal better with discipline, and improve or change instruction. Tonya, for instance, recollected:

> I have worked only for 2 or 3 years during the Soviet Union times. First of all, I was sent to a school with strong pedagogical cadres, there were many experienced teachers. What I really liked is a system of support, starting with the principal and ending with my colleagues, teachers who were more experienced than I was. I felt support and a willingness to help a novice teacher. I think it played a major role for me, because if I were sent to a different school where attitudes towards novice teachers were different, I would have never achieved what I achieved so far. (Tonya, 17:6, 38)

Another teacher, Lyuda, added that despite a strict order and authoritarian leadership in the provision of mentoring services, she learned from experienced teachers how to work properly. She agreed that mentoring had good results and had influenced her teaching career in a positive way.

Post-Soviet Societal Changes and Teacher Collaboration

Answering the questions about the influence of external societal changes on teacher collaboration after the collapse of the USSR, the participating teachers made reference to the degree of the perceived impact and discussed various transformations in the nature and format of teacher collaboration. A detailed description of their responses is provided in sections below.

The Degree of Perceived Societal Impact

Teachers' opinions about the degree of the influence of post-Soviet societal changes on teacher collaboration ranged from "insignificant" to "very significant". A small number of participants believed that societal changes were of little impact on teacher collaboration in their schools. Their comments mainly related to the *personal* side of collective work and relationships among teachers. They argued that such aspects of collaboration as mutual help and support are independent of society and teachers continue to work together the way they had worked before. "I think collaboration is outside of society. That's what we brought out of our families, our upbringing. That warmth, that flame is brought from our home; we bring it here to share with each other", stated Ilona (3:21, 70). Another respondent posited:

> I think there were insignificant changes in this area, because teachers are quite kind and considerate people and have always tried to help each other and treat each other in a friendly manner in the times of the Soviet Union and nowadays. I am a representative of an older generation, but when a young specialist comes to school, I try to share my experience with him, show something, invite to my lessons, give advice on how to do certain things, etc. I think little has changed in this area. People are people. (Roksolana, 10:11, 22)

Quite a few teachers stressed that such a factor as 'upbringing in the spirit of collectivism' was instrumental in the fact that teachers of an 'old school' (as some of them termed it) collaborate in the same manner despite all the changes. According to Lina, Makarenko's principles of collective from the Soviet era still guide teachers' work:

Person remains the same, be it in the Soviet or other times.... [R]elationships were good], because it is a teachers' collective, and it is impossible to exist without such relationships. Our work is joint in nature. I look and acquaint myself with instructional methodologies of other countries, and I can tell that every teacher works for himself for herself there. Those Makarenko's principles of collective used to guide and still guide our work. We are so close that we know every little detail about each other, even about each other's salary (which is unheard of anywhere in the world). Thus, those collectivistic principles remained. (Lina, 18:11, 30)

Several experienced teachers agreed that they still live with an old way of thinking: "First think of the Homeland [Soviet Union], and then about yourself." (Lyuba, 4:19, 96). Volodymyr concluded that that relationships between colleagues in schools remained the same as they were in the Soviet times, ranging from collaboration to unacceptability and competition.

The majority of focus group and interview participants, however, indicated (both directly and indirectly) in their responses that post-Soviet societal changes had a significant effect on the nature of teacher collaboration. As Lyuba put it, "One can't live in society and be outside of society" (4:18, 44). Most teachers argued that the *nature*, *content* and *format* of their joint work with colleagues have undergone "very significant" transformations.

Societal Impact and Subsequent Transformations in Collaboration

The participants in this study outlined a number of differences in the ways in which school teachers worked together in the Soviet Union and independent Ukraine eras. Respondents believed those differences were both direct and indirect results of the societal influences on schools in general, and teachers in particular. Their responses related to the change in content of collaboration with the introduction of new tasks and requirements; voluntary participation in collaborative activities; changed format of collaboration; increased administrative control; impacts of material welfare and financial difficulties on teachers' willingness and ability to collaborate; transformations in teacher relationships; division among teachers; and, shift in the perceptions of the notion of "collective".

Changes in the content of collaboration.
Teachers articulated that the content of teacher collaboration had changed. First of all, they referred to the tasks and requirements assigned to their school by educational authorities, both national and in-school administrators. New tasks and requirements differed from the ones fulfilled by a school collective in the Soviet times:

At that time, we were fulfilling different tasks assigned to our collective and tried to help each other. The time passed; now, there are other tasks. Again, we are carrying them out with the same staff; we are trying to help each other in solving the problems that are set by the government. (Nina, 2:24, 182)

Several participants reminisced that pedagogical councils and staff meetings in the Soviet times had always started with the discussion of tasks and requirements set by the Communist Party.

As for the pedagogical council meetings, they differ from what they used to be like in the Soviet times. Before, we were given a theme of the lecture and asked to comment on it after the presentation. Usually, nobody wanted to participate; therefore, several teachers were appointed to present. They would sit in the corner and tremble, as they had to say something following the lecturer's speech. (Antonina, 11:10, 52)

In addition, a few respondents emphasized a significant decrease in the number of teacher assemblies of different kinds, such as staff meetings and pedagogical meetings, in comparison with the Soviet times.

Voluntary participation in collaborative activities. Respondents indicated that unlike the obligatory participation in school activities exercised in the Soviet times, participation in collaborative activities in Independence era became more voluntary-based. Several teachers tied the absence of ideological pressure and political context of the collaborative activities to a greater eagerness to participate on the part of teachers:

> [Unlike the Soviet era pedagogical council meetings], nowadays, teachers want to get involved and volunteer to participate, because issues discussed at those meetings are usually very topical and urgent to us as teachers. If teachers dislike something, they can request to change the topic or discuss it at some other time. Teachers can also bring in a motion for discussion of different issues, ranging from instruction to general life in school, youth development, student leisure, neighborhood and community issues and activities, etc. (Antonina, 11:10, 52)

In a number of schools, it was indicated that unlike before, greater participation from teachers was encouraged and promoted by the school administration. However, it was not based on the use of administrative force; participation was voluntary: "If someone doesn't want to do something that is not included in the list of professional responsibilities, such as being part of the collective or participating in different activities, that person can always refuse, and it will not affect relationships with others" (Arkadiy, 14:13, 64).

Voluntary participation in collaborative activities was perceived to be the direct outcome of the freedom of speech. Many teachers noticed a greater openness in expressing of individual opinions in the school collective. Roksolana commented:

> There is more openness; no one is afraid to express his or her point of view. Before, if you looked at the collective, it seemed like every member of the collective had the same views. No one knew each other's thoughts, but from what they said you could think they had the same views. Now, teachers have different points of view and express different opinions. Very often, these are opposite of views, but no one judges others for that. That's considered to be absolutely normal. It has to be like that. (10:13, 70)

Moreover, in teachers' experiences it was not a gradual change, but a sudden one.

Changes in the format of collaboration. Along with freedom of expression, the participants experienced freedom for instructional innovations. The analysis of teachers' responses affirmed that the introduction of new collaborative activities for teachers was especially obvious in the schools of a "new type", such as lyceum and gymnasium. While most of the forms of cooperative work in regular schools remained the same as in the Soviet times, elite schools had initial freedom to incorporate innovations in the area of collaboration in their work. When schools of a new type were being established, they had a certain degree of freedom as there was no regulatory basis of legal policies that clearly outlined and prescribed school activities. Therefore, elite schools (lyceums, gymnasia) had possibilities to experiment with pedagogical work and do something new and original. They were built on the principles of creativity and self-actualization – something not connected with former Soviet command-type pedagogy:

> Teachers came to us with understanding that we were an elite school, a school of a new type. They came to work here with the feeling that they can realize their potential, that they will not be cowed down, that they will be able to collaborate with colleagues, build their world of pedagogy, and see their pedagogical ideals fulfilled here that were impossible to be fulfilled in general secondary schools…. They hoped for mutual understanding, contact between teachers, students, and parents based on different principles. I would call it 'the school of happiness' for teachers. (Arkadiy, 14:8, 20)

The format of collaboration in these schools sought to emphasize "[teacher] relationships with the room for creativity, freedom of action, the right to make mistakes in pedagogical experiments, and freedom for innovations" (14:8, 20). Arkadiy also provided a description of new collaborative activities established in their school:

> In order to implement changes in collaboration, we try to introduce more group-work activities, both for students and teachers; organize various staff meetings and seminars that would stir up teachers' interest towards their profession, because along with material welfare, teachers need to think about professional growth, professional development, and professional self-actualization; introduce more interactive methods of teaching; transfer relationships between teachers, students, and parents from the subject-object to subject-subject level, where communication is done on equal terms. (14:8, 22)

All of these factors stimulated interest towards such elite schools among teachers in regard to self-actualization and ability to carry out not only mechanical instruction, but also creative and experimental work. However, as the participants pointed out, this freedom was gradually leveled off with the introduction of the uniform legislative system and policies for all schools, including elite schools, in the middle of 1990s.

Increased administrative control. After the initial period of democratization, when schools were allowed to use creativity in the process of collaboration, starting with the last years of the 20th century, many teachers felt that the old Soviet authoritarian mentality gradually tried to "grip them in its vice again". These respondents were particularly concerned about the most recent several years when they experienced increased bureaucratic control in the planning process and organization of staff meetings, actions of in-school administration, and policies of national and municipal authorities in education, such as Ministry of Education and Department of Education. Teachers indicated that time for collaboration became insufficient due to increased paperwork and requirements to account for all aspects of school work:

> Unfortunately, we do not have enough time. We used to communicate very often before. Now, we simply do not have time due to the fact that we encounter more problems and deal with excessive paperwork. This paperwork wastes our time; it takes away the time that could be spent on collaboration with colleagues. (Antonina, 11:9, 48)

Some focus group participants assumed that this phenomenon was connected with the return to power of people who used to work in Soviet times, who had wanted to rule again and establish the same "Soviet school" working procedures in the education system of independent Ukraine.

Changing work relationships between generations of teachers. Many of the interviewees asserted that the lack of collaboration between younger and older generations of teachers was related to the abrupt transition in society from one system of values and beliefs to another. In the older teachers' views, the younger generation of pedagogues came to school with significantly different values, worldviews, and, in most cases, different attitudes towards work and their colleagues. The older teachers expressed concerns that younger teachers were more reluctant to work together with their colleagues and to take on active roles in the school collective. "They want to finish their lessons faster and go home" or "They don't know what it means to devote their personal time after classes to the public", were some of the most common responses about the work of younger colleagues. Lyuba affirmed: "The older teachers are more prone to being involved in the collective, but the young ones are not drawn toward the collective anymore" (4:21, 150). The reason for that was that older teachers were brought up in a collectivistic society, while younger teachers grew up in a more individualistic environment. However, some representatives of the older generation confirmed that when there was a need, the younger teachers worked closely together:

> I would say that younger generation of teachers is more individualistic, but if there is a need for something to be done, there is complete collaboration among all of them. For instance, we were holding a principals' seminar and there was a direction about what should be done

115

and how it should be done. They worked in close collaboration. They all supported each other. (21:29, 137)

Some suggested that with technological developments, younger teachers are able to draw necessary information from a variety of sources; therefore, they may have a lesser need for mentoring from more experienced colleagues. Another reason for limited cooperation between generations of teachers, voiced by a few participants, was that younger teachers did not pay much attention to the collective because of time and commitment issues: many of them worked at several jobs in order to "get out of a scrape" and survive in difficult economic conditions.

Impacts of material welfare. Interestingly enough, material welfare of teachers and financial instability were deemed as the aspects that exerted the most significant impact on teacher collaboration. Many of the respondents argued that a variety of social and material aspects had significant negative influence on the willingness and ability of many teachers to collaborate with their colleagues. Larysa (L) and Antonina (A) explained:

L: Different social and material reasons influence collaboration as well. They *do* influence, and influence it greatly.

A: Yes, we want to talk to others, learn more, watch something, observe others, but then you get a subconscious thought, 'Why am I sitting here, there is no money in the house, I need to 'get out of a scrape', and you look for extra ways to earn that money. (5:22, 153)

Others also confirmed that school teachers were more preoccupied with survival than their professional duties. For some of them, teaching became a hobby:

The problem is that the majority of teachers do not think about how to teach something during the lesson; they think about how to earn some extra money. The fact is that often a teacher has more than one job. Therefore, teaching is like a hobby for many people, while almost all of them have another job on the side. One needs to have a side job in order to survive. (Iryna, 21:9, 34)

As was also mentioned by Iryna, she used to participate in an interschool teacher group, but due to the fact that many teachers worked at two or three jobs, the groups fell apart and collaboration between schools ceased. Another respondent added that societal changes influenced personal collaboration among teachers in terms of their financial ability to get together for celebrations and holidays. "Before, we could afford to work and celebrate all holidays together in the restaurant. Nowadays, we can't afford this, because we will have to pay a pretty penny for it" (Antonina, 11:8, 28).

Transformation in teacher relationships. Several of the respondents perceived material and financial instability to have been instrumental in transforming the nature of relationships among teachers. Lyubomyra observed that relationships used to be closer and kinder, and communication between colleagues was much better before:

Now, teachers become annoyed if others possess something better. For example, when they introduce teacher ranks and titles, it irritates some teachers, because not every teacher can achieve a title or rank with his or her work. To some degree, these things irritate colleagues. For some reason we became more exasperated, cruel, envious to colleagues who do better at work. Relationships are like that now, but they used to be kinder and nicer, much nicer. There was no division between those who have teacher ranks and those who do not. It was a little different. Maybe the conditions of life have affected us so much that we have become embittered and resentful. (12:9, 38)

When asked whether the above described phenomena were the result of the influence of societal changes on relationships among teachers, Lyubomyra replied:

> Yes, because some families have a better material welfare, and it is noticeable at work. Such teachers enjoy greater freedom at work, teach only the required hours of instruction and go home. Therefore, they feel better than those who are not 'socially defended', who live on scarce means. It is difficult for them; therefore, relationships with colleagues become different to some degree. (12:9, 42)

She drew parallels between the nature of collaboration outside and inside the school walls, indicating that change in the relationships in society greatly influenced relationships between teachers in school:

> Before, people used to be happier, friendlier, and closer with others. Nowadays, I observe that people do not visit each other, do not invite others to visit. Talking to other teachers, I can see that teachers do not go out or visit others. The only times when we do is when they obligate us to go to the concert or function with students. Otherwise, our route is 'school - home - school'.... In addition, I see that people are exhausted; we do not feel that life will become better. Everyone stews in one's own juice and tries to survive. Therefore, there is no collaboration as such. We used to go to the forest on weekends to pick mushrooms with teachers in those 'communist' times. There is nothing like that anymore: everyone stays at home and stews in one's own juice. (12:6, 117)

Several other teachers supported this point of view, stating that relationships in society became distant, even between family members. Iryna concluded that relationships became business-like:

> Everything is done in a businesslike manner: gainful and remunerative relationships became more popular and people started respecting only those people who are beneficial to know. Relationships among people, that were based on respect, knowledge and high moral qualities, become worse and worse with every day. (Iryna, 21:5, 157)

Furthermore, participants believed that disunited and alienated relationships led to isolation, both in society and in schools. "Unfortunately we started 'hiding in the corners', we rarely see each other – only at pedagogical council or staff meetings; that's it. It is impossible to meet in an informal atmosphere around the table and share our troubles or joys", Lyubomyra shared (12:10, 46).

Division among teachers. Some of the respondents also noticed that the decline in material welfare and change in relationships resulted in division among teachers. They stated that collaboration among all teachers in the collective gradually disappeared: "We used to get together in our Assembly Hall, but then something changed - either we became older or something changed in our pockets - and we started getting together in groups, big or small" (Lyuda, 23:24, 96). Teachers started getting together in groups based on affiliation with specific organizational divisions, as well as personal factors, such as similar interests or social status. Lyubomyra noted:

> Somehow, we became divided. We became divided into our department, grade parallels, secondary and elementary divisions in our schools. You find colleagues to whom you can pour out your heart, and that is how we get divided into groups. There is no collectivity in us, or heart-to-heart conversation among teachers. (12:10, 46)

Another respondent, Arkadiy, noted that such division had not been present in the schools before:

> The [societal conditions] influenced the school in the way that teacher coalitions started emerging in the collective. When we just started working in this school, there was nothing like that; the whole collective used to be like one family. Gradually, those material and moral problems started pushing teachers toward the establishment of the micro-groups in the collective, based on common economic or social status. Teachers formed those micro-groups to influence communication among teachers. (14:8, 26)

Some respondents alluded to the fact that teachers started communicating and working together with those colleagues who they felt could be of some benefit to them. One participant called it "cliquing": "It's not a collective, it's a clique" (Rimma, 8:13, 82).

Shift in the perceptions of the collective. The analysis of teacher responses indicated that perceptions of the notion of *collective* have changed. One teacher mentioned that such change resulted in the lack of collective support in problem solving:

> It seems to me that such a notion of collective, as it used to be before the collapse of the Soviet Union, doesn't exist anymore. In that time, the notion of collective meant that people got together, discussed different questions in pedagogical councils (that are not frequent now), discussed other questions. For example, students' behavior was discussed collectively by teachers... as distinct from one teacher racking his brains over how to deal with certain students now.... These problems exist everywhere, and each teacher solves them alone. There is no such notion as collective. (Rimma, 8:13, 78)

It was believed that these changes in perceptions were directly related to the decrease of collectivistic values in society.

Many participants believed life has changed so substantially, that societal interests did not trump personal interests of teachers any more: "The interests of the collective used to be higher, but we have stopped talking about 'think first about Motherland, then about yourself' a long time ago" (Adelya, 6:15, 111). Generally, teachers agreed that the collective had been in the foreground during the Soviet era:

> Collective spirit in the 'old', Soviet school was higher, because of the 'socialist competition'. Sometimes we sacrificed our everyday classroom work in order to show the achievements of our collective. At the same time, we were losing in the increase of knowledge and training skills... (Viktor, 15:7, 28)

According to most interviewees, collectivism was gradually disappearing, and individualism was becoming more apparent in society and in schools. It was especially obvious in the work of the younger generation of teachers: "You know, we can observe a reverse phenomenon: a feeling of collectivism gradually disappears. Now, young teachers won't say, 'Let's do it together.' This feeling of collectivism gets lost" (Lyuba, 4:20, 106). Moreover, some comments referred to the complete denial of collectivistic views and sole emphasis on individualistic views in the times of independent Ukraine. Instrumental in this seemed to be the Ministry of Education emphasis on the "Individuality Oriented Approach", which entailed individual approaches to teaching and professional development of a teacher (Kolotylo, 2005). According to the document analysis, the priority for innovations in the content of educational process became humanization of education, based on common human values and emphasis on the person's individuality (Department of Education and Science of Chernivtsi Regional State Administration, 2003). The successful realization of this goal depended on the teacher: "individuality-oriented approach to education starts with the individuality of a teacher.... In other words, individually-oriented education is a change in the viewpoint of a teacher" (p. 24). Thus, greater emphasis on individuality in schools seemed to have led to a gradual decline of collectivistic values.

Future of Teacher Collaboration

Besides the discussion of the societal influences that teacher collaboration had already undergone, the participants outlined their predictions about the direction in which it will head and changes in the society that will shape collaboration in the near future.

Prospective Direction of Collaborative Work

Many of the respondents were unsure about the direction in which teacher collaboration will develop. They believed this feeling was connected with a general sense of uncertainty in which direction Ukrainian society will move and a gradual loss of hope for the "brighter future". A majority of the participants believed that future development of collaborative relationships will depend on the willingness and priorities of the new generation of teachers:

> It will depend on those teachers that come to school: if they want something new and good, they will work closely together; if they are indifferent, there will be no collaboration…. There are indifferent teachers, but somehow they do not stay in the school for long, they leave after one year of working in the school. On the other hand, there are young teachers in our department who are creative and want to work. Wherever there is a will, there is a way. (Roksolana, 10:12, 50-54)

However, many of the respondents believed that younger teachers' priorities will continue to be different from those that older teachers hold. Iryna commented:

> Society will influence schools when the generation of teachers that are working in the school now will leave. When they leave, I am afraid it will be a *disaster* in education. It seems to me that totally different people will come into teaching profession, with different priorities. We still have those priorities of the Soviet system of education. On one hand, we said they were bad. Yes, relationships were different, they were less open, but for the most part those relationships were sincere and genuine; we sincerely helped each other. Nowadays, it is more and more obvious that the sincerity in relationships disappears. Other priorities take over, such as wealth and others…. It seems to me that in the future people will become more selfish and egotistical, and those 'Soviet' relationships will gradually disappear. (Iryna, 21:3, 141)

Thus, it was perceived by most experienced teachers that collaboration would decrease with the tendency towards prevalence of individualistic values in the younger teachers' work and retirement of the generation of pedagogues brought up in collectivistic views.

Societal Conditions and Perspectives of Collaboration

Despite the prevalent sense of pessimism regarding the future of collaborative work, teachers hoped that it would improve with the presence of favorable societal conditions. Many participants outlined a number of transformations that, in their view, were necessary for collaboration in Ukrainian schools to move in the "right direction". They addressed such issues as teacher status and authority, material welfare, spirituality and morale, balance between collectivism and individualism, and greater collaboration in society. Their recommendations are presented in accordance with the frequency of mention and degree of importance outlined by teachers.

First of all, most participants indicated the need for improvement of *teacher status* and increase of *teachers' authority* in society. Several of them advocated for a public service [public capacity] workers' status for teachers:

> Why some bureaucrats that sit in the Chernivtsi Regional State Administration [Governor's Office] or some other administration and do some paperwork are considered to be public officers? And we, people who form the generation that will be our leaders in the near future, are not public officers. In this regard, teachers should be first to obtain the status of a public officer. (Sonya, 13:2, 74)

Also mentioned was the need to restore the prestige of the profession of a teacher:

> This should not be restored by one-time actions, such as an award or a new program (without proper funding). There should be constant action to increase the authority of a

teacher. Teacher's authority needs to become stronger in order to increase the authority and power of knowledge. The power of knowledge needs to increase in the society, and not the authority of the person who doesn't need knowledge to earn money…the authority of a specialist who needs knowledge and training, and, thus, needs qualified teacher. This would change attitudes towards school and teacher. (Arkadiy, 14:6, 78)

Another respondent believed that teachers' authority in society would not increase until society realizes that teachers are the "doctors of human souls", and the way people live in the society largely depends on teachers: "A doctor cures the body, but a teacher cures the soul. We educate, we put something into the souls of these kids. Therefore, we have to be treated accordingly, so that we could feel that others need us" (Lyuba, 4:14, 216). Societal trust and valuing of professionalism were also perceived as pivotal in restoring teachers' authority.

Secondly, respondents made references to the *material welfare* of teachers. They believed stability in economic, social, and political areas will allow teachers to be more financially and socially secure, and concentrate solely on their work:

If I have enough, I will want to live, communicate, help others, and I will feel better and happier in this life. Otherwise, we live isolated lives with our own problems. It seems to me that all my colleagues have big problems. I realize that there is no life without problems, but these are constant, global problems: how to *survive*. (Lyubomyra, 12:7, 121)

It was suggested that material welfare and social guarantees will help teachers view their work differently:

Collaboration will happen if teachers see that teaching is the sense of their life. However, at this time, it is not the sense of our lives - right now, after you have finished teaching six classes a day, you turn around and go somewhere where you can earn money. It would be good to earn money at your place of work, developing programs, and be paid well for those programs. (Iryna, 21:18, 78)

It was concluded that security in terms of material well-being of teachers would promote teacher creativity, professional development, and collaboration among colleagues.

The respondents regarded higher levels of *spirituality and morale* as necessary prerequisites to positive future influence of society on schools and teacher collaboration. Several teachers believed that improvements of both material and spiritual aspects in society were important for teacher collaboration.

Material - because we have to eat every day, and spiritual - because, as they say, in ancient times leaving home for war, a warrior always took weapon, bread, and a song. I think morality can be compared with that song…. Spirituality and morality are very important; they keep the soul from getting sick. The worst thing that can happen is when your soul hurts. (Mariya, 20:7, 175)

Mariya concluded that there should be a harmony in combination of spiritual and material welfare. She also suggested that future collaboration in schools needed to be organized according to a higher moral standard.

According to many respondents, collaboration required a *balance between collectivism and individualism* through equal emphasis on individuality and collectivity in schools. It was perceived that extreme emphasis on either collectivism or individualism was not desirable for effective teacher collaboration:

The prevalence of collective views, according to Makarenko, corresponded to the system that existed at that time. I didn't accept it then, because any societal development has to consist for both individualistic and collectivistic factors. Moreover, during the last 15 years, the prevalence of individualistic factors with the complete denial of the collective needs was a large drawback for our future development. Because, as we live in the 21st century, ignoring those who are around us, either on the left or on the right, as well as their interests, in my opinion, is a hindrance to the development of modern social science. Only through common efforts and consideration of individual interests something can be achieved. Therefore, teacher collaboration is necessary and imperative. (Volodymyr, 3:25, 136)

Teachers agreed that the collective consists of individualities, and both collective and individual interests needed to be taken into consideration in order for collaboration to develop.

Finally, teachers believed that *greater level of collaboration* among people outside of school will have a positive impact on teachers' collective work. As an example, one respondent stated that greater collaboration between teachers in the after-school hours regarding personal matters will positively affect professional collaboration in the collective: "I would like to see us not only focused on our job, but also focused on getting to know each other outside of workplace" (Lina, 18:18, 70). Other participants affirmed that if the culture of cooperation, mutual help, support, and understanding develops in the Ukrainian society, it will transfer onto working cultures of teachers, administrators, and students in the schools.

Summary: Post-Soviet Societal Changes' Influence on Teacher Collaboration

This chapter described participants' perceptions of the impact of external societal transformations on teacher collaboration after the collapse of USSR. In their responses teachers discussed the nature of teacher collaboration in the Soviet Union times, which was based on the principles of collective work, possessed political and ideological background, and boasted a well-established system of supports for novice teachers. Though some participants perceived the degree to which societal changes influenced collaboration to be "insignificant", a vast majority of interviewees indicated (both directly and indirectly) that societal changes exerted significant impact on teachers' collaborative work. Among the most significant transformations respondents named changes in content of collaboration with the introduction of new tasks and requirements; increased voluntary participation in collaborative activities; changed format and new activities of collaboration; increased administrative control; impact of decreasing material welfare and financial instability on teachers' willingness and ability to collaborate; transformations in teacher relationships; division among teachers; and, the shift in the perceptions of the notion of "collective". They also provided their views and recommendations regarding the future impact of societal factors on teacher collaboration. Participants believed that collaboration among teachers tends to decrease with the prevalent individualistic values in society and among younger teachers. In order for collaboration in Ukrainian schools not to degrade, participants expressed the need for a higher stature of teachers and schools within society, material and financial security, emphasis on spiritual and moral values, balanced between collectivism and individualism, and greater collaboration in society in general.

Chapter 8

SCHOOL PRACTICES AND COLLABORATIVE WORK

I am always guided by this principle: a person has the right to be the one he or she chooses to be. (Iryna, 21:27, 129)

As evident from preceding discussions, external societal change factors fairly significantly contributed to the transformation in internal school practices. Participants in this study provided an in-depth description of a number of internal factors and practices that, in their views, shaped the current nature of collaborative work among teachers. As most of their responses related to the changing cultures in their schools and increased micropolitical activity of school members, this chapter contains the summary of their perspectives according to these two categories. Teachers' perceptions of the future direction of internal school practices that may influence collaboration conclude this chapter.

The Perceived Impact of Elements of School Culture on Collaboration

In order to engage participants in discussion of the impact of school culture on collaboration, I employed Schein's (1985) conceptualization and categorization of elements of school culture in framing focus group and individual interview questions. Therefore, the themes from the discussions of elements of culture perceived to influence the ways in which teachers collaborated with colleagues were grouped, according to Schein's terminology, into three categories: *school culture artifacts*, which included celebrations, rituals, traditions, ceremonies, heroes and heroines; *espoused values, norms, and beliefs*; and taken-for-granted, *basic underlying assumptions*.

The Role of School Culture Artifacts

Data analysis revealed some variations in the number of school culture artifacts between participating schools. However, most of the teachers indicated the presence of the same or similar traditions, ceremonies, and rituals in their schools. Interestingly enough, some of the organizational culture artifacts had existed in schools since the Soviet times; others were introduced after the collapse of the USSR.

The respondents indicated that all of them, starting with the "First Bell" and ending with the "Last Bell" ceremonies (marking the beginning and the end of the school year), were important for schools and served an ultimate purpose of bringing teachers together through common planning and organization. Roksolana stated, "If there is a holiday celebration organized, then one teacher or one class is not enough. Therefore, we collaborate" (10:25, 46). Another respondent, Olena added, "Not a *single* holiday is held without teachers getting together to discuss how to celebrate that holiday" (1:32, 246).

Many participants paid significant attention in discussions to the process of setting up school *celebrations* for statutory, national, and religious holidays. Along with the national Ukrainian holidays, revived after the collapse of the Soviet Union, schools started celebrating holidays of national minorities. Olena shared about celebrations of Jewish holidays in their school:

> Once a month, teachers' collective and a graduate class or some younger students, meet for Sabbath. This is a tradition of our school. Every Friday, we observe Sabbath in one of the classes with parents and school staff. If we hold Passover celebration in one of the classes, we celebrate it in the staffroom, too. (Olena, 1:32, 256)

All of the respondents from a different school emphasized the importance of Romanian spring holiday called "Martisor", when on the first day of March, staff wish each other health and happiness and exchange a little charm or decoration tied up with red and white woolen threads; these, they can wear on their cloths, or on their wrist. Many of the respondents believed that such traditions helped schools and people in them to preserve their national identities.

School-specific *ceremonies*, such as school anniversaries and awards nights were also discussed. In one school, interviewees reminisced about preparations for the celebration of their schools' centennial anniversary. In a different school, teachers organized a choir for the 20th anniversary of the school:

> Last year we had to organize a teachers' choir. Was it not collaboration? It was hard: some didn't have time, others complained about something else. But when it came to the matter, we organized a good choir.... This was a collective thing. Everyone sang. The principal didn't attend the practice once, twice, and I told him, "If *you* don't attend, there will be no choir. You have to attend." And he did attend and sing. (Lena, 7:29, 107-111)

Much attention was paid to teacher collaboration in the process of planning and organizing of sports ceremonies in an elite school: "We have sports ceremonies - once a year we have a Sports Night, where we sum up accomplishments of our athletes. All teachers help with organization of this function" (Arkadiy, 14:7, 36).

Most frequently mentioned school *rituals* were those of initiation and graduation. Initiations were held as solemn ceremonies, in which teachers, students, and parents took part. School graduations were often organized by teachers in a special manner: "We have a great celebration on the 'Graduates' Day', when the graduates have to pass under the traditional embroidered towels that are held by their parents" (Tonya, 17:18, 92). Besides graduation, very important for teachers were annual "Graduates' Meetings", when they looked forward to see their former students who remembered, visited, and supported their schools.

Through these rituals, teachers endeavored to promote parental involvement and family traditions in schools. One school started a custom called 'Family', a family holiday when parents and teachers gathered together for a celebration: "Parents' committees of each class are gathered together with teachers, and there is a celebration with the students' concert. It's held as a thank-you activity for parents for their active participation in the school life; their financial, moral, and material support" (Inessa, 8:19, 241). In another school, a participant established a tradition to gather grandparents and parents for a family holiday called "Guelder-rose Day":

> We sit around the tables and listen to grandparents sharing their knowledge and experiences from the past, they tell students about their childhood and youth, traditions, customs. You know, it is quite interesting, and children and parents are excited about such holidays. (Lyubomyra, 12:20, 92)

This holiday eventually grew into a school tradition supported by administration and other teachers. Through this holiday, teachers tried to establish the connection between older and younger generations.

Some of the *traditions* that were the same in all schools were so-called "Subject Days", when a certain month or week was dedicated to a specific subject. Volodymyr explained: "I held a 'Law Week' in the school, and all [teachers] helped out with it. In March, we'll have 'Shevchenko Days'; then we will pay more attention to philologists or traditions of literature and language" (19:16, 90). Another common tradition is "Teacher's Day". On that day, students greet teachers and choose the best teacher by means of interviews, talk shows, and skits. During the celebration of "Teacher's Day" there is a so-called 'Self-government Day', when senior students teach the lessons, and teachers play the role of students. Such lessons are not regular lessons: "Students want to center us out and show how we load them with assignments. In our turn, we show them their pranks and bad behavior behind the desks. It is interesting for them to be in our shoes for a day" (Antonina, 11:21, 114). Despite the fact that the majority of activities on "Teacher's Day" were organized by students, the background planning for this holiday had always been the collective responsibility of teachers.

Teachers did not leave aside the discussion about the *heroes and heroines* of their schools. They shared with pride about outstanding teachers and administrators from their schools who achieved great accomplishments and recognition as pedagogues. Lyubomyra reminisced about a good working atmosphere in their school when it was built in 1989:

> [We] had a creative, good principal. We studied in the university and worked in the school together; he was a creative person, dedicated to school. We were taught to love school and teaching in school. He had many different creative ideas, and it was motivating for us to go to school every day expecting something interesting to happen in the school. He organized very interesting round-table discussions and different creative methodological associations. (12:17, 78)

Another teacher emphasized that teachers in their school still followed the collaborative relationships that have been established by the former vice-principal: "She taught teachers to work and to be responsible for their areas. Nowadays, it doesn't matter if anyone supervises us or not, we still work according to those standards" (Iryna, 21:8, 28). In their discussion, teachers viewed their school heroes and heroines as role models in hard and effective work, as well as collaboration with colleagues.

The Role of Values, Beliefs, and Norms

The responses indicated that the most prevalent values, beliefs, and norms that guided relationships among teachers in their schools were seen to be those common to all humankind: *respect*, *kindness*, *love*, *patience*, *help*, and *compassion*:

> We exercise kindness, love and respect to your neighbor, sense of responsibility and friendship; in other words, common human values. It seems to me that it has to be like that everywhere in the ways people communicate with others, think of others, greet others. These are the elements of common culture. (Lyuba, 9:20, 62)

For the majority of teachers, the most important value was mutual respect among teachers and between teachers and students. Collaboration was also ranked high for some teachers: "The most important value for me is collaboration. This value is prevalent in our school, and it should be. Also, respect towards each other - it is present, and should always be present. As well as, consideration and tolerance toward the opinions of others" (Volodymyr, 19:17, 94).

Work relationships of teachers seemed also to be shaped by the fact that their behavior is observed by students who perceive teachers to be role models:

> First of all, we teach children, therefore, we have to act as intelligent people. We have to act accordingly and teach students to act that way. I tell my students, "… I want you to become 'humans' first, and then 'students'. Your assignment mark is not everything in this life. Your human qualities are most valuable in life". Therefore, a teacher who says such words to students has to be a *role model* for them. She has to think about what she says, how she behaves, what attitudes she has towards colleagues and students. It is a very important thing. It is impossible to demand from colleague or student something that you do not do or do not want to do. You have to show positive attitudes of a polite, well-bred, and intelligent person. Then, you will be a teacher, and not some kind of fishwife. (Sonya, 13:12, 70)

Participants added that teachers tried to instill common human values in their students through good work ethics and conscious fulfilling of their everyday responsibilities.

Despite the overall positive role of the values, norms, and beliefs in guiding collaborative relationships between teachers, several participants hinted at the existence of negative factors. They stated that they tried to follow the common human values and moralities in their work, but society, material welfare, and environment made significant "amendments":

> So far, material values and wealth are foremost to teachers; everyone tries to do their best to survive in this world. I suppose, if our material welfare were higher and if we were valued more in the society, then we would start thinking more about spirituality, integrity. Otherwise, it is hard to talk about this. Our spirituality is at the very low level, both among teachers and students. (Lyubomyra, 12:19, 88)

These respondents regretted that the shift from spiritual to material values and norms often affected their collaboration and relationships with others.

The Role of Basic Underlying Assumptions

When asked to characterize the most common constituents of their schools' organizational cultures, participants easily related to such factors as ceremonies, traditions, values, and norms (as discussed above). An explanation of the reasons why those things were done in their schools in certain ways and how they influenced teacher collaboration posed a more challenging task for them. One of the underlying assumptions that most teachers agreed upon was *belongingness to a school collective*. Most teachers believed that the length of time teachers spent working together influenced the degree to which the culture of their school was bound. In one school, teachers argued that they could not live without their school collective where they have worked since their youth:

> This is our life; we are set up that way. Secondly, it's much easier to work in the collective. I have something to compare with. Last year, we sent our Grade 1 students to the kindergarten building, because we didn't have room for them here… Though that was a new collective for us, we managed to join it. However, we felt the difference. Here, in school, you have a colleague, a mentor, a person with new ideas; but when we went there … we were new to it, we couldn't feel that collective. Therefore, we could not fit into that collective as opposed to here, in school. We have human relationships, we are friends with each other's families, and we are like one family. (Lina, 18:13, 48)

The similar story was shared in a different school, where all respondents mentioned the fact that most of them moved to this school as a closely bound collective from the neighboring school (when new school was built) and have been working together since the opening of the school in 1986. Another assumption mentioned by many of the participants was *cultural background*. Identification with certain national cultures of teachers (for example, Ukrainian, Jewish, or Romanian backgrounds) was also perceived to have significant impact on the school culture through specific ways of working, behaving, and teaching.

Micropolitical Factors Influencing Collaboration

Participants were asked to dwell upon a number of micropolitical issues outlined by the conceptual framework of this study. Judging from their responses, it became possible to assert that micropolitical activity in schools increased after the collapse of the USSR. During the Soviet era, teachers seemed to constitute one "gray mass", while the period of Independence established conditions necessary for the development of differences in opinion and multiple perspectives, clash of interests, and division among teachers. This section presents participants' discussions about power and influence; coalitions and interest groups among teachers; micropolitical strategies to achieve group or personal goals; difference of opinion and arguments; conflicts and conflict resolution; and, individual and collaborative working preferences of teachers. In addition, they also elaborated on the impact of external, macropolitical factors on micropolitics in school.

Power and Influence

From the discussions, it was evident that all participating teachers tried to use power and influence to achieve individual or collective goals in their schools. However, most teachers indicated that such power was mainly exercised at the teacher level – in grade parallels, departments, or methodological associations. They believed that more often than not teachers did not have enough power to influence administrative decisions and bring about change in schools. Volodymyr, for example, stated that school administration has everything under control, and teachers do not have much influence on their decision-making: "We need to understand that a principal occupies an absolutely different position.... Therefore, I don't think that there exists an extremely democratic principal (or vice-principal) who will allow teacher collective to have their way in decision making process" (19:12, 58). Another respondent added:

> We are sometimes forced to go and clean the neighborhood (which no one likes); it has to be done because of the orders from above. Also, we are forced to buy tickets to go to the Philharmonic Hall - we have to buy them and take kids there. Also, we are forced to make contributions to the Red Cross. (Lina, 18:23, 96)

Lina concluded that there still existed a command type relationship between administration and teachers, as teachers were forced to obey what they were told. This sometimes resulted in powerlessness of teachers: "I follow the lead of administration in the [organization of school work], whether I agree or do not agree with them. I see it as work and I have to work in that direction" (Lyuda, 23:29, 128). Loss of hope was also reflected in some teachers' comments: "We used to believe more that we could change things. Now, there is some kind of apathy and hopelessness. We lost hope in changes" (Antonina, 11:19, 102).

Thus, teachers' power and influence were limited to certain areas within the school. First of all, as Lina sharply phrased it, "a home room teacher is a *god* and *king* in his or her classroom" (18:23, 96). The prevalent majority of teachers felt they were empowered to make decisions (without prior agreement with administration) that pertained to their classroom matters (such as syllabus, student behavior, parent-teacher interviews, etc.), as long as they were appropriate and coincided with the policies, regulations, curriculum, and programs of study. Lyubomyra commented:

> In my classroom, I can make decisions without agreeing them with vice-principal, as long as these are appropriate decisions. For example, I decided that I needed to organize parent-teacher interviews yesterday, because I saw that children are going out of control and their learning and behavior is getting worse and worse. I decided to have them yesterday, and I did. Whatever I planned for the interviews, whatever issues or problems I wanted to discuss with parents were up to me, I don't have to agree them with the vice principal, because I saw the need for them. Certainly, there are curriculum, programs of studies, and calendar plans approved by school administration and Ministry of Education, and I can't make decisions that do not coincide with the set direction.... There are calendar and educational plans that we have to agree with school administration, but if there are urgent issues that need to be resolved, I make my own decisions. (21:25, 129)

The main areas in which these teachers felt empowered to make their own decisions were classroom instruction methodologies and techniques, organization of leisure time for students, planning of school functions, and organization of methodological association meetings.

Discussing the sources of their power and influence (both on other teachers and administration), the respondents made mention of experience, knowledge, age, professional abilities, personal traits of character, and position. Experience, age, and knowledge were most frequently identified as the main sources of the respondents' power. Experienced teachers felt that by sharing their experiences and skills acquired over the years they gained influence in teacher collective. Lyubomyra posited:

[Other teachers] listen to my opinion, because of the number of years that I've worked in school: there is acquired knowledge, experience, publications, and accomplishments. Therefore, if I have anything to say, colleagues listen to me. Besides, my works are used and implemented in other classes, especially by younger colleagues. (12:24, 125)

Her colleague added, "There is a saying, 'A person first works for the authority, and then authority works for a person'. I think my authority works for me now" (Roksolana, 10:14, 78). This notion of *earned authority* emerged out of a number of interview discussions. Mariya noted:

I think I have some power, because every person is an individuality and has to gain a foothold. You have to earn the authority; no one else can do it for you. A person has to earn the respect of colleagues, parents, students. I think my opinion is listened to because of the authority that I earned. I adhere to the opinion that I need to 'take a step back' in order to learn the situation better. I don't have any dictatorship power, but I think my colleagues pay attention to my points of view. (20:31, 127)

Teachers indicated that authority was earned by professional abilities as a teacher, as well as personal talents, attitudes, and traits of character. Mariya commented about her personal convictions that helped her gain authority among other teachers and administration:

I always think twice before doing anything, never make hasty decisions, and always try to act when everyone is in agreement with my decisions. Some people take radical changes very painfully, and I am one of them. It seems to me that people want others to be like them and act the way they think is appropriate. I always try to smooth any rough edges in relationships with others, because it depresses and dispirits me. I value professionalism and passion for work in people, because some people slack at work, they simply come to work to earn money and do bare minimum of what is required of them. (Mariya, 20:31, 131)

Other personal characteristics that were viewed as contributing to the increase of teachers' influence included openness and sincerity, hard work and dedication, persistence and persuasion in arguments, and organizational abilities. These characteristics received fairly similar emphasis in teacher responses throughout the individual interviews.

Several of the respondents discussed power drawn from occupying certain positions in the school, such as department head, head of a methodological association, vice-principal, or principal. One of the respondents, a school vice principal, stated:

When I just started working here, the source of my power was based on my position. Now I hope that in the last three years my colleagues learned more about me and approach me with the questions of counseling or help. I think that I can influence their decisions and communicate with them not just because of my position, but also because of the authority that I gained in these years. (Tonya, 17:21, 108)

A number of participants observed that teachers who had more power or control over other teachers behaved differently according to their personality and their position. Some became spoilt by the top-office position; others still had great relationships of mutual respect with others in the collective. Most teachers believed that being assigned to a superior position spoilt people, even more than money. Lyudmyla even quoted Ukrainian proverb to support her point of view, "If you want to get to know the person, assign him or her to be a superior" (1:40, 426). Thus, power and influence of individual teachers affected their collaboration with colleagues.

Coalitions and Interest Groups

Data analysis revealed that gaining power and influence to achieve desired outcomes in school was one of the reasons teacher coalitions formed in schools. When asked to dwell upon the existence, formation, and functions of coalitions in their schools, the respondents expressed various views. Several of the participants denied existence of any coalitions in their schools. However, the majority of teachers agreed that coalitions existed in their schools in one form or another. Volodymyr posited, "They exist in any school, not just ours. They always exist; a larger social entity breaks into smaller parts" (19:15, 82). Moreover, coalitions were perceived to influence collaboration among teachers in both positive and negative ways as elaborated below.

The majority of respondents perceived coalitions with a negative connotation, such as "undercurrents", "unpleasant relationships", "cliques", or "heated tempers". One respondent thought of coalitions as groups pitted against others:

> I would assume that there are some coalitions, because our school is big, and you can't disregard that. … However, I would say that they are formal and informal at the same time, because we get together according to our friendships or our collaboration within the departments. You can call these coalitions, but I think of coalition when you have some group of people going against another group. There are no groups going against each other in our school. I would call them groups or departments. Our work pushes us to communicate with those closest to us. (Lyuda, 23:25, 100)

Another participant supported this with the statement that there was a period of time when it was very difficult to work due to revolutionary moods and tempers in school. Despite the prevalent negative perceptions, a significant number of respondents viewed coalitions as formal or informal groupings fulfilling professional duties in a collaborative manner with positive outcomes for the schooling process.

Teachers' responses indicated that coalitions were formed according to a number of factors. The most frequently mentioned were age and experience. Participants stated that they often observed groups of older, middle aged, and young teachers communicating and working together. Also, it was common for more experienced and novice teachers to join together into separate groupings. Despite the fact that coalitions were often based on formal school's structural arrangements, such as departments, methodological associations, grade parallels, elementary or secondary school levels, most of them were informal in nature, organized according to common interests, views, goals or likings. Interestingly enough, there was a mention of three teacher coalitions formed according to the language and nationality principles in one school. There was also observed a tendency towards "depoliticizing" of the notion of coalition in discussions with teachers.

Such unofficial coalitions were perceived as normal phenomena in school life by most of the teachers:

> There are some [coalitions]. You have to understand, it's a staff of 30 people. It's impossible for 30 people to be friends at the same time. People gather according to their interests.…It is normal for adults: 30 people cannot have one common interest. There are some subgroups in the school. (Lyuba, 9:10, 110)

Many teachers felt that despite their prevalent unofficial status, coalitions exerted significant influence on one another and general decision making in school. An example of such influence was provided by one of the participants:

> I know of coalitions in one of the departments. Teachers disagree with scheduling, because they want to have a normal teaching load for a good salary. Therefore, language teachers grouped together as some of their problems were left unresolved. We do not have anything like that in the elementary school, because we have the same number of teaching hours for all teachers. (Lyubomyra, 12:23, 113)

Lyubomyra concluded that coalitions were more prone to appear at the secondary school level, rather than in elementary school. This assumption was supported by the majority of participants, who also added that coalitions tend to develop in larger school staff. In their views, secondary schools tended to have larger and more disconnected staffs, while elementary schools usually had smaller family-like teacher collectives. A teacher from a large school even mentioned a popular saying among their staff: "Don't get together in groups of more than 3 teachers! … You know, every principal thinks that if teachers get together during the break, then it means that they talk about something negative, something that he did not do right" (Lina, 18:32, 52). Therefore, school size was perceived as instrumental for the development of coalitions.

Micropolitical Strategies

The analysis of responses revealed that the process of collaboration among teachers was affected by the use of individual or group strategies with the purpose of obtaining power and fulfilling their interests. These micropolitical strategies varied from school to school. Participants observed that in some schools teachers squabbled openly to prove their points; in others, teachers reported the use of "cultured" and respectful strategies to achieve their goals. One of the approaches outlined in several focus group discussions was openness and direct contact between the involved parties. Important in this approach, as Lena stated, was the need to leave one's self an escape route in case of a conflict. However, young teachers in one school emphasized that telling the truth in someone's face or bringing teachers into a direct conflict as a strategy to resolve the issue would not work in their collective, which predominantly consisted of female teachers:

> If there are any negative attitudes towards certain teachers - it happens sometimes, we have witnessed that - there is a circle of close people with whom I can share my opinion. I would never bring myself to a direct conflict, only because we are all educated people. Maybe, it would be better to tell it in someone's face, but in a female collective, nothing good will come out of it. (Nadya, 8:12, 219)

Thus, participants in this particular focus group (all – female teachers) preferred to wait and let the steam out in such situations.

The young teachers' focus group discussions addressed the issue of micropolitical strategies more than in other groups. Disagreements within their teacher collective were perceived as working situations. Depending on personality, some teachers could loudly prove their points, while others got offended and took it close to heart. Many participants in this group believed that various working situations taught them who and how they should talk to:

> There are people in our collective who are very incommunicative and reserved; they are not bad or rude, but they are silent all the time. And you have to work with such people, say 'hello' and 'good-bye'. It does not mean that that person is bad, and I don't want to communicate with that person. Maybe she doesn't think that I am bad either.... For some people you are a pleasant person to communicate with, and for others you are not. (Rimma, 8:12, 229-233)

Teachers indicated that *time* allowed them to reconsider their behavior and know with which issues and with whom they can take more liberties or be more reserved. Hence, many respondents often preferred to keep silent and think twice before saying something not to offend others. Several respondents preferred also to act according to the "golden rule": treat others as you would like them to treat you.

Participants from the young teachers' focus group also discussed a strategy of pretending to be ignorant and approaching older teachers for help in a pleasant manner. Ability and skills to communicate with others influenced the effectiveness of such approach. Nadya commented:

> I have never approached other teachers in an insolent manner, I always approach them nicely. I pretend to be completely ignorant and say, 'I would like to observe you in the class, you are such a good teacher, I've heard so many things about you. Can I sit in the back of your classroom? I want to learn from you'. I think it's impossible to refuse me in such request. This is a psychological question. It's about teacher's communicability, sociability, attitudes to others. (8:26, 169)

130

An interesting observation was made by Nadya's colleague, Tasya. She noticed that strategies that teachers used in communication and collaboration with others reflected the way they treated students in classroom:

> I tried to characterize teachers by looking at students. [Teachers in the elementary school] are close to children, because they need to be taken care of, etc. Maybe, that's why they treat other people humanly, too. However, if you look at the secondary school, there are teachers who act like a gendarme in classroom, and that is how they communicate with other people too. No matter how you approach them and say to them, 'You are a nice teacher, please help me'. They will say 'No' anyways. There are people like that, aren't there? (Tasya, 8:26, 175)

Younger teachers concluded that it was easier for them to seek help from a younger teacher from an elementary school rather than from more experienced secondary school teachers.

Argument and Difference of Opinion

According to the responses, the process of joint work among teachers was often marked by arguments and differences in points of view. Describing the manner in which these phenomena were perceived and handled in their schools, many of the respondents noted that everyone has the right to express his or her personal opinion. According to Mariya, if teachers hold different opinions in the collective, they can stick to them and others do not try to impose their own views on them. "Even if something is said or done, it is not done without any grounds or proofs or in a very direct manner" (20:32, 135). Her colleague, Iryna, added that she taught her students and tried to follow the view that every person had the right to be individual in his or her opinions:

> I am always guided by this principle: a person has the right to be the one he or she chooses to be. If someone does anything wrong, my task is to help that person, tell her; but it's her choice what to do. I always tell my students, 'You have the right to be the one you choose to be. What I can do is show you the diversity, but it's up to you to choose how you act. It's your right; only yours'. (21:27, 129)

However, respondents identified several conditions for different opinions to be taken into consideration. First of all, points needed to be valid or worthy of notice. Lyuda emphasized: "We are all educated people and we understand that our views have to be based on some reality. If that point of view is valid, teachers will listen to it, as well as administration" (23:28, 124). Secondly, teachers could adhere to their opinions as long as "their views did not harm the functioning of the school or norms followed by the majority of the collective" (Tonya, 17:23, 116). And lastly, their points should be of some benefit for the school.

Several comments indicated that relationships between administration and teachers were to a certain extent collegial, and that teachers could freely voice their disagreement with the policies and regulations set by administration. Lina explained:

> We do not always agree with our principal: he has his own views, we have our views. As they say, 'Truth is born in the argument'. If you can express your own opinion in the school (even if it is contrary to what administration thinks) and you are understood, then that school is a good place to work. (18:21, 84)

Furthermore, Lina perceived the difference of opinion as an important factor to help avoid groupthink: "Difference of opinion will keep us from saying only yes to what others say. If you don't agree, you have to express your opinion... A person cannot only agree; it's impossible, because she will be like a robot" (18:25, 104). She also added that difference of opinion does not always have to grow into a conflict; however, it often does.

Conflict

The majority of participating teachers perceived conflict as inevitable part of the collaborative process. "School is a big home and a big family, and every family has conflict of interests. If this happens in the family, what do you expect in the school with so many teachers?!" Lyubomyra stated (12:21, 100). Another teacher added, "I am not a conflictive person by nature, and I think that conflict certainly has to be present, just like in any literary work, but it doesn't mean that it has to be a quarrel or broil like we see at the bazaar" (Lyuda, 23:31, 136). Most of the teachers agreed that conflicts, either major or minor, still existed or used to exist and had a significant impact on the way teachers collaborated in their schools. Their responses regarding the frequency with which conflicts arose varied from "often" to "seldom", with the majority stating that most of the time those were not serious conflicts. Minor issues, arguments, and disagreements were not considered to be conflicts.

The notion of conflict was perceived differently by the respondents from different schools. In general, it was viewed as a "blatant fact", a signal that someone was discontented, or something went wrong and needed to be resolved. For many of the respondents, conflict had clearly outlined positive or negative connotations. Moreover, comments about the negative nature of conflict were prevalent in discussions. Several teachers stated that from their experience conflict is always negative, because it consumes everyone and should not take place in the process of working together. Iryna justified her point with the statement that conflict among teachers sets a negative example for students:

> [Conflict is] negative! Negative, because if we, teachers, cannot have normal relationships, we show a negative example to children. Children can't respect a teacher that cannot build up good relationships with others. On the one hand, we have no rights to be poorly dressed or be in a dismal mood; we have to be role models in everything. Neither do we have the right to say anything bad about anybody or show it by our behavior in relationships with each other. We have to behave so that children could see us and say, 'Yes, I will behave myself in the same manner'. This is an extremely important issue in relationships with others. (21:26, 125)

"Wherever there is conflict, there are nerves", added Antonina (11:16, 90). Other comments also suggested that some teachers did not believe that any of school issues should be solved through conflict. Proponents of positive characteristics of conflict argued that it allowed for natural selection or survival of the fittest. Lina believed that "without a strong opposition one can not have a strong country; without a conflict one can not have a strong school" (18:25, 104).

There were respondents who argued that conflict can be both positive and negative, depending on the nature and outcomes. Sophia's perceptions depended on the heart of the problem or conflict:

> Sometimes it can be positive, for example, if there is a dispute over a new textbook or teaching methods, and somebody disagrees or doesn't see expediency in using it, and then when you show its effectiveness during the open lesson or that person will see positive results after some time of using it, then you can convince a person in its expediency... The negative aspect of a conflict would be when a person is extremely ambitious without having grounds to be such; we have some teachers like that, not many, but we have them. Then conflicts arise, because you see that what that teacher does in class is wrong. He thinks it is right, and tries to prove you wrong. (22:17, 60)

Another respondent explained that outcomes of conflicting situation shaped her perceptions:

> If conflict arises over a serious work or instructional issue, and it is solved in a normal way and it doesn't impact other people, then it may be viewed as positive. However, if the conflict grows over the limits, and other people are involved and impacted by it, then it is

negative. Conflict probably has less positive characteristics, because it is more negative by nature, but you always have to look for something good in each bad thing. (Lyuba, 9:9, 106)

Sonya, an instructor of "Civil Education", stated that in her course she teaches a lesson about conflict and explains to students that conflict is not always bad. She noted that conflict can be very positive, depending on the way it is resolved:

Conflict can be a push towards something positive, quality changes that will lead to better results. If a conflict doesn't arise, everything will slowly get rotten. It all depends on the situation and the cause of the conflict. It can be both positive and negative. Usually, we have this association or stereotype that conflict is always bad. It is not. Conflict is not always negative. If it arises in human relationships between teachers, certainly, it can't be completely positive and can have negative results. If it has to do with professional issues, then argument or conflict regarding differences in opinions about instruction can be positive in nature. (Sonya, 13:11, 66)

Thus, conflicts that led to changes were considered by most teachers as being positive. "Truth is born in the argument" was a common statement respondents used to justify this point.

Conflicts that arose in schools were either professional or personal in nature. Professional conflicts arose when teachers tried to persuade each other or administration regarding professional issues, such as methods of instruction, student upbringing, and organization of school activities and functions. One of the examples was a conflict situation between teachers and administration regarding the obligatory use of the uniform for secondary school students:

For example, discussion has started recently about the need for uniforms in the secondary school. Not all teachers agree with that, because they are used to casual clothes and it is better for them than having to control their dress code all the time. Controlling the dress code will take much effort and time, and not all teachers want or have time and energy to do that. (Lyubomyra, 12:22, 104)

Also mentioned were conflicts between teachers and administration in regard to scheduling and distribution of work hours. Moreover, distribution of work hours was seen as directly related to material welfare – which teachers would get more teaching hours to make more money.

Participants believed that the majority of conflicts flare up due to traits of character, temper, ambitions, or beliefs of teachers. Several respondents stated that every collective has scandalous people who like conflict, always disagree with everything, or dislike everything. Antonina recollected one conflict situation in their school:

There is one teacher who is very canny, doesn't communicate with anyone, deems herself smarter and greater than others. For many years, teachers tried to prove to her that is she is not better than them, but they suffered defeat and now everyone keeps together, while she is alone. It is a bad example, but unfortunately, we have this in our school. School administration tried to resolve this conflict, but they didn't succeed. It depends on the person's character, she is quite old and it's probably impossible to change her. (11:15, 86)

Very often, such conflicting people did not "take root" [stay] in the school collective and quit, because teaching profession required extreme patience:

The job of a teacher is hard by nature; we are always under pressure from administration, parents, and students.... If a person has a specific purpose to get involved in conflicts, they seldom stay in school. They usually leave teacher's position, because it requires patience. There is a saying that a gymnast asks [God] for flexibility, and a teacher asks for patience. (Mariya, 20:33, 139)

In several individual interviews, participants concluded that despite some conflicts, misunderstandings, and discontentment among teachers during the process of joint work, they realized the need to come to an agreement and work as one collective, because all of them worked for the same cause – educating students.

Conflict Resolution

The participants outlined a number of factors that affected the ways conflicts were resolved in their schools. Quite a few of the participants indicated that conflict resolution depended on individuality and the type of conflict. Sophia explained that one needs to know each teacher, each individual in the collective:

> Sometimes, you need to use harsh words with some teachers; with others you need to come to an agreement and find common language. It all depends on the individuality! I think there can't be any universal way to solve the problems. As an administrator and teacher, I always try to consider every detail. (Sophia, 22:16, 56)

Lena added, "Just like every teacher needs to know peculiarities of each student to avoid conflict situation and make classroom work more effective, so one needs to know teacher collective very well. All of us are individuals, and very often we are maximalists" (7:22, 168). It was also suggested that as teachers are professionals and experts in their fields, they know and understand why certain conflicts arise or what certain teachers try to achieve by arguing and proving their opinions to others.

A few respondents believed that school size played a significant role in conflict resolution; it was easier to solve the conflicting situations in a small school rather than in a large school complex. This was due to the family-like atmosphere and positive school climate where teachers knew each other well. Religious beliefs and convictions also helped some respondents in resolving conflicts with other teachers. "It happened so that in the second half of my life I thoughtfully came to God, and sometimes, when emotions are negative and there are certain irritants that I do not agree with, I need to come to my senses, and I turn to God", stated Lena (7:21, 159). Lena added that she always started by resolving a conflict within herself; after that she had the right to demand anything from other parties involved in the argument. Many teachers mentioned that they did not prioritize or dramatize conflicts; whenever arguments or conflicts arose, common goal – teaching and upbringing – came up as a mediating factor that made them realize what was worth fighting for.

Most responses indicated that teachers preferred approaching or confronting others *directly* and *openly* in order to resolve issues and conflicts. They did not support indirect approaches in which others acted tactlessly and complained to administration or other authorities without first addressing the issues with colleagues whom they had something against. Furthermore, the majority of participants stated that conflicts were usually resolved in a calm, tactful, and sober-minded manner without screaming, shaking of fists, squabbles, or rows. Sonya commented:

> If conflict does arise, it needs to be resolved in a calm atmosphere. I think our principal was right when he said once, "I wanted to tell you about this today, but I know that I need to 'cool down'. I will tell you about this at the next staff meeting. Moreover, I think it will be the right thing, because right now I can tell you many different things". I think he was absolutely right. We do not scream at each other; teachers do not tear each other's hair, thanks God; everything is done in a civilized and intelligent manner. (13:11, 62)

Discussion and explanations helped teachers avoid scandals or strenuous relationships as a result of conflicting interests. Another conflict management technique identified by a few participants was avoidance. They argued that conflicts are either resolved or outlived. Some participants shared that they used to let those who liked conflicts to "push them around", but then eventually learned to ignore them; therefore, conflicts go out as quickly as they flare up.

The data analysis revealed that most conflicts among teachers were resolved informally, when conflicting sides looked for a resolution of problematic situations. However, if the sides did not meet half-way, then formal committees, trade unions, and administration became involved and tried to bring the conflict to a compromise or consensus. In most of the schools there seemed to exist a number of levels for problem solving. Several of the participants stated that whenever conflicts arose, teachers tried to settle the matters at their level first. Tonya asserted:

> First of all, we try to solve the problems among ourselves. If there are problems that we can't solve ourselves, we can address the school administration. I don't think we had any issues that we had to go even higher to solve them. Everything is solved within the school walls - among ourselves or with school administration. (17:20, 100)

Arkadiy, a principal in one of the elite schools, observed that when teachers directly involved in conflict could not come to resolution, their colleagues often helped:

> There is a friendly, amicable conflict resolution, when teachers understand that collaboration is more important than continuation of the conflict. I do not remember any long-term conflict during my work in the lyceum. Usually, conflicts are resolved in 2 or 3 days. As a rule, these conflicts are emotional. There are no conflicts regarding the scheduling process, because it is done collegially, teachers come to agreement among themselves about the classes, times, and workload they are willing to take from what is available. (14:10, 46)

In one of the schools, participants indicated that the school psychologist worked on revealing the origin of conflict: "If there is a 'malignant tumor' in the student collective, parent collective, or teacher collective, we consult with the psychologist, distribute surveys, in order not to resolve the problem, but to find its sources. It is easier to prevent the problem than to deal with its consequences" (Viktor, 15:13, 60). To a certain degree, it was also a responsibility of administration to prevent or resolve conflicts. One principal noted that his task was to make a teacher collective into an efficient, hardworking, and non-conflicting unit in order to expect positive work results in school. Despite the fact that administration played a significant role in resolving conflict situations in schools, it was mostly used as a last resort. Many teachers, however, gave credit to school administration for preventing conflicts from flaring up.

Working Preferences

Responding to the question about the amount of time spent working together or working alone during the school day, the majority of participants indicated that teachers' work was predominantly individual. The most commonly mentioned proportion was 80% individual work and 20% collaboration. The majority of the day was spent on individual work such as instruction and preparation. The rest, on average from one to two hours a day, for most teachers was equally divided between collaboration with their colleagues or working alone.

Many respondents assigned such working proportions to individual preferences of teachers, which in turn were shaped by the prevalent individual nature of teachers' work. Lyuba argued that every subject teacher has his or her own peculiarities. Therefore, she deemed collaboration as impossible in some cases:

> I go to my lesson with my own individual plan and program. We can't work together during instruction….lesson instruction is solely teacher's responsibility, of course. Who else can be present with me in my lesson?... In terms of instruction, there is less collaboration. It's not because we don't want to collaborate! It's because of the specificity of teacher's work. (9:21, 66-74)

Another respondent also reflected upon the specific nature of her work as a pedagogue:

> Teacher's work is individual in nature, … and no matter how many advices I can get, I still have to put it through my mind. I have my own style of work; though others do things differently, they may not fit my style of work. A combination of individual and collective work can be observed during the school-wide events. However, teacher's work is individual and differs from others. (Mariya, 20:28, 115)

Mariya added that some days she did not have any contact or collaboration with other colleagues at all; other times, she preferred to be silent for a while during the break and have some rest instead of discussing issues with colleagues.

Most participants supported the viewpoint that working preferences depended on the individuality and predispositions of teachers. In general, the majority of teachers in participating schools preferred working together in the collective, because "collectively work is done with greater enthusiasm and energy, in a cheerful and friendly atmosphere" (Arkadiy, 14:14, 50). However, there were some incommunicative teachers who preferred working in isolation. "Some like to work alone, and do work in isolation, but I think it's more difficult that way", stated Lina (18:29, 132). Furthermore, Roksolana argued that teachers had the right not to collaborate if they preferred so:

> I prefer working individually: I - child, I - class. If there are any debatable issues, I contact one or more colleagues or I raise that question at the methodological association meeting. In principle, I constructed my lesson, I see it that way and I want to organize it accordingly. This is my right; I don't need any collaboration in that. On the other hand, I can borrow something from my colleague and use it in my instruction, but it is not always the case. Sometimes, it works out perfectly for my colleague, but it won't work for me, or vice versa. It depends on personality. (Roksolana, 10:30, 140)

Different preferences were observed in the way preparation time was perceived: for some it was joint work, for others – isolated activity. Majority of participants, however, indicated that preparation time was more individual type of work.

Macropolitical Impact on Micropolitical Interactions

An important aspect that came out of discussions with teachers was the impact of external, macropolitical, factors on micropolitical interactions in schools. A number of participants indicated that they became more politicized as a result of political events in Ukraine that had greatly affected their school collectives. I experienced it firsthand, when teachers showed high interest in national politics in most of our conversations, especially in the focus groups. Most of the participating teachers expressed great knowledge in political developments in Ukraine and often digressed from the subject of collaboration to politics during the focus group and interview discussions.

High "politicization" in society significantly affected relationships among teachers. According to the responses, political events often influenced the way teachers worked together if they adhered to different political views. It was especially noticeable during the 2004 Presidential Elections in Ukraine:

> Just like in the society, our collective was split into two different groups. Even three groups, but those were people who were skeptic and indifferent about the elections….There weren't any big arguments, at least in our elementary school. All of us respected the view of other colleagues, because everyone has the right for his or her opinion. (Tonya, 17:13, 72)

Other respondents noted that all of the political events and developments in Ukraine, especially after the "Orange Revolution", affected collaboration among teachers; they perceived such events as their personal wins or losses. Moreover, political events served as a means to bring teachers together to discuss, argue, or express concerns about political life of the country.

Internal Factors and Future Development of Collaboration

Along with the discussion of the internal school practices that influenced teacher collaboration, the participants outlined several conditions that were necessary, in their view, for greater degree of collaboration in their schools. Their responses are presented according to the degree of emphasis and importance. *First of all*, they believed that there was a need for a common system or theory, which would guide collaborative school work among teachers in schools. *Secondly*, they indicated the need for family-like relationships and cooperation without destructive quarrels and conflicts in order to decrease the number of teachers leaving their jobs. *Thirdly*, participants would like to see some kind of creative intellectual competitions for teachers (similar to the 'socialist competitions' in the Soviet times) that would provide teachers with some rewards and incitements to compete (in a good sense). Such competitions, according to respondents, had the potential to promote staff collaboration, especially between younger and older teachers. And *lastly*, as stated in many schools, participants felt the need to relieve the load on schools, make schools and classes smaller in order to facilitate collaborative activities among teachers. Olena argued: "If any changes should take place in the system of education in Ukraine *now*, then the very first thing to do is to *unload* the schools, *unload* the classes, because it's physically impossible to teach forty kids in class, or run the school of 1500 students" (1:46, 209). Thus, participants viewed "overload" to be an important barrier to collaboration, removal of which would increase the productiveness of joint work among teachers.

Summary: Internal Factors' Impact on Teacher Collaboration

This chapter provided an outline of participants' perceptions regarding internal factors and school practices that shape the nature of collaborative work among teachers. School culture was seen to play a very important role in establishing and sustaining collaborative relationships among teachers. Holiday celebrations, ceremonies, rituals, and traditions served an ultimate purpose of bringing teachers together through common planning and organization. Despite the fact that most frequently mentioned values, beliefs, and norms that guided teacher relationships were common human values and moralities, teachers observed a decline and shift from spiritual to material value systems. Though it was more difficult for participants to outline the underlying assumptions behind collaborative work among teachers, respondents seemed to emphasize belongingness to a certain collective, degree of which depended on the length of time teachers worked together. Also, collaborative work was influenced by teachers' cultural background or their association with certain national cultures.

Various aspects related to micropolitics were also deemed to have significant impact on collaboration. The process of joint work among teachers often involved formation of coalitions to obtain power and influence and use of micropolitical strategies, arguments, and conflicts to achieve group or personal goals. Interestingly enough, conflict resolution served as one of the forms of teacher collaboration. Individual and collaborative working preferences of teachers were shaped by individual characteristics of teachers, as well as predominant individual nature of teachers' work. Wrapping up the discussion of micropolitics, respondents elaborated on the impact of external, macropolitical factors on micropolitics in school. Finally, participants outlined several conditions that were necessary, in their view, for greater degree of collaboration in their schools.

Chapter 9

BRINGING PUZZLE PIECES TOGETHER

You see, you asked the questions that have been on our hearts for a long time. Not often do others find interest in what is on our hearts and what hurts in our souls. We came with pure hearts and souls to your interview, and you will have to make conclusions out of what was said... (Stella, 7:21, 163)

One of the most rewarding feelings for me is the feeling of completion of the project, study, or assignment. This is especially relevant at times when I complete the work on a jigsaw puzzle, with all pieces in place, secure and interlocked, which allows me to see the whole picture. In this chapter, I bring all pieces of this research together, with an attempt to do justice to the research data and show the reader the "big picture" of this study. I begin this chapter with an overview of the problem, purpose, methodology, and findings of the study. The major themes that emerged from this study are discussed, followed by implications for theory, practice, policy, and methodology. The chapter concludes with my personal reflections about this research journey.

Summary of the Study

Post-Soviet societal changes and teacher collaboration have been my interests for some time. Therefore, it seemed logical to conduct an in-depth study combining these two areas of interest. Moreover, I was encouraged by the findings of my previous research (Kutsyuruba, 2003) that indicated a need for collaborative relationships and culture among teachers in Ukrainian schools. Is collaboration a wide-spread practice among teachers in Ukrainian schools? What are the professional teacher relationships like in Ukrainian schools? Did relationships between school members change or do they continue to reflect a top-down, centralized model of schooling characteristic of educational systems in the Soviet Union? How did post-Soviet societal changes affect education? Did societal changes have any impact on teacher collaboration in Ukrainian schools? Can a collaborative culture in Ukrainian schools be developed *instrumentally* or do certain conditions *enable* its development? Questions of this nature required study, and the unprecedented post-Soviet societal changes in Ukraine provided a valuable case in point.

The purpose of the study described in this book was to examine teachers' perceptions of the impact of societal changes on teacher collaboration in schools within the period of independence of Ukraine (1991 – 2005). This study provided a description of teacher experiences in a context of large-scale philosophical, ideological, social, political, and economic changes of the post-Soviet era, and the teachers' interpretation of the impact of related changes upon teacher collaboration in Ukrainian schools.

Several research questions gave focus to the study. They were divided into two subgroups. First, questions inquiring into teachers' perceptions of the nature of post-Soviet societal changes: *What are teachers' perceptions of the nature of post-Soviet societal changes? What is the perceived general impact of post-Soviet societal changes on Ukrainian schools?* Second, questions regarding the impacts on teacher collaboration: *What is the nature and state of teacher collaboration in Ukrainian schools? What are teachers' perceptions of the impact of external societal changes on collaboration among teachers? What are the internal practices that influence teacher collaboration in schools?*

This study primarily dealt with ill-structured problems, characterized by many decision makers, numerous possible alternatives, competing definitions of the problem, and conflicting values to guide decision-making. Therefore, according to White (1999), it was appropriate to adopt a naturalistic orientation to this study. "Naturalists assume that there exist multiple realities which are, in the main, constructions existing in the minds of people…. [and] naturalist assumptions are more meaningful in studying human behavior" (Guba & Lincoln, 1999, p. 142). Within the naturalistic paradigm, an interpretive constructivist approach to methodology, which recognizes the mutual creation of knowledge by the researcher and researched (Guba & Lincoln, 1994; Lincoln & Guba, 2000; Schwandt, 2000), prompted the use of qualitative methods of inquiry.

The data collection techniques of document analysis, focus group interviews, and individual interviews were utilized. The Ministry of Education, Department of Education, and school policies and procedures that pertained to teacher collaboration issued during the period of 1991-2005 were reviewed, analyzed, and translated into English. The participants in this study were elementary or secondary school teachers in the city of Chernivtsi, Ukraine. All participants were volunteers and had been in the teaching profession within the education system of Ukraine during the period of time from 1991 to 2005. In total, fifty-five teachers participated in this study. Eight focus group interviews were conducted with two to eleven participants in each group. After the focus groups, fifteen individual interviews were conducted with selected focus group participants. Transcripts of all focus group discussions and individual interviews were translated into English by the researcher. This process took a considerable amount of thought and time. Translated transcripts were coded with the help of ATLAS.ti qualitative data analysis software. Important issues that emerged were then grouped into themes and analyzed using the same software. The use of these methods provided the study with a rich, descriptive, and generous amount of information.

Overview of the Findings

The following section provides a brief summary of the findings related to the research questions raised in the study. Teachers' perceptions and document analysis data are organized into the following categories: nature of post-Soviet societal changes; impact of post-Soviet societal changes on schools; nature and state of teacher collaboration; impact of external societal changes on teacher collaboration; and, influence of internal school practices on teacher collaboration.

Nature of Post-Soviet Societal Changes

The analysis of data revealed that the collapse of the Soviet Union was seen by the school professionals as a major catalyst for change. Societal changes were perceived as possessing a "double-sided" nature, with both positive and negative outcomes for the participants' personal and professional lives. Different types of societal transformations (*economic, ideological, philosophical, political*, and *social*) were discussed from both positive and negative perspectives.

In their discussion of *economic* changes, respondents reflected upon advantages and disadvantages for the country in general, and their lives in particular. The factors leading to positive changes in the economy were seen to include development of entrepreneurship, permission to open private businesses, opportunities for additional income, permission to go abroad, and relative economic stability in the recent years. Rebuilding of the economic system, transition to the new economic relationships, inflation, instability, unemployment, industrial decline, government corruption, inadequate financial remuneration, and delays in salary payments were viewed as the negative characteristics of economic transformations in Ukrainian society. As a result of these changes, schools had to survive without appropriate funding, support, and resources from the government. Moreover, societal attitudes toward schools and teachers changed due to the fact that teachers' job lost its prestige and financial advantage. Therefore, many educators (especially male teachers) left their teaching jobs in search of more lucrative careers.

Most *ideological* transformations were connected to the collapse of the Communist Party ideology. This ideology, dominant in the Soviet society, exerted ideological pressure on education through pre-service and in-service training for educators and ideologically-laden youth organizations, consisting of three echelons – Zhovtenyata, Pioneers, and Komsomol. As the majority of responses suggested, the collapse of the Soviet ideological system led to the weakened ideological pressure and changes in the system of moral values and ideals in the independent times.

Post-Soviet societal events and phenomena resulted in transition to different philosophies, perspectives, and systems of norms, values, and beliefs in the society. Most frequently mentioned *philosophical* changes were national identity issues, development of Ukrainian language instruction, and establishment of national schools. These aspects were regarded by most participants as contributors to the increased freedoms, such as freedom of conscience, freedom of expression and speech, and freedom of religion. Some respondents, especially younger teachers, emphasized a shift from collectivistic to individualistic views in the society.

Contemplating about *political* changes after the collapse of the Soviet Union, the majority of teachers indicated that the issue of gaining Independence was one of the most significant changes in their lives. Many perceived it to be instrumental in developing democracy, freedom of speech, establishing of the national language policies, and opening country borders. Political transformations at the government level led to a change in the political order, government structure, multi-party system, and reforms. Government inefficiencies were evident through the lack of support and care for common people and disorder at the governmental level. Some participants also expressed mixed feelings about the relatively recent political developments related to the Orange Revolution and Presidential Elections of 2004, stating that their expectations were not fulfilled by the outcomes of these political changes.

For most of the respondents, changes in the *social* sphere were perceived to be the worst, as people lost their former ways of life and were forced to adapt to the new social realities. Quite a few teachers felt that relationships in communities and families became more hard-hearted and colder as a result of people becoming more isolated and withdrawn. They recognized the lack of connection and communication between parents and children that influenced students' upbringing, attitudes towards others, and achievement in schools. Of extreme concern for many was the fact that a significant number of students were being brought up by grandparents, relatives, or parents' friends because their parents went to work abroad. Many responses suggested that moral and spiritual, as well as physical, health of the nation had deteriorated. Moreover, a decrease in social guarantees for population and changing economic relationships led to greater stratification according to socio-economic levels in the society.

Impact of Post-Soviet Societal Changes on Schools

All participants observed a direct impact of societal transformations on the system of education. The shift in societal views and perspectives and transformations in economic, political, and social spheres in the years of Independence were seen as instrumental in bringing change to Ukrainian schools. However, for some respondents, the transition from the old, Soviet, system of education to the new, Ukrainian, system has not yet been completed. Respondents outlined several periods of transformation. The initial transitory period was marked by instability, lack of solid foundation, lack of direction and goals, and changing requirements. This period resulted in 'school democratization', characterized by rejection of the ideological aspects of the Soviet education and shift in the focus and goals towards new perspectives. The time of 'school democratization' was perceived to have led to greater freedom and flexibility in the choice of instructional materials, freedom of conscience, and freedom to implement certain instructional methodologies. Paradoxically, many of the respondents observed a tendency toward a more rigid control and increased supervision of instruction, as well as overwhelming paperwork, in the recent years.

Major educational reforms included the establishment of Ukrainian language as the main language of instruction; the emergence of elite schools and schools with specific instructional profiles; the switch to a 12-year school system; reviewing of the grading scale and marking procedures; and the introduction of new school curricula and programs of studies. These reforms elicited mixed feelings in many participants, as they were perceived to have both positive and negative outcomes for schools. Some of them were believed to be introduced haphazardly, without proper preparation or foundation for innovation. Most importantly, all participants felt that attitudes towards education and teachers in society deteriorated and exerted negative influence on their ability to provide high quality instruction to students. Schooling and teachers' work became more difficult because the authority, prestige, and reputation of schools were lost and teachers' social status degraded.

Nature and State of Teacher Collaboration

First of all, participants differentiated between the professional and personal sides of teacher collaboration. *Professional* collaboration was seen as a formal part of school life, which dealt with academic or organizational issues. *Personal*, or informal collaboration, was perceived to be related to issues of everyday life in schools. However, it was believed that both of these aspects were integral parts of the same phenomenon. Moreover, teacher collaboration was compared to a *lubricant* that kept all links of school mechanism working smoothly.

The nature of teacher collaboration was viewed as possessing both positive and negative characteristics. Teacher collaboration was guided primarily by a mindset of mutual help, a building block of joint work among teachers. Other guiding principles were framed within mindsets of lifelong learning in personal and professional realms, interpersonal communication, and teacher and administrative leadership. Along with perceived benefits, there were also challenges that were seen to limit the extent of collaboration. The lack of time to participate in collaborative activities was seen to be the most significant limitation to effective collaboration. Less frequently discussed, albeit very significant, were challenges related to limited communication and cooperation between teachers of different age groups, "forced" or "mandated" collaboration, lack of resources, and lack of a formal system of collaboration.

A number of ways in which teachers collaborated were outlined by the participants. Some of these collaborative activities were representative of teachers' work in all schools, while others occurred only in several schools from the study. Furthermore, these activities also varied in the degree of occurrence in individual schools. Most frequently mentioned were common planning of activities and common sharing of instructional materials. Teacher collaboration was very often linked to their work in "methodological associations", i.e., formal groups of teachers of a specific subject, as well as pedagogical councils and school-level staff meetings. These activities were extremely important for establishing greater integration between subject areas and cooperation between teachers through sharing, planning, and professional development. Evident also were such forms of collaboration as cooperation between subject and homeroom teachers and mentoring between novice and experienced teachers. Much attention was paid to interdisciplinary integration and classroom intervisitations and observations. And finally, participants stressed that external collaboration with teachers from other schools in the city as well as colleagues from other regions of Ukraine was a vital part of their professional activity.

Impact of External Societal Changes on Teacher Collaboration

The nature of teacher collaboration in the Soviet Union times seemed to be based on the principles of collective work, to possess political and ideological background, and to boast a well-established system of supports for novice teachers. It was apparent that collaborative relationships and work were guided by the notion of *collective,* prevalent in all spheres of Soviet school system. Although a few of the participants perceived the degree to which societal changes influenced teacher collaboration to be insignificant, the majority of interviewees observed significant differences in the *nature, content,* and *format* of teacher collaboration in independent times as compared to the Soviet era.

Among the significant transformations, the majority of respondents named new tasks, guidelines, and requirements for teachers, characterized by withdrawal of ideological pressure or politicized context of collaborative activities. Increased *voluntary* participation in teacher-oriented school activities was seen by many participants as a direct outcome of the freedom of expression. Along with the freedom of speech, teachers experienced freedom for instructional innovations and creativity that led to new orientations to collaborative activities (especially in the first few years of Independence). However, starting with the last years of the 20th century, many teachers felt that old Soviet authoritarianism "gripped them in its vice" through increased bureaucratic control and paperwork in the planning and organization of collaborative activities in schools. An abrupt transition from one system of values and beliefs in society to another changed work relationships among staff and lessened cooperation between younger and older generations of teachers. Instrumental in such change was also the decreasing material welfare of teachers. Many teachers believed that material and financial instability in society generated more distant and colder relationships regarding professional and personal issues among teachers. One of the most noticeable outcomes for the respondents was the division and formation of cliques in teacher collective (usually based on common economic and social status), which was not evident in the schools before. Several participants attributed such transformation to the general shift from collectivistic to individualistic values and norms in society.

Despite the general sense of uncertainty about the future direction of collaboration, many believed that collaborative relationships would depend on the priorities and values of the new generation of teachers. In order for collaboration in Ukrainian schools to increase, almost all participants believed that it is necessary to improve teacher status and teachers' authority in society. They also voiced a need for economic, social, and political stability in Ukraine to secure teachers' material well-being, which they thought would promote teacher creativity, professional development, and collaboration among colleagues. Not only material, but also spiritual well-being of society was deemed important for the future of teacher collaboration. According to many respondents, greater collaboration in Ukrainian schools required a balanced emphasis on individualism and collectivism, as well as greater level of collaboration in society.

Influence of Internal School Practices on Teacher Collaboration

Along with the external societal change factors, participants believed that a number of internal factors contributed to the changing nature of collaborative work among teachers. Internal factors and school practices that shaped the nature of collaborative work among teachers related to elements of organizational culture and micropolitical interactions of school members.

According to most participants, various components of school culture played important roles in establishing and sustaining collaborative relationships between teachers. Holiday celebrations, ceremonies, rituals, and traditions were perceived to serve an ultimate purpose of bringing teachers together through common planning and organization. Teachers' responses indicated that some of these school culture artifacts had been established in schools in the Soviet times; others were introduced after the collapse of the USSR. National Ukrainian, Jewish, and Romanian holidays, traditions, and ceremonies constituted a significant part of overall number of celebrations in different schools. Several comments suggested that teachers continued to follow the collaborative relationships that had been established by the former school teachers or administrators - their heroes and heroines. The most frequently mentioned values, beliefs, and norms that guided teacher relationships were common human values and moralities, such as respect, kindness, love, patience, help, compassion, and tolerance, as well as the fact that students perceived them to be role models. Despite the overall positive picture, teachers observed a decline in values and morality and a shift from spiritual towards material priorities in their work. Participants easily related to more visible aspects of school culture like artifacts and values, but explanation of the reasons of "why things were done a certain way" in their schools posed a more difficult task. Taken-for-granted underlying assumptions for collaboration among teachers were perceived to be *belongingness to a certain collective*, which depended on the length of time teachers worked together, and *cultural background*, or their association with certain national cultures.

Teacher collaboration, as many participants observed, seemed to be also susceptible to the influence of increased micropolitical activity in schools after the collapse of the Soviet Union. Teachers used to constitute one "gray mass" in Soviet schools, while independent times established conditions conducive to the development of differences in opinion and multiple perspectives, clash of interests, and division among teachers. The process of joint work among teachers often involved formation of coalitions to obtain power and influence, and use of micropolitical strategies, arguments, and conflicts to achieve group or personal goals. Interestingly enough, conflict resolution served as one of the forms of teacher collaboration. School and staff sizes played significant roles in conflict resolution: the smaller the school or staff, the easier it was to solve the conflicting situation. Of great importance for the respondents was the impact of external, macropolitical factors on micropolitics in schools: political events brought teachers together to discuss, argue, or express their concerns, and their political views often affected working relationships with colleagues. Finally, participants believed that such conditions and practices as a common theory of collaboration, family-like relationships, intellectual competitions for teachers, smaller class sizes, and reduced instructional loads were necessary for greater degree of collaboration in their schools.

Discussion

The following sections align major themes that emerged from the analysis of the research findings with the research literature and conceptual framework for this study. These themes include the perceived move from a modernist to postmodernist orientation in Ukrainian society; views of school as a microcosm of society; dimensions of postmodern dilemmas and paradoxes; teacher collaboration in the context of drastic societal change; understanding culture and the micropolitics of collaboration; and, perceived prerequisites for collaborative culture development.

From a Modernist to Postmodernist Orientation

Analysis of the data has pointed to the fact that Ukrainian society experienced a shift from a modernist era of the Soviet Union to an era of Independence characterized by increased influence of postmodernist thinking. The collapse of the Soviet Union, which served as a major catalyst for this transition, resulted in significant transformations in economic, ideological, philosophical, political, and social spheres. According to Hargreaves (1994), postmodernity is a social condition in which economic, political, organizational, and personal lives become organized around very difference principles than those of modernity. Some of the societal conditions of the age of postmodernism are transparency of cultural and national backgrounds, global information revolution, increased travel and mobility, interdependent economy and trade systems, political uncertainty and economic instability, and multiple perspectives on living, thinking, and believing in the world (Furman, 1998). Participants in this study observed and found themselves amidst many of these conditions in the fast-changing, compressed, complex, and uncertain society.

The most prominent observation among participants was the ability to hold and express multiple perspectives. Ukrainian society seems to be in transition from a Soviet era of foundational truth and unified perspective to a society of plurality, diversity, and interdependence. Philosophically and ideologically, broader and faster dissemination of information was seen to place "old ideological certainties in disrepute as people realize there are other ways to live" (Hargreaves, 1994, p. 9). After the collapse of the Communist Party ideology, the weakened ideological pressure in the independent times led to the shift in the system of moral values and ideals. As Kononenko and Holowinsky (2001) argued, political and cultural changes in Ukraine have resulted in a collapse of the former system of values and beliefs and created a need for a new system.

Participants' responses in this study supported this view; they believed that change in the philosophical perspectives that guided societal relationships resulted in the deprecation of the old "Soviet" system of values, norms, and beliefs. The old system was based on the Marxist-Leninist *collectivism,* in which individualism was not allowed and the individual's interests were always considered secondary to the interests of the collective and the society (Keltikangas-Jarvinen & Terav, 1996; Makarenko, 1967). For many, the change was especially evident in the gradual disappearance of the *collectivistic* views and increased emphasis on the *individualistic* perspectives in the society. Respondents believed that life has changed so substantially, that societal interests did not trump personal interests of people anymore. However, most of the participants pointed to the fact that the new system of norms and values had not yet been fully established and was still in the process of transition. The Ministry of Education of Ukraine (1999) recognized the lack of attention to the development and implementation of new social ideology as one of the most significant areas of regress, or absence of positive changes. Furthermore, a number of respondents believed that monetary values prevailed in the society, as people strove for money and material welfare. According to Turner (1990), monetarization of values is one of the main characteristics of the modernist age. Thus, despite many of the characteristics of the move towards postmodernist perspectives, societal conditions still possessed features of modernity.

Another characteristic of postmodern worldview, *the collapse of belief* or the growing suspicion that all belief systems are social constructions (W. T. Anderson, 1990), was observed in general awareness of otherness which was deemed unimaginable and impossible in the Soviet era. Such factors as freedom of conscience, freedom of religion, and freedom of speech respectively led to greater recognition of multiethnicity and national minorities, greater expression of religious beliefs and convictions, and liberation and ability to share different opinions and access to published information that was forbidden in the Soviet times. In postmodern society, people experience "a shift from a small number of singularities of knowledge and belief to a fluctuating, ever changing plurality of belief systems" (Hargreaves, 1994, p. 56). Some teachers claimed that society became more liberated and people were no longer afraid to express their opinion, even if they were criticizing government decisions. At the same time, other teachers felt that despite the fact that people were given the right to freely express their opinions, they did not really have a say in what was happening in the society.

All teachers indicated that Ukrainian society experienced *economic* transformations unheard of in the Soviet era, such as transition to a market economy and the capitalist system, development of entrepreneurship and small businesses, open borders and more widespread ability to travel abroad for leisure, business, or employment. Economically, postmodern societies are characterized by the decline of the factory system and development of economies that are built around the production of smaller goods rather than large ones, services more than manufacturing, information and images rather than products and things (Hargreaves, 1994). However, general unpreparedness for these changing realities resulted in uncertainty and instability, industrial decline, unemployment and corruption, and decrease in the material welfare of the population.

In the *political* realm, participants believed that Ukraine's independence and sovereignty were instrumental in promoting the development of democracy and freedoms of speech, conscience, and religion. Political aspects of postmodern societies include decentralization, flatter decision-making structures, blurring of roles and boundaries (Hargreaves, 1994) and political disorder and uncertainty (Furman, 1998). However, despite the change in the political order and introduction of decentralized government structures, the Ukrainian political system was often deemed inefficient and corrupt.

Changes in the *social* sphere were perceived by the respondents as having the most negative connotation, because people lost the former ways of living and had to adapt to the new social realities. Most significantly, society was affected by the transformations of social relationships in families and communities. Participants indicated that relationships became hard-hearted and colder as people seemed to be more isolated and withdrawn. Hargreaves (1994) argued that in the restructured postmodern world, the "lack of permanence and stability can also create crises in interpersonal relationships, as these relationships have no anchors outside themselves, of tradition or obligation, to guarantee their security and continuance" (p. 9). Instrumental factors in such degraded social relations were economic instability and relative easiness to cross the borders that forced parents to go abroad in search of employment and leave their children to be brought up by relatives or friends. As a result, families of migrant workers often fell apart, and their children lacked in proper upbringing and did not perform well in schools. A general decline in the process of proper upbringing of children in families and tendency toward deteriorated communication, respect, obligation, and connection among family members seemed to contribute to the societal moral and spiritual degradation. Social sphere transformations were perceived to be closely connected to the economic changes: limited financial abilities and loss of free medical care contributed to the poor "physical health" of the nation, while a decrease in social guarantees resulted in the greater socio-economic differentiation in society.

School as a Microcosm of Society

In the light of the previous discussion, an important issue is whether schools have remained intractably modernist in the midst of an increasingly postmodern world (Giroux, 1994). Hargreaves (1994) noted that schools and teachers are being affected more and more by the demands of the increasingly complex and fast-paced, postmodern world: "challenges and changes facing teachers and schools are not parochially confined to education but are rooted in a major sociohistorical transition from a period of modernity to one of postmodernity" (p. 23). As the country made a transition from a totalitarian Marxist Leninist ideology to democracy and pluralism, changes that occurred at the societal level greatly affected education (Zhulynsky, 1997). The post-Soviet Ukraine faced the new, unexplored terrain of postmodernism.

The majority of the participants' answers directly or indirectly indicated the impact of societal changes on the schools. School was described as a mini-system, a mini-model, or a barometer that reflected absolutely all events in the society. Similarly, documentary analysis revealed the evidence of direct impact of societal transformations on the system of education (Department of Education and Science of Chernivtsi Regional State Administration, 2002). According to the participants in this study, the shift in societal views and perspectives, as well as transformations in economic, political and social spheres, in the years of Independence were instrumental in bringing about changes (both positive and negative) to the Ukrainian educational system.

The role of the state in initiating change was widely recognized by the participants. Analysis of the documents revealed that declaration of Ukraine's intention to transform into a democratic state with the regulated market economy gave birth to the strategic plans to reform education as part of a nation-wide transformation (Ministry of Education of Ukraine, 1999). As Wanner (1998) pointed out, due to the capacity and potential of education to articulate and instill new norms of social and cultural behavior in the newly formed country, the system of education was one of the first spheres to be subjected to the reforming process. In addition, most participants viewed school system changes as natural consequences of the events in society and requirements of time and the new era, characterized by increased intellectual capacity, creativity, and liberation of the student population.

According to the Ministry of Education National Report (1999), the vector of changes in education focused on transition from the "Soviet school" model to the democratic European one. The majority of respondents however, argued that despite the numerous changes, many characteristics of the Ukrainian system of education were the same as the Soviet command-type school system, and the transition had not yet been completed.

The process of change was slow and some reforms have not taken root in the education system due to a number of reasons. First, the most important reason was perceived to be the fact that it was difficult to move away from the system of education in which schools and teachers have been inculcated for more than seventy years. This was especially the case with more experienced teachers, who were "products of their epoch" (Arkadiy, 14:5, 70), and many of them seemed unwilling and unable to keep pace with the fast changing realities. Participants' responses related to Dyczok's (2000) argument that the pace of change and reforms in Ukraine was slow because many educators and administrators were products of the previous education system and not familiar with alternative models. As Wanner (1998) found, the formal structural aspects of Soviet education were easier to reform than the practices instilled by the values of the Soviet system. Second, economic crisis, inflation, significant cuts in educational budgets, lack of resources, and delays in payments for educators negatively affected the progress of reforms and forced schools into the survival mode. Moreover, the third reason was the need for more time to implement innovations offered by reforms in the educational sphere. Finally, participants believed that initial endeavors lacked the unity of direction and foundation to build upon. Many of the reforms were perceived to be introduced haphazardly and without proper preparation, attempting to destroy and discard the existing base without a clear idea of how to create the foundation for future development. As Volodymyr concisely put it, "it was thrown away as garbage" (19:6, 30).

The nature of educational reforms in Ukraine was fragmentary and yielded only a partial transition to the new paradigm of education (Ministry of Education of Ukraine, 1999). If one could depict the respondents' perceptions of the school system transformations in the graphical representation, it would be a parabola or a bell curve (see Figure 4). First, teachers observed a period of school democratization, characterized by rejection of the ideological aspects of the "Soviet school" and shift in the focus and goals of education. This period led to establishing of schools of a new type, introduction of new curricula, removal of politically and ideologically-laden subjects, greater freedom in the choice of instructional materials and teaching methodologies, and increased creativity in teachers work. The positive outcomes of this period were the democratization, decentralization, and deideologization of education and acceptance of pluralist perspectives in education and society. Following this period, came the time when most participants experienced increased administrative control, overwhelming red tape and paperwork that reduced creativity and turned teaching into "papermania" (Zinaida, 6:3, 40). These years became the period of stagnation and partial losses of the achievements of the initial reforms (Ministry of Education of Ukraine, 1999).

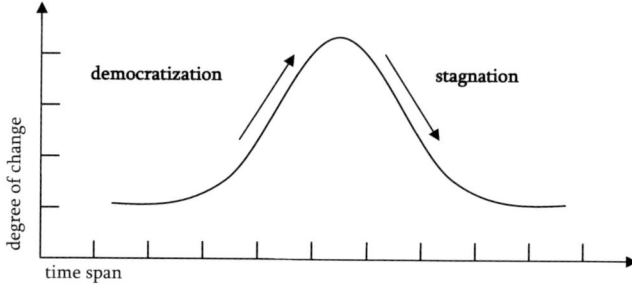

Figure 4. The impact of societal changes on Ukrainian schools: A temporal view.

In sum, aligning the respondents' comments with Maxcy's (1994) perspective allows one to conclude that system of education of Ukraine was caught on the cusp of a new era, the one between a modernist paradigm, characterized by uniform requirements, centralized planning and administration, and concern for bottom-line result, and the postmodern pattern with fast institutional changes marked by decentralization, pluralism, and system restructuring. Despite the fact that certain educational aspects successfully transformed according to the requirements of the new postmodern era and enabled further development of the system, many components remained true to the characteristics of the modernist school system and were detrimental for further transformations.

Dimensions of Postmodern Dilemmas and Paradoxes

Situated amidst the changing realities and transition from modernist to postmodernist paradigms in society in general and in the system of education in particular, teachers found themselves facing various tensions and dilemmas that had immense influence on their work. These were perceived as unanticipated consequences that emerged as a result of various societal changes. In addition to the dilemmas, it appeared that participants struggled with embracing the meaning of several contradictions or paradoxes that were characteristic of teachers' work in this period of transition. The analysis of participants' responses revealed the following four dimensions around which dilemmas and paradoxes were organized: professional commitment in uncertain times; balancing individualism and collectivism; division between generations of teachers; and conflicting freedoms and constraints.

Professional Commitment in Uncertain Times

The first dilemma that stood out from the discussions was the decisive test of professional commitment amidst the decline of material welfare and deterioration of societal attitudes. Many of the participants believed that their professionalism and commitment to teaching were rigorously tested by the post-Soviet transformations and part of the reason for this they believed has been the declining material welfare. A number of respondents believed that transition to different economic relationships were influential in changing the societal status of teachers. Due to extreme inflation and opportunities to earn more money outside of schools, many teachers needed to work at two or three jobs to provide for their families. Being forced into the survival mode because of annulled Soviet bank-book savings, low teacher salaries, and considerable delays in salary payments, many teachers eventually left teaching for more lucrative careers and entrepreneurship. A combination of all of these factors resulted in the deterioration of quality of teaching and deprofessionalization (Wanner, 1998). Those who remained faithful to teaching despite many "temptations" to follow the example of their former colleagues seemed to be more preoccupied with survival and material encumbrance than professional duties, such as instruction and professional development. Teachers had less time and opportunities for individual professional development, studying of new sources of educational information, and performance of additional measures to increase student achievement (Ministry of Education of Ukraine, 1999).

Being active members in societal development, the majority of participants believed that deteriorating attitudes towards schools and education in general in society also exerted a negative influence on their ability to provide quality instruction to students. Their responses indicated that authority, prestige, and the reputation of teaching profession have been lost in the independent times, which sharply contrasted with the Soviet era when teachers used to be held in such respect that people often took hats off and bowed upon encountering them on the streets. Many respondents stated that generally educators did not enjoy high stature within society and often experienced disrespect, distrust, abuse, abjection, and humiliation. Most often teachers tied the deteriorated attitudes towards education to the general defiance towards all authority, permissiveness, depreciation of education, and monetarization of values in Ukrainian society. However, several of the participants attributed such change in attitudes to the general shift in teacher's role in society: teacher became a less significant source of information and authority for students in the informational society. As Hargreaves (1994) suggested, the knowledge explosion led to a proliferation of expertise that began to reduce people's dependence on particular kinds of expert knowledge and created a collapse of certainty in received wisdom and established beliefs.

Balancing Individualism and Collectivism

The second dilemma was related to the balance between *emerging individualism* and *engrained collectivism*. As the vast majority of participants observed, the decline of collectivistic values and gradual shift toward individualistic values in society found their reflection in the system of education. Most of the respondents were brought up under the influence of the Soviet propaganda era (both as students and teachers) and had been inculcated in the notion of collective for the greater part of their lives. The communist political system based on Marxist-Leninist collectivism, relied of the notion of collective by Makarenko (1967), who maintained that individual's interests should always be secondary to those of the collective or the society. Many of the respondents indicated that life has changed so substantially that societal interests did not trump personal interests of teachers anymore and individualism became more apparent in society and in schools. In their view, instrumental in this shift were changing societal system of values and beliefs, as well as political and philosophical directions from the government. With the collapse of Soviet school system, education in independent Ukraine intended to eliminate the authoritarian pedagogy put in place by a totalitarian state, which led to the suppression of individuality of all participants in the education process (Ministry of Education of Ukraine, 1992). Therefore, in place of uniformity and collectivism, policymakers pursued an educational program through an individualist approach by cultivating individuality among students and teachers (Wanner, 1998). Similarly, document analysis revealed that local educational authorities in Chernivtsi region emphasized the provision of favorable conditions in schools for the development of individuality (Department of Education and Science of Chernivtsi Regional State Administration, 2002). Being the products of the Soviet "collectivistic" epoch, many teachers struggled with the prevalent individualistic culture and often refused to understand and accept new values imposed on them by society. These tensions also pertained to the acceptance of reforms in education, as a few teachers in one focus group were skeptical about innovations in educational system and argued that totalitarian Soviet system gave absolute knowledge. This was especially evident in the conversations with the older teachers who found it hard to work together with younger colleagues within entrenched cultures of individuality and perceived differences in value systems.

Division between Generations of Teachers

Stemming from the previous discussion is the third dilemma encountered by participants – the division between teachers related to their age and experience. The vast majority of the participants in this study (about 95%) were experienced teachers who had been working in the schools since Soviet times. In fact, several teachers had been in the teaching position for forty years. Only about five percent of the respondents were young teachers, whose teaching experiences were solely within the context of independent Ukraine and ranged from several months to a few years. What became evident in most focus group and interview discussions was the tension between older and younger teachers in all participating schools. Representatives of both generations argued that communication and collaboration between them posed a significant challenge in schools. A great number of responses suggested that this challenge was related to the abrupt transition in society from one system of values and beliefs to another. The reason for this is that the hierarchical bureaucracies that characterized the life of most adults are being called into question; this creates confusion and imbalance in the relationships of generations of teachers (Lieberman & Miller, 2004). Different generations of teachers were believed to be attached to opposite values and ideals based on their upbringing and common interests. Older teachers were found to be more prone to collectivism and cooperative work, and seemed disapproving of the views of the younger teachers (often called "the youth"). Participants in the young teachers' focus group, in turn, were more oriented towards individualism and stated that they experienced undue pressure and discouragement on behalf of their older colleagues. The most commonly voiced reason for such differences was that older teachers were brought up in a collectivistic Soviet society, while "the youth" grew up in a more individualistic post-Soviet environment. Hence, the process of schooling often suffered because of challenges related to differences in age and experience of staff.

Paradox of Conflicting Freedoms and Constraints

In addition to the above-discussed dilemmas, many participants seemed to grapple with a paradox related to the interplay between freedoms and constraints, flexibility and rigid bureaucracy in their work. On one hand, with the introduction of reforms in education, many participants reported that they obtained greater freedoms and flexibility in the selection of instructional materials and methodologies, curriculum planning, interpretation of instructional materials, and expression of personal points of view regarding the process of schooling. Due to the greater freedoms and flexibility in instruction in the independent times, many participants believed their work and instructional approaches became more effective, interesting and creative. As a matter of fact, it was indicated that in the independent Ukraine, at a certain point of time, there had been more freedom in curriculum than in other countries. This seemed to be an immense difference from the Soviet times, when teachers, according to Roksolana, had to act as a steel mechanism or as a robot. As Limerick, Cunnington, and Crowther (2002) argued, flexibility and freedom are characteristics of postmodern theory, in which individuals are freed from the imperatives and restrictions of structures, because they have been discredited and demolished. "They are freed of constraints imposed by their recorded social and cultural history, free of artificial hierarchies and structures, and free to be different, to be themselves" (p. 13). Interestingly enough, this was only partly true of the participants' experiences.

As partially discussed elsewhere in this chapter, many of the respondents observed a tendency toward a more rigid control of teachers' work in recent years. Requirements and commands from Ministry of Education seemed to grow in frequency with every year, and teachers sensed that too much was demanded from them, and they were controlled and supervised more than necessary. Many teachers felt that old Soviet authoritarianism authority returned and was gradually putting a "tight reign" on them again. They were especially concerned about the increased paperwork, excessive reporting, and bureaucratic control in the actions of in-school, municipal, and national educational authorities. As several focus group participants assumed, this phenomenon may have been related to the return to power of the "old guard" who wanted to establish the same "Soviet school" working procedures in the system of education of independent Ukraine.

The paradoxical relationship of these aspects, it seems, is related to the arguments of *professionalization* and *intensification*. The arguments around professionalization emphasized the struggle for and the realization of greater teacher professionalism through extensions of the teacher's role, making teaching more complex and more skilled (Lieberman & Miller, 1990; Nias et al., 1989; Rosenholtz, 1989). The second argument of intensification highlights major trends toward deterioration and deprofessionalization of teacher's work, portraying teaching as more routinized, deskilled, and increasingly controlled by prescribed programs, mandated curriculum, and increased accountability and paperwork (Apple, 1989; Barth & Guest, 1990; Densmore, 1987; Hargreaves, 1994; Larson, 1980). According to the intensification thesis, teachers' work has become increasingly intensified, with teachers expected to respond to greater pressures and comply with multiple innovations in the education system. However, participants' responses in this study indicated that the interplay of creativity and constraints deemed to be a paradox generated more by the changing societal realities than by any reforms in the school system. As Hargreaves (1994) put it, paradoxes like this make postmodernity not only such a fascinating phenomenon, but also one that can be immensely difficult to understand.

Collaboration in the Context of Drastic Change

Amidst the uncertainties of transitional period in society and educational system, teachers believed that working together in the school *collective* helped them deal with outcomes of drastic change. Overall collaboration in school was perceived by many respondents as a vital and essential component for existence of any school organization. Moreover, it was compared to a "lubricant" that kept all the "links" of a school "mechanism" working smoothly for the same cause: educating new generations. Collaboration became one of the core requisites of the postmodern society (Fullan, 1993) and a cornerstone of postmodern organizations in which problems are unpredictable, solutions are unclear, and expectations are intensifying (Hargreaves, 1994). Teacher collaboration was deemed by all participants to be an integral component of collaboration between all stakeholders in the school.

The Nature of Collaboration in a Period of Transition

From the responses, the notion of teacher collaboration appeared to possess a "double-sided" nature, consisting of professional and personal facets, or in other words, *levels of collaboration*. Professional, or formal, level of collaboration was seen to deal with academic and organizational issues, while personal or informal collaboration related to everyday situations in schools that involved personal issues of teachers. Discussions of personal level of collaboration included aspects of non-professional nature, without which, as participants argued, professional collaboration could not exist. In other words, these were seen as *antecedents* of professional collaboration that provided teachers with the foundation or grounds for effective joint work regarding professional school issues. Some of the examples of such antecedents were mutual material and financial help in dire straits, friendly advice, emotional support in unfortunate circumstances (such as death or illness), encouragement, common celebrations of holidays, to name a few. An important antecedent was a general harmony in school – the effectiveness of teacher collaboration was perceived to depend on the level of harmony among pedagogues. Interestingly enough, most of the participants' responses about the nature of collaboration referred to these antecedents first, and then to its professional elements. Hence, these findings suggest that in the times of uncertainty and changes, perhaps, the *personal* aspect of collaboration has more importance for teachers than the *professional* one. Most importantly, the majority of participants believed that in order to understand the meaning of collaboration, one needs to look at both professional and personal aspects as integral parts of the same phenomenon.

The principles that guided collaborative work among teachers can be classified according to four mindsets: a mindset of *mutual help*, a mindset of *lifelong learning*, a mindset of *communication*, and a mindset of *leadership*. As the most frequently mentioned, the mindset of *mutual help* was considered a building block of teacher collaboration, both in personal and professional contexts. Its professional constituents involved mutual advice, assistance, and sharing of experience and instructional materials. This aligns with the view that collaboration involves sharing resources, whether they are time, availability, knowledge, advice, or materials with others (Friend & Cook, 2000). However, it should also be noted that quite a few respondents experienced a lack of resources after the collapse of the USSR. In order to conduct lessons, they often had to borrow instructional materials from their colleagues, as those were limited or unavailable due to insufficient funding. Though such sharing of the materials may seem as a collaborative activity for some, for participating teachers that was a challenge. As for the non-professional and personal issues of mutual help, they included material, financial, or moral supports. Hargreaves (1994) found that greater collaboration provides moral support by strengthening resolve, permitting vulnerabilities to be shared and aired, and carrying people through failures and frustrations that accompany change.

Lifelong learning emerged as another important mindset of collaboration. Participants believed that all teachers, including novice ones, have valuable aspects regarding teaching, upbringing, or approaching students that others may learn from them. Collaboration seeks to promote learning (Hargreaves, 1994) and reflective dialogue among teachers (Louis et al., 1996; Putnam & Borko, 1997).

A third mindset of collaboration emerging from the perceptions of participants was *communication*. Unlike Schrage (1990) who argued that individuals that are merely communicating are not collaborating, the frequency of participants' responses indicated that communication and discussion were viewed as the best means to collaborate with colleagues in the school. This pertained to meaningful communication that included sharing experiences, problems, successes, and achievements within the school collective. Communication was also perceived as a strategy to avoid isolation and ensure continuous progress. Friend and Cook (2000) differentiated between communication itself and the nature of interpersonal relationships occurring during the interaction and the ways in which individuals communicate with each other.

The fourth mindset demonstrated by the participants was *leadership*, which consisted of two aspects: *teacher leadership* and *administrative leadership*. Having a teacher leader was deemed important for ensuring joint work in the collective. Collectives needed a "natural leader" to whom others turned the most, who was respected and tacitly recognized by others as a leader, and who was willing to collaborate, show initiative, and encourage others to do the same. Lieberman and Miller (2004) emphasized the role of teacher leaders in establishing collaboration, establishing professional learning within communities of practice, and reshaping school culture. Another key aspect for collaboration was administrative leadership or involvement in establishing collaborative relationships and organization of activities in the schools. Participants in a "school of a new type" (i.e., elite school) especially appreciated leading by example on behalf of their principal, who was personally involved in school renovations in the summer. As Reeves (2002) suggested, the value of *leadership modeling* far exceeds the impacts of memos, seminars, and suggestions about ways to collaborate. In Deal and Peterson's (1999) view, modeling values through the demeanor and actions is an example of *symbolic leadership*.

Post-Soviet Shift in the Essence of Collaboration

As the data analysis revealed, the nature of teacher collaboration in participants' schools has undergone several significant changes as compared to the Soviet era. According to the respondents, school cultures during the Soviet era were highly collective in nature: all participants of the Soviet school process were required to be the same, or in the words of one of the participants, to constitute "one gray mass". In the modernist view, cultures are considered to be overly bounded and integrated structures that emphasize homogeneity and sameness of its constituents (Furman, 1998; Gerholm, 1988; M. E. Henry, 1993). Collaboration in the Soviet schools was seen to resemble the characteristics of a *groupthink*, the uncritical conformity to the group decisions, unthinking acceptance of the latest solution, and suppression of individual dissent (Fullan, 1993). The notion of the *collective* (Makarenko, 1967) was of the highest priority, and teachers' individual interests had to be subdued to the interest of the school collective. Therefore, collaboration in the Soviet era meant that teachers had to participate in all school activities and "go all out in school," setting everything else aside as secondary. Besides, collective work required conformity and a unified perspective; therefore, as one participant framed it, it often looked like every member of the collective had the same views. From the responses, the content and format of the majority of the school collaborative activities at that time appeared to be politically and ideologically-laden. Teachers reminisced that collaboration was used by Communist Party committees in schools as a means for uniting school collective (usually accompanied by a rigid supervision and control over teacher participation). At the same time, a well established system of mentorship seemed to serve as a tool of socializing novice teachers into the unified culture of school collective.

Discussing the degree of perceived impact of the post-Soviet societal changes on teacher collaboration, some of the teachers (especially, those who called themselves 'old school') stressed that such a factor as 'upbringing in the spirit of collectivism' was instrumental in the fact that they collaborated in the same manner despite all the changes. This sentiment parallels the arguments of Mal'kova (1988), Monoszon (1988), and Sukhomlinskii (1981) that the Soviet educational system expected individuals to develop a collective, rather than a personal identity. According to the respondents, Makarenko's (1967) principles of collective from the Soviet era still guided the work of teachers who were brought up with the Soviet values and beliefs. However, these comments mainly related to the personal side of collective work and relationships. The majority of responses indicated that the nature, content, and format of their joint work with colleagues (both in personal and professional sense) had undergone significant transformations.

The new tasks and requirements of the reforming school system seemed to modify the content of collaboration, which detracted from the former political or ideological bases and was oriented towards new guiding principles of education: nationality, morality, and individuality (Ministry of Education of Ukraine, 1992). Many participants also observed an increased voluntary participation in teacher-oriented school activities. Friend and Cooke (2000) viewed voluntary participation as one of the characteristics of effective collaboration, stating that school professionals have to choose to carry out collaborative activities. Many participants noticed that greater freedom of expression in society induced greater openness in expressing and parity in acceptance of different individual opinions in the process of collaboration. This sentiment reflects the postmodern conception of collaboration, which is based on the feeling of responsibility to cooperate with others who may be different, as the center of collaboration has shifted from sameness to acceptance of otherness and cooperation within difference (Furman, 1998; Slattery, 1995). Effective collaboration requires parity among participants, in which every person's contribution is equally valued and each person has equal power in decision making (Friend & Cook, 2000). Along with freedom of speech, the respondents experienced freedom for instructional innovations that led to the new format of collaborative activities based on the principles of creativity and self-actualization – notions that were not usually associated with the former Soviet command-type pedagogy. Hargreaves (1994) described collaborative relationships to be development-oriented, as teachers are committed to work together on their own or externally mandated initiatives.

Despite the fact that most of the collaborative activities in the schools were "inherited" from the Soviet school system, some of them differed substantially in many components. Teacher collaboration was often linked to collaborative planning and sharing of instructional resources in methodological associations, as well as pedagogical councils and staff meetings. However, these initiatives were relieved of the "political and ideological burden" of the Soviet past and aimed at the development of creativity and voluntary participation among teachers. The function of a *methodological association* very closely resembled the notion of *professional learning community*, with teachers questioning the status quo, seeking new methods, testing those methods, and then reflecting on the results (DuFour & Eaker, 1998). These associations served to establish interdisciplinary integration and cooperation between teachers through sharing, planning, and professional development. Evident were also such forms as subject and homeroom teachers' cooperation, classroom intervisitations in the form of "open lessons" and peer observation. Though mentoring was present to a certain extent, its effectiveness was limited by the peculiarities of inter-generational relationships discussed elsewhere.

Along with the positive changes in the content and format of teachers' collaborative work, many participants raised concerns about several negative effects of post-Soviet societal changes that pertained to teacher collaboration. First of all, the relatively recent increase in bureaucratic control over various aspects of schooling negatively influenced collaboration among teachers. Many of the participants felt pressure and authoritarianism in the organization of some collaborative activities among teachers, which they termed "mandated" or "prescribed" collaboration. This mirrors the notion of *contrived collegiality* (Fullan & Hargreaves, 1996), characterized by a set of formal, specific, bureaucratic procedures to increase the attention being given to joint teacher planning, consultation, and other collaboration activities. As many participants indicated, time for collaboration became insufficient due to excessive paperwork and unreasonable accountability to various levels of administration. Similar to Hargreaves' (1991) and Leonard and Leonard's (1999) arguments, most respondents considered lack of time and overload to be the most significant limitations. Though one of the claimed benefits of collaboration is reducing overload (Hargreaves, 1994), the respondents in this study did not feel the relief in their workload as a result of changes in the process of collaboration.

Secondly, material welfare of teachers and financial instability had a significant negative influence on the willingness and ability of many teachers to collaborate with their colleagues, because many school teachers were more preoccupied with survival and providing for their families than their professional duties. Moreover, the increased socio-economic differentiation in society was instrumental in transforming relationships among teachers from being close and friendly to distant and competitive. Such disunited and alienated relationships led to isolation among teachers, or as Lyubomyra phrased it, "stewing in one's own juice" (12:6, 117).

Thirdly, collaboration appeared to be affected by increased division and formation of cliques in the collective based on common economic and social status, affiliation with specific structure within school. Gradually, collaboration among *all* teachers in the school was disappearing, and many participants attributed this to the general shift from collectivism to individualism in society. This was particularly noticeable in deteriorated relationships and lack of cooperation between older and younger generations of teachers. Collaboration among these entities was perceived to suffer due to the differences in systems of values and beliefs, attitudes, and approaches to instruction. There seems to be a contradiction with the argument that in postmodern organizational context "persons are able to approach one another freely through *the recognition of difference*" (Murphy, 1988, p. 612). Despite the fact that differences between generations of teachers were recognized, they appeared to be too great to overcome for establishing effective collaboration among the parties in the school environment.

Finally, collaboration in some schools was seen to be "*unsystematic*" or *random* in nature and occurred only if there was an urgent need to get things done. Perhaps, this was an outcome of the general uncertainties and multiplicity of directions of the transition period in the system of education. There seemed to be no broad-range, formal system that would encourage teachers to collaborate, share experiences, and thereby increase the level of professional growth. Earl and Lee (1998) suggested that successful collaboration is a function of *urgency-agency-energy*, in which urgency is the need to make a difference, agency is collaboration that focuses on inquiry and coherence, and energy is ability to achieve desired outcomes. For the respondents, teacher collaboration seemed to have urgency and agency to a certain degree, but lacked energy to accomplish tasks. Moreover, one of these participants regretted that schools did not have a solid theory that would coordinate teachers' collective work in the instructional process. Effective collaboration needs to be based on mutual goals – specific and important enough to maintain teachers' shared commitment (Friend & Cook, 2000).

The themes, as depicted, showed that participants perceived changes that occurred in the area of teacher collaboration as a result of post-Soviet transformations from both positive and negative perspectives. Their responses reflected general sense of uncertainty regarding the future direction and a gradual loss of hope for the "brighter future" in society. However, despite the prevalent sense of pessimism about the future of collaborative work, many teachers hoped that it would improve with the presence of favorable societal conditions. As Walker (2006) argued, in a world of postmodern collapse of belief, a world without solid truth, standards, or ideals, a world devoid of social cohesiveness, educators need to foster hope as leaders of future generations of leaders in society.

Understanding Culture and the Micropolitics of Collaboration

As evident from the above mentioned themes, collaboration has the tendency to increase the complexity of organizing and managing school organization. Therefore, as Pounder (1999) argued, a single lens, framework, of disciplinary approach is an inadequate aid to understanding such complex organizational phenomenon. This study attempted to make sense of the nature of collaboration through two lenses: organizational culture and micropolitics.

Post-Soviet School Culture and Teacher Collaboration

The cultural perspective means the use of organizational culture and a frame of reference for the way one looks at, attempts to understand, and works with organizations (Ott, 1989). Besides informal understanding of culture as "the way we do things around here" (Deal & Kennedy, 1983; Deal & Peterson, 1999), a formal understanding presents it as historically transmitted explicit and implicit patterns of meaning (Geertz, 1973; Schein, 1985). The findings of this study showed that various explicit and implicit components of school culture significantly influenced the ways in which teachers collaborated with colleagues in their schools.

Utilizing Schein's (1985) levels of culture, the explicit nature was manifested in *school culture artifacts* (celebrations, rituals, traditions, ceremonies, heroes and heroines), and *espoused values, norms, and beliefs*. Judging from teachers' responses, some of the cultural artifacts had been established in schools in the Soviet times; others were introduced, either by administration or teachers, after the collapse of the USSR. It appeared that holiday celebrations, ceremonies, rituals, and traditions served an ultimate purpose of bringing teachers together through common planning, organization, and participation. Moreover, several comments suggested that teachers in several schools continued to follow collaborative relationships established by the former school teachers and administrators, whom they viewed as heroes and heroines. Artifacts are easy to apprehend but difficult to interpret without knowledge of the deeper level, *espoused values*, or statements and beliefs about the way things are done in school and how people are supposed to behave (Schein, 1985). Review of teacher responses revealed that despite the fact that teacher relationships in their schools were primarily guided by common human values and moralities (e.g., respect, kindness, love, patience, help, compassion, and tolerance), there was a decline in the system of values and beliefs and a shift from spiritual towards material priorities in their work. This shift often negatively affected relationships and, subsequently, collaboration among teachers.

The implicit nature of school culture is manifested through an invisible flow of taken-for-granted assumptions that give meaning to people's actions and shape their interpretations (Deal & Peterson, 1990; Stolp & Smith, 1995). This explains why participants easily related to more visible levels of school culture, but struggled with explanation of the reasons behind them. One of the underlying assumptions that most teachers agreed upon was *belongingness to a school collective*. This assumption seemed to be tied to the historically transmitted notion of collective (Makarenko, 1967). Despite all the recent developments and increased emphasis on individualism, collective spirit appeared to be still powerful due to its dominance in school cultures for more than seventy years. It became the underlying social meaning, and it continues to shape teachers' views on their work, behavior in schools, and relationships with colleagues (Deal & Peterson, 1999). This may be the reason for struggles in collaboration between older and younger generation of teachers. A somewhat unexpected finding was that *cultural background* was considered to be another underlying assumption. As national minorities were oppressed in the Soviet times, identification with certain national cultures of teachers (for example, Ukrainian, Jewish, or Romanian backgrounds) must have gained importance after the collapse of the Soviet Union, and were also perceived to have significant impact on the school culture by guiding working relationships and behavior of teachers.

Increased Micropolitical Activity as a Consequence of Change

Micropolitical processes and structures tend to intensify during periods of change in schools (Blase, 2005). During the research, it became evident that micropolitical activity in schools increased after the collapse of the Soviet Union due to the observed development of differences in opinion and multiple perspectives, clash of interests, and division among teachers. This was partly due to the impact of external, macropolitical factors. Researchers (Blase & Blase, 2002; Malen, 1995; Mawhinney, 1999b; Townsend, 1990) confirmed that macro level factors (or factors external to schools), significantly influence the micropolitical character of schools. Responses in this study affirmed that teachers became highly politicized as a result of various societal transformations (mainly political), which often influenced the way teachers worked together if they adhered to different political views. As the majority of participants observed, this was in sharp contrast with the Soviet era, when teachers seemed to constitute one "gray mass" and were not allowed to deviate from political views of the communist ideology. Other reasons seemed to be the socio-economic differentiation that led to increased divisiveness in the collective, and philosophical transformations like freedoms of speech and conscience that led to acceptance of multiple perspectives in schools. Thus, schools became political entities where school members (individual or groups) developed micropolitical strategies to achieve their own personal and school goals (Bacharach & Lawler,

1980; Bacharach & Mitchell, 1987; Iannaccone, 1975). Increased micropolitical activity seemed to have significant implications for collaboration among teachers.

In order to understand decision making in the process of collaboration, one needs to understand political power and the strategies that individuals and groups used to gain such power (Pettigrew, 1973). Participants emphasized experience, age, and expertise as the main sources of their power in schools. For Miller and O'Shea (1991), these constituted two warrants for teacher leadership: leadership through experience and leadership through knowledge. The notion of *earned authority*, that emerged from discussions, depended on teachers' professional abilities, personal talents, attitudes, and traits of character. *Positional authority,* obtained by teachers from occupying certain positions in the school, seemed to have a deteriorating affect on collaboration among teachers, as many believed that "superior position spoilt people even more than money". In postmodern view, power is not vested in the top but resides with individuals and evolves from the dynamic collaboration and problem solving of the group (Sackney et al., 1999). However, most participants in this study noted that their power and influence were mainly exercised horizontally, at the teacher level; most teachers did not have enough power to influence administrative decisions. One participant stated that there still existed a command-type relationship between teachers and administration, and teachers only felt empowered to make decisions regarding issues that pertained to their classroom matters. According to Marshall and Scribner (1991), these were characteristics of ongoing negotiations of boundaries and turf between the administrator zone and the teacher zone in schools. Several participants believed they had the right not to participate in collaborative activities if they preferred to work and plan alone. As Hargreaves (1994) argued, the protection of individuality and discretion of judgment of such teachers is also a protection of their rights to disagree and reflect critically on the value of collaboration.

The work of Hoyle (1986) and Gronn (1986) revealed that school personnel use both overt and covert micropolitical strategies within schools to use authority and influence to fulfill their interests. The issue of micropolitical strategies was most frequently addressed by the young teachers' focus group. This might be attributed to the fact that novice teachers had to use various tactics (often very elaborate) to approach experienced teachers for help with instruction or upbringing that they would not be able to obtain otherwise. These tactics depended on personality, as teachers learned with which issues and with whom they could take more liberties and be more reserved. Strategies mentioned in this research varied from school to school: in some schools teachers squabbled openly; in others, they used respectful strategies to achieve their goals. As Mangham (1979) argued, micropolitical strategies can ultimately serve as an impetus for creation of collective meaning among individuals and groups within organizations.

Gaining power and influence to achieve desired outcomes was seen as one of the reasons teacher coalitions formed in the participating schools. School members often form shared objectives and micropolitical strategies with other school members, i.e., coalitions, in order to achieve successful and preferred decision outcomes (Bacharach & Lawler, 1980; Bacharach & Mitchell, 1987). Despite the prevalent negative perceptions of coalitions as "undercurrents and cliques", a significant number of participants viewed them as formal or informal groupings that formed in an endeavor to bring about change to the schooling process. The majority of coalitions discussed by the respondents were formed according to the factors of age and experience, methodological association or department, common interests, and language and nationality. Interestingly enough, participants observed that coalitions were more prone to develop in larger staffs than smaller staffs, and in secondary schools as opposed to elementary schools.

Political interactions in organizations include both cooperative-consensual and conflictive behaviors, and are reflected in individual behavior as well as organizational structure (Blase & Blase, 2002). Arguments, differences of opinion, and conflicts were seen as having both positive and negative connotations, depending on the nature and outcomes for the effective process of joint work. Rows and squabbles were perceived as possible negative outcomes. An important positive outcome was reaching a balanced representation of opinions to confirm their validity. Participants outlined three conditions necessary for any point to be accepted into consideration in the process of collaboration: it needs to be valid and worthy of notice; it needs to adhere to the shared norms in the collective; and, it needs to be of some benefit for the school.

Conflict was perceived as an inevitable part of the collaborative process, both in personal and professional contexts. A significant number of participants perceived interpersonal conflict to be a "blatant fact", a signal of discontent in the collective. Professional conflict, on the other hand, was prone to be viewed as a constructive phenomenon, capable of invoking change and preventing school culture from its stagnant state. "Truth is born in the argument" was a common belief among teachers. Interestingly enough, resolution of conflicts was perceived as one of the forms of teacher collaboration. In one school, the whole collective worked together to find the sources of the conflict, as they believed "it was easier to prevent the problem than to deal with its consequences" (Viktor, 15:13, 60). To a certain degree, it was a responsibility of administration to prevent and resolve conflicts through collaboration with teachers in order to maintain positive work environment in schools. As some posited, school and staff sizes played significant roles in conflict resolution: it was easier to resolve conflict in a small school rather than in a large comprehensive school. Many attributed this to a family-like atmosphere of small schools in which teachers knew each other and worked well together. Most importantly, some participants mentioned that whenever arguments or conflicts occurred, common goal of teaching students came up as a mediating factor that forced them to realize what was worth fighting for. I find this argument related to the point of view that micropolitical strategy of collaboration, along with micropolitical strategy of conflict (Blase, 1991; Townsend, 1990), generates in teachers a sense of shared accountability for outcomes of their decision-making (Friend & Cook, 1996).

Characteristics of the Prevalent Types of School Culture

This study was mainly concerned with cultures of teaching that help give meaning, support, and identity to teachers, their work, and relationships between them and their colleagues (Hargreaves, 1994; Waller, 1932). Though this study did not provide an opportunity to study the culture of each of the participating schools in depth, teacher responses and observations allowed me to discuss in general the prevalent themes regarding two dimensions of cultures of teaching in these schools: content and form. Hargreaves (1994) asserted that content consists of attitudes, values, beliefs, habits, assumptions, and ways of doing things that are shared within a teacher group; the form consists of the characteristic patterns of relationships and forms of association between members of the cultures. Viewing collaboration through two lenses, cultural and micropolitical, allowed for discrimination between different types of school culture.

Researchers (Fullan, 1993; Hargreaves, 1994; Huberman, 1993; Little, 1990; Lortie, 1975; Peterson & Brietzke, 1994) have differentiated between non-collaborative, pseudo-collaborative, and collaborative school cultures. Characteristics of all of these types of culture were present in focus group and interview discussions.

Some of the responses related to non-collaborative cultures, characterized by individualism and isolation, conservatism in educational approaches and unwillingness to change, and presentism, or focusing on immediate, rather than long-term issues in schools (Lortie, 1975). The majority of respondents from all schools indicated that their work was predominantly individual in nature (in the form of instruction and preparation), constituting on average of eighty percent of the overall working time during the day. Most of them neither had time, nor was collaboration possible in some cases. Though classroom isolation offers many teachers a welcome measure of privacy, it also shuts out possible sources of feedback and support (Hargreaves, 1994).

Tensions between generations of teachers also revealed features of non-collaborative cultures: younger teachers argued that older teachers were unwilling to change their instructional approaches (as required by new trends in education), while older teachers believed that younger teachers were more individualistic and reluctant to work together with their colleagues. (As an example, they stated that young teachers were not devoted to teaching; they wanted to finish their lessons faster and go home). Furthermore, increased intensification of work resulted in unwillingness or inability (due to stress, exhaustion, and burnout) of some teachers to be involved in collaboration with their colleagues. Little (2002) believed that schools often intensify isolation of teacher by the way they organize time, space, and responsibilities.

Data analysis has made is possible to affirm that the majority of participants' responses about collaboration in their schools related to the characteristics of pseudo-collaborative cultures, that seem collaborative in context, but lack collaborative substance (Fullan & Hargreaves, 1996). First, teachers commented about the culture of *balkanization* (Hargreaves, 1994). Increased division among teachers in all participating schools after the collapse of the Soviet Union resulted in the creation of groups (or cliques) according to common interests and affiliations with certain structures within schools, as well as coalitions competing for influence in teacher collectives. Teachers started communicating and working with those colleagues who were perceived to be closer "in spirit", age and experience, and socio-economic status.

Secondly, respondents described the presence of cultures of *comfortable collaboration* (Fullan & Hargreaves, 1996) or *independent artisanry* (Huberman, 1993) in several schools. This was particularly visible in the responses of several teachers who indicated the lack of formal system of collaboration in their schools. Teacher collaboration was random and occurred only when there was an urgent need to get things done. Such cultures focused on the immediate, short-term problem solving to the exclusion of long-term solutions.

Most frequently discussed were the traits of the third type of pseudo-collaborative culture, *contrived collegiality*. In the majority of schools, participants discussed planned or mandated collaborative activities on behalf of school administration. This process was double-edged with positive and negative comments from the respondents. On one hand, collaborative activities were interesting, development-oriented, and relieved teachers from the burden of organizing them; on the other hand, they were concerned with the "prescribed" nature, authoritarianism in organization, and pressure on teachers to participate in those activities.

Finally, teachers' responses demonstrated the presence of characteristics of *collaborative cultures* in their schools. Some comments described support networks of professionals who shared problems, ideas, materials, and solutions. This was especially noticeable in, but not limited to, the schools of a new type, where teachers' work was characterized by creativity, innovation, flexibility, self-actualization, and lifelong learning. Another example was a large school complex in which sharing of experience, instructional materials, and expertise was set up as a well-working system. These cultures seemed to take a form of a *moving mosaic* (Hargreaves, 1994), extending beyond traditional boundaries (particularly between administration and teachers) and allowing teachers to recognize their collective strength. Almost in all participating schools, participants recognized difference of opinions, or as Fullan (1999) termed it, the value of dissonance inside the collective and outside the organization, in society-at-large.

Prerequisites for Collaborative Culture Development

Despite the fact that some schools possessed the characteristics of collaborative cultures, the majority of characteristics of participating schools' cultures in the study were connected with pseudo-collaborative type. A strong collaborative culture seems to be a necessity for every school, and schools in Ukraine are not an exception. This brings us to the argument in the beginning of this study as to whether collaborative cultures are developed instrumentally from inside or certain societal conditions are necessary to shape it from the outside. As Schein (1985) argued, culture is created through external adaptation to survive in and adapt to the environmental changes, and internal integration of its processes to ensure the capacity to survive and adapt. The findings of this study reinforce the suggestions that collaborative school cultures require both internal shaping and external conditions. Collaborative cultures, then, take the form of a moving mosaic (Hargreaves, 1994), characterized by acceptance of otherness and cooperation within difference (Furman, 1998).

Internal Shaping of Collaborative Cultures

Collaborative cultures are not easy to develop (Fullan & Hargreaves, 1996; Little, 2002; Rosenholtz, 1989); they are shaped by the way principals, teachers, and key people reinforce and support underlying norms, values, beliefs, and assumptions over a period of time. The process of shaping a collaborative culture involves reading the existing culture and identifying aspects of the underlying norms and assumptions that serve the core mission and meet the needs of the school. Collaborative cultures seem to be built around important *antecedents* of collaboration, such as mutual help, emotional support, harmony, and friendly advice. The building blocks of collaboration, such as mutual help, lifelong learning, communication, and leadership, need to be supported on a constant basis. Identified as the major underlying assumptions in the participating schools, school administration may use the notion of a collective (not as a tool, but as a condition of education as Krasovetsky (1995) argued) to provide the necessary balance between the emerging individualism and engrained collectivism in order to accommodate the needs of various generations of teachers. Similarly, another underlying assumption of *cultural background* may be used to meet the collaborative needs of teachers from different nationalities.

Shaping a collaborative culture also requires reinforcing and celebrating those aspects that support development of joint work and changing the folkways and norms that destroy collegiality. Reinforcing of issues as common planning and organization of school functions, difference of opinion and constructive conflict, and professional work in methodological associations would be favorable for the evolution of collaborative school cultures. The participants in this study also outlined several areas that required improvement in their schools if collaboration were to be developed to a greater extent. First, they believed there was a need for a common system or theory that would guide deep collaboration among teachers. Second, they indicated the need for family-like cooperation without destructive quarrels and conflict. Third, they prized intellectual competitions organized by school administration to stimulate teacher participation, professional development, and creativity. And fourth, they felt the need to relieve the instructional load, undue pressure, and bureaucratic requirements on behalf of administration to allow for more time to be spent on collaboration.

Societal Conditions Conducive to the Development of Collaborative School Cultures

Collaboration at both the school and societal levels became one of the core requisites of postmodern society (Fullan, 1993). Participants in this study considered collaboration in schools to be closely dependent on the collaboration in society-at-large. They outlined a number of conditions that in their view were necessary for the development of collaborative cultures in their schools. First of all, most participants indicated the need for improvement of teacher status, increase of teachers' authority, renewal of trust, and value of professionalism in society. Second, they believed that stability in material welfare and social guarantees would allow teachers to be more financially and socially secure and concentrate solely on their professional duties. Third, teachers regarded higher levels of spirituality and morale in society as necessary prerequisites to collaborative relationships in teacher collective. Fourth, collaborative cultures required a balance between collectivism and individualism in order to prevent isolation on one hand, and groupthink on the other. And finally, teachers believed that greater levels of collaboration among people outside of school will have a positive impact on teachers' collective work. Their responses mostly addressed the personal side of collaboration; however, some comments pertained to professional collaboration as well. Participants affirmed that if the culture of cooperation, mutual help, support and understanding develops in Ukrainian society, it would transfer onto the culture of teachers.

Implications of the Study

Based upon the results of the study, the following section presents implications for theory, practice, policy, future research, and methodology.

Implications for Theory

The initial conceptual framework as described in the literature review (see Figure 3) incorporated a number of theoretical constructs suited for the concepts under study. The purpose of understanding teacher collaboration in Ukrainian schools was a central theme of this framework. Discussion of collaboration was situated within a discourse of postmodernism as a social theory, utilizing constructive postmodern perspective as an analytical tool. This perspective allows building upon the existing foundation, adopting the previous achievements in the area of collaboration, and applying a new lens, defining collaboration as a network of persons who may differ but who are interdependent. Two distinct levels, macro (society) and micro (school) depicted the impact of large-scale post-Soviet changes (economic, social, political, ideological, and philosophical) on schools and teacher collaboration within them. Review of teacher collaboration at the micro (school) level relied on two disciplinary frameworks: the organizational culture perspective and the micropolitical perspective. The concept of collective, pervasive in the Soviet society and school system, was regarded as a basis for establishing collaborative school cultures. The final part of the framework included implications for actions, i.e., development of collaborative school cultures, through a two-fold process: instrumental shaping and responding to societal conditions. Inherent in this framework was the belief that a collaborative school culture was necessary for schools in Ukraine to adapt to the uncertainties and transformations of the post-Soviet era.

The revision to the initial framework on the basis of this study (see Figure 5) would include several significant issues that need to be considered for better understanding of the theoretical constructs under study. This study highlighted the ongoing struggle between forces of modernity and postmodernity in post-Soviet Ukrainian society. The process of transition from modernist to postmodernist perspectives is time-sensitive, painful, and unpredictable. Gains of deideologization and freedoms of conscience, speech, and religion are counteracted by economic decline, political instability, and social insecurity. Despite the declared transition from the Soviet era of modernism to postmodernity, the Ukrainian society possesses many characteristics of the modernist society.

Both collectivism and individualism are important for the discussions of collaboration. Abrupt transition from collectivistic to individualistic systems of values and beliefs removes the foundation for teachers to rely on in their collective work. Individualism and collectivism represent the extremes of a continuum between a system of order, stability, sameness, and conformity and a condition of uncertainty, instability, flexibility, otherness, and difference. Emphasis on either of the opposites may lead to isolation and privatism on one side or groupthink and uniformity on the other. Discourse on collaboration requires a balanced representation of these opposing perspectives.

Collaboration among teachers in schools is susceptible to transformations at the macro (societal), as well as micro (school) levels. Macro transformations affect the *nature* of teacher collaboration in a direct way through changing societal realities, while *content* and *format* are usually influenced indirectly through the impact on school structures, reforms and policies, and teachers' values and beliefs.

A focus on understanding the essence of collaboration in the times of uncertainty, instability, loss of hope, and devaluation of truth reveals personal and professional sides of collaboration. During periods of rapid and radical change, personal aspects of collaboration tend to gain more significance than the professional ones, and these serve as antecedents for the development of professional collaboration. The building blocks of collaboration in unstable times are mindsets of mutual help, lifelong learning, communication and leadership.

This study highlighted the need for better understanding of the role of teachers' lives outside of school in the process of establishing collaborative relationships in schools. Material welfare, spirituality and morale, social security, societal attitudes, and changing fabric of social relationships exert significant impact on teachers work. If teachers' needs in these areas are not met, professional side of their collaboration with colleagues tends to suffer. When teachers feel financially, materially, and socially secure, their work gains orientation toward professionalism and professional development.

160

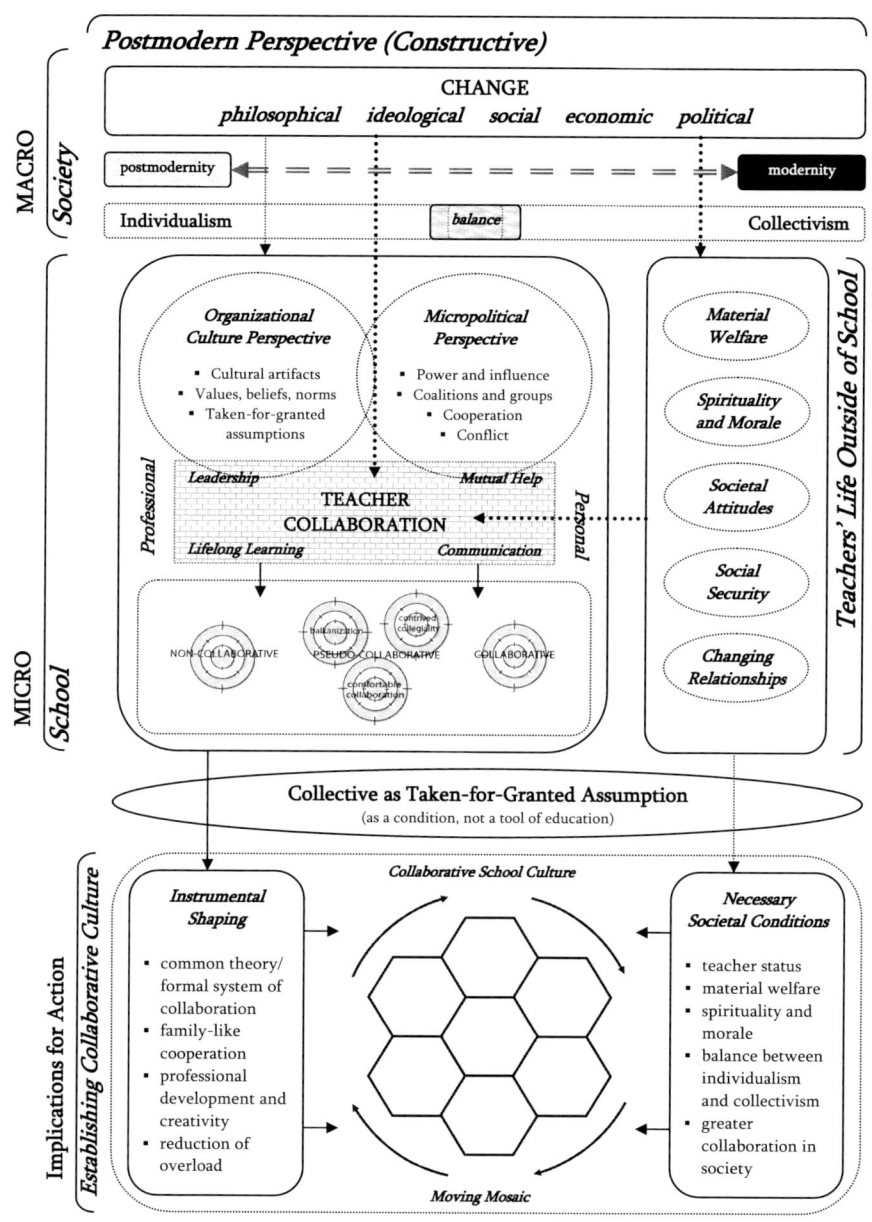

Figure 5. Revised conceptual framework.

The development of collaborative cultures is a two-fold process that involves both instrumental shaping on the part of teachers and administrators, as well as necessary societal conditions. Instrumental shaping, according to participants, involved common theory or formal system of collaboration, family-like cooperation, collaborative activities aimed at professional development and creativity, and reduction of overload and bureaucratic requirements. Societal conditions conducive to the development of collaborative cultures include improvement in teacher status, spirituality and morale, balance between individualism and collectivism, and greater collaboration in society. When both of these prerequisites are present, collaborative cultures in schools in postmodern society take the form of a *moving mosaic* (Hargreaves, 1994).

Implications for Practice

Based on the results of this study, the following recommendations are made to help establish collaborative cultures in schools.

As various societal transformations affect the work and lives of all teachers, it is essential that a much greater effort be made on the part of the government to establish economic and political stability in the country, improve material welfare and social security of teachers, foster spirituality and morale, and help increase value of education and teachers' status in the society by recognizing the contributions that teachers make in educating and upbringing future generations of citizens. For a higher stature in society, teachers should be assigned a status of public service [public capacity] workers. Schools should be more prepared to respond to teachers' needs in times of societal changes. Responses point to the need for raising teachers' salaries, valuing teachers' work, fostering teachers' status, improving student discipline, and enhancing moral and spiritual principles. The study has made it possible to affirm that both material and spiritual aspects of teacher collaboration need to be taken into consideration. Stability in material and social spheres allows teacher to concentrate of carrying out of their professional responsibilities, while spirituality and morale provide teachers with moral support.

Despite the fact that time and life required change on the part of teachers, many teachers were reluctant to change their attitudes and instructional strategies. Teachers need to adapt to the new realities in education by being constantly involved in collaborative and professional development activities with their colleagues. Continuous encouragement and development of creativity and self-actualization in schools need to become an integral part of the system of education in order to improve the effectiveness of instruction. This is especially true for professional development and retention of younger generation of teachers. To encourage creative work among teachers, senior levels of educational administration should reduce control, supervision, and undue requirements for reporting and paperwork. Reduced workload and paperwork would allow professionals to reach their fullest potential in teaching through increased time for professional development and collaboration with colleagues. Collaborative initiatives like methodological associations, interdisciplinary integration, and intervisitations and mutual observations should be fostered by the administration. Voluntary participation and involvement should be encouraged and promoted. Teachers should be provided with the support in terms of resources and time. Schools should provide teachers with proper funding for methodological materials and visual aids to expedite sharing of materials and exchange of ideas in the process of collaboration among teachers.

Overall school collaboration is a vital and essential component for existence of any school organization. Teacher collaboration should become an integral component of collaboration between all stakeholders in the school. Collaboration needs to be a priority in schools in the times of rapid and radical changes, given the related need for teacher support, affirmation, and empowerment. In the times of transition, personal aspects of collaboration seem to be more significant for participants and are regarded as antecedents of professional collaboration. Personal collaboration needs to be fostered in schools to provide a solid foundation for professional collaboration. Mutual help, lifelong learning, communication and leadership should be used as building blocks of collaborative work. It would be beneficial to give consideration to the development of deeper collaboration in place of mandated or prescribed "pseudo-collaboration". Participants were discontented with undue pressure and authoritarianism and clearly expressed desire for greater freedom and flexibility in organization of collaborative activities.

Collaboration requires a balance between collectivism and individualism. As participants noted, extreme emphasis on either collectivism or individualism is not desirable for effective teacher collaboration. Much attention should be paid to the divisiveness and grouping into coalitions in the teacher collective. There seems to be a call on the part of the respondents to eliminate the tensions between the older and younger generations of teachers to reach lasting and deep working relationship between them. Enhancing mentorship practices would help accomplish greater collaboration between experienced and novice teachers.

Reinforcing and celebrating rituals, traditions, and ceremonies that support development of collaborative cultures in schools would be beneficial. Similarly, differences of opinion, valid arguments, and constructive conflicts should be encouraged in schools. It would be useful to avoid or change such practices as squabbles, rows, and unconstructive conflict that destroy collegiality. In conflict resolution, the common goal of educating and upbringing students should be the mediating factor that will make teachers realize what is worth fighting for.

Implications for Policy

Although some policy implications are provided in the previous sections, in order to inform policy makers in their understanding of how schools respond to rapid and radical societal changes, the following recommendations are made.

It has been noted that the initial reform endeavors lacked the foundation to build upon, the unity of direction, and consistency in requirements in their pursuit to discard the old policies as unnecessary without a clear vision of the new system of policies. Schools require more time to implement innovations offered by reforms in the educational sphere.

The process of implementation of reforms takes time and thought. Many of the reforms in the system of education were perceived to be introduced haphazardly, without the appropriate theoretical and practical foundations. Therefore, proper preparation, sound judgment, and consultations with teachers should be seen as crucial steps in the future implementation of school reforms and policies.

Teachers' rights should be observed in order to revive the prestige and authority of teaching profession. Besides, teachers required a relief from the immense pressure put on them to provide high quality education and be responsible for students' upbringing and achievements. School administration needs to outline that students' upbringing is not only the school's responsibility, but it is primarily an obligation on the part of the family.

A discourse should be developed which recognizes the importance of multiple perspectives, acknowledges differences of values and beliefs, but which strongly nurtures the values of mutual help, mutual respect, tolerance, morale, and spirituality among all stakeholders in the schools.

A common theory or system of collaboration should be developed among teachers and fostered in schools to substitute the *random* nature of collaborative work among teachers with a *systematic* collegiality. Participants were convinced that such framework would uncover the fullness of teachers' potential for collaboration through constant and consistent involvement in collaborative work with colleagues.

Implications for Methodology

This study utilized a constructivist research paradigm oriented to the production of reconstructed understandings of the social world. The researcher and respondents in this paradigm are both the co-authors and co-constructors of the knowledge. The main implication of this study for methodology is the difficulty associated with co-construction of knowledge between the participants and researcher involving the use of different languages and translation. Paraphrasing

Denzin and Lincoln (1994), as a researcher I faced a *double standpoint epistemology* or the act of *coming clean twice*. What is meant by this is that, first, I had to understand the meaning of data in the original language; and second, I had to make sure that readers would understand it in the target language. Not only did I have to choose words from a semantic and semiotic perspective, but I had to use linguistic techniques, paraphrases, and constructions to find the translation that would be the closest in meaning to the one used in the original language. The majority of the interviews and focus groups were conducted in Ukrainian, with the exception of two that were in Russian. Being proficient in both the original and translation languages, sometimes I still struggled with choosing the most appropriate translation. This especially pertained to the use of metaphors, idioms, and proverbs. However, language proficiency is not enough. The researcher or the translator needs to be closely familiar with the terminology specific to the field of study. For the researcher, it is preferable to do the translation himself/herself and avoid the use of translators, an additional step in the process of deciphering data that presents an extra layer of challenge if one wants to *come clean* in a research involving translation and use of multiple languages. However, external *translation audit* as a check of appropriateness and consistency of the researcher's translation should be a requirement for the study of this nature.

Reflection on the Research Journey

When I reflect upon the highlights of this research journey, I often recollect the very beginning of this undertaking when I wondered if I would have enough data to complete the study. My worries turned out to be groundless, as the research produced a body of inquiry and results that were much larger than anticipated. Handling such a great amount of data presented an immense challenge. Although the process of data analysis was lengthy, tiring, and at times, frustrating, it turned this research into a journey full of fascinating findings and unexpected discoveries.

In retrospect, it was interesting to observe the ongoing struggle between the forces of modernity and postmodernity in post-Soviet Ukrainian society. Gains of deideologization and freedoms of conscience, speech, and religion were counteracted by economic decline, political instability, and social insecurity. Societal transformations were seen as having direct impact on the system of education, resulting in a difficult transition period from the old Soviet to the new Ukrainian system of education. It was fascinating to discover a *parabolic* representation of participants' perceptions of changes both at the societal and school levels, in which the euphoria of change and related positive transformations were eventually displaced by struggles and prevalent negative attitudes. This notion relates to the *implementation dip* (Fullan, 2001), i.e., the tendency for new initiatives to go through a period of decline after the initial change.

Despite the fact that collaboration among teachers in schools was found to be susceptible to transformations at the micro (school) level, the realities and impacts of macro (societal) influences were ubiquitous. Macro transformations affected the *nature* of teacher collaboration in a direct way through changing societal realities, while *content* and *format* were influenced indirectly through the impact on school structures, reforms and policies, school culture, and micropolitical interactions among professionals.

A fascinating discovery was that in times of uncertainty and radical changes, personal aspects of collaboration seem to gain more significance than the professional aspects. Material welfare, spirituality and morale, social security, societal attitudes, social relationships, and shift in the systems of values and beliefs exerted significant impact on teacher collaboration. It was pointed out that discourse on collaboration required a balanced representation of individualistic and collectivistic perspectives. From this research, it is possible to conclude that the development of collaborative cultures in Ukrainian schools needed to be a two-fold process, involving instrumental shaping on the part of teachers and administrators and an understanding of the inevitability of societal conditions that can influence professional interaction.

It was not until the end of the data collection for this study that I realized its importance not only to me as a researcher, but also to those teachers who agreed to participate in focus groups and interviews. As I was analyzing the data and writing the findings into the report, the comment of one of the participants was constantly reminding me about the responsibility given to me by the participants. This comment was intentionally placed as an epigraph at the beginning of this chapter:

> You see, you asked the questions that have been on our hearts for a long time. Not often do others find interest in what is on our hearts and what hurts in our souls. We came with pure hearts and souls to your interview, and you will have to make conclusions out of what was said... (Stella, 7:21, 163)

To be honest with the reader, at times, this responsibility seemed to be too much for me to handle. Looking back at this research journey, I hope that I managed to cope with such a great responsibility to understand and convey participants' perceptions to the reader in a fair manner.

And finally, I would like to end with the discussion of the item with which this book project started – the photo of scattered pieces of a jigsaw puzzle, intentionally placed on the cover page. To me, it represents a duality of meanings: first of all, it symbolizes the times of uncertainty and radical change that left Ukrainian society in general, and schools and teachers in particular, with enormous amount of puzzle pieces that needed to be put together; secondly, it represents my research journey at the beginning, with a great many puzzle pieces that needed to find the right place for me to see the whole picture of this study. I hope that the reader was able to see that "big picture" with me. At the same time, the study described in this book presents a number of new questions that require answers as well. And so, other jigsaw puzzles await...

REFERENCES

Achinstein, B. (2002). Conflict amid community: The micropolitics of teacher collaboration. *Teachers College Record, 104*(3), 421-455.

Anderson, G. (1991). Cognitive politics of principals and teachers: Ideological control in an elementary school. In J. Blase (Ed.), *The politics of life in schools: Power, conflict, and cooperation* (pp. 120-138). Newbury Park, CA: Sage.

Anderson, W. T. (1990). *Reality isn't what it used to be: Theatrical politics, ready-to-wear religion, global myths, primitive chic, and other wonders of the postmodern world.* New York: HarperCollins.

Apple, M. (1982). *Education and power.* London: Routledge Keagan Paul.

Apple, M. (1989). *Teachers and texts.* New York: Routledge & Kegan Paul.

Aronowitz, S., & Giroux, H. A. (1991). *Postmodern education: Politics, culture, and social criticism.* Minneapolis: University of Minnesota Press.

Atkinson, P., & Silverman, D. (1997). Kundera's *Immortality*: The interview society and the invention of self. *Qualitative Inquiry, 3*, 304-325.

Bacharach, S. B., & Lawler, E. J. (1980). *Power and politics in organizations: The social psychology of conflict, coalitions, and bargaining.* San Francisco: Jossey-Bass.

Bacharach, S. B., & Mitchell, S. M. (1987). The generation of practical theory: Schools as political organizations. In J. W. Lorsch (Ed.), *Handbook of organizational behavior* (pp. 405-418). Englewood Cliffs, NJ: Prentice Hall.

Bacharach, S. B., & Mundell, B. L. (1993). Organizational politics in schools: Micro, macro, and logics of action. *Educational Administration Quarterly, 29*(4), 423-452.

Ball, S. J. (1987). *The micro-politics of the school: Towards a theory of school organization.* London: Methuen.

Barrot, J. E., & Galvin, P. F. (1998). The politics of supervision. In E. F. Pajak (Ed.), *Handbook of research on school supervision* (pp. 310-336). New York: Simon and Schuster.

Barth, R. S., & Guest, L. S. (1990). *Improving schools from within: Teachers, parents, and principals can make the difference* (1st ed.). San Francisco: Jossey-Bass.

Batelaan, P., & Gundare, I. (2000). Intercultural education, co-operative learning and the changing society. *Intercultural Education, 11*(Supplement), S31-S34.

Bauer, M. I. (2001). *State and perspectives of education in the region in the context of the project of the National Doctrine of Development of Education in Ukraine in XXI century.* Chernivtsi, Ukraine: Department of Education and Science of Chernivtsi Regional State Administration.

Berg, B. L. (2001). *Qualitative research methods for social sciences.* London: Allyn and Bacon.

Biesta, G. (1995). Postmodernism and the repoliticization of education. *Interchange, 26*(2), 161-183.

Blase, J. (1998). The micropolitics of educational change. In A. Hargreaves (Ed.), *The international handbook of educational change.* (pp. 544-557). London: Kluwer.

Blase, J. (2005). The micropolitics of educational change. In A. Hargreaves (Ed.), *Extending educational change: International handbook of educational change* (pp. 264-277). New York: Springer.

Blase, J. (Ed.). (1991). *The politics of life in schools: Power, conflict, and cooperation.* Newbury Park, CA: Sage.

Blase, J., & Anderson, G. (1995). *The micropolitics of educational leadership.* London: Cassell.

Blase, J., & Blase, J. (2002). The micropolitics of instructional supervision: A call for research. *Educational Administration Quarterly, 38*(1), 6-44.

Bogdan, R. C., & Biklen, S. K. (1992). *Qualitative reserach for education: An introduction to theory and methods* (2nd ed.). Needham Heights, MA: Allyn & Bacon.

Bolman, L. G., & Deal, T. E. (1997). *Reframing organizations: Artistry, choice, and leadership* (2nd ed.). San Francisco: Jossey-Bass.

Botyuk, S. (2007, May 17). Hunger for love. *Doba*, p. 7.

Boyd, W. L. (1991). Foreword. In J. Blase (Ed.), *The politics of life in schools: Power, conflict, and cooperation.* (pp. vii-ix). Newbury Park, CA: Sage.

Burns, T. (1961). Micropolitics: Mechanisms of institutional change. *Administration Science Quarterly, 6*, 257-281.

Cabinet of Ministers of Ukraine. (2000). *"On secondary educational institutions", Decree of the Cabinet of Ministers of Ukraine, N 964.* Kyiv, Ukraine: Author.

Cabinet of Ministers of Ukraine. (2002). *State Program "Teacher".* Kyiv, Ukraine: Author.

Cavanagh, R. F., & Dellar, G. B. (1996, April). *The development of an instrument for investigating school culture.* Paper presented at the Annual Meeting of the American Education Research Association, New York.

Center for a Postmodern World. (1990). *Position paper on postmodernism.* Claremont, CA: Claremont Graduate School of Theology.

Chepil', O. G. (2005, September 2). Problems and ways to improve socio-economic protection of participants in the educational process. *Regional Education (Newspaper of the Department of Education and Science of Chernivtsi Region State Administration)*, p. 7.

Clegg, S. R. (1990). *Modern organizations: Organization studies in the postmodern world.* London: Sage.

Cohen, L., Manion, L., & Morrison, K. (2000). *Research methods in education.* London, UK: RoutledgeFalmer.

Cooper, M. (1988). Whose culture is it anyway? In A. Lieberman (Ed.), *Building a professional culture in schools* (pp. 45-54). New York: Teachers College Press.

Creswell, J. W. (1998). *Qualitative inquiry and research design: Choosing among five traditions.* Thousand Oaks, CA: Sage.

Cyert, R. M., & March, J. G. (1963). *A behavioural theory of the firm.* Englewood Cliffs, NJ: Prentice Hall.

Dalin, P., Kleekamp, B., & Rolff, H. G. (1993). *Changing the school culture* (1st English ed.). London: Cassell.

Deal, T. E., & Kennedy, A. A. (1982). *Corporate cultures: The rites and rituals of corporate life.* Reading, MA: Addison-Wesley.

Deal, T. E., & Kennedy, A. A. (1983). Culture and school performance. *Educational Leadership, 40*(5), 14-15.

Deal, T. E., & Peterson, K. D. (1990). *The principal's role in shaping school culture.* Washington, DC: U.S. Department of Education, Office of Educational Research and Improvement.

Deal, T. E., & Peterson, K. D. (1999). *Shaping school culture: The school leader's role.* San Francisco: Jossey-Bass.

Densmore, K. (1987). Professionalism, proletarianization and teachers' work. In T. Popkewitz (Ed.), *Critical studies in teacher education: Its folklore, theory, and practice* (pp. 130-160). London: Falmer Press.

Denzin, N. K., & Lincoln, Y. S. (1994). Major paradigms and perspectives. In N. K. Denzin & Y. S. Lincoln (Eds.), *Handbook of qualitative research.* (pp. 99-104). Thousand Oaks, CA: Sage.

Denzin, N. K., & Lincoln, Y. S. (2000a). Introduction: The discipline and practice of qualitative research. In N. K. Denzin & Y. S. Lincoln (Eds.), *Handbook of qualitative research* (2nd ed., pp. 1-28). Thousand Oaks, CA: Sage.

Denzin, N. K., & Lincoln, Y. S. (Eds.). (2000b). *Handbook of qualitative research* (2nd ed.). Thousand Oaks, CA: Sage.

Department of Education and Science of Chernivtsi Regional State Administration. (2002). *Materials for August conferences of teachers in Chernivsti region: Methodological recommendations for subject instruction and upbringing in 2002/2003 school year.* Chernivtsi, Ukraine: Chernivtsi Regional Institute of Post-Diploma Pedagogical Education.

Department of Education and Science of Chernivtsi Regional State Administration. (2003). *Methodological recommendations for organization of educational process in general secondary schools in 2003/2004 school year.* Chernivtsi, Ukraine: Chernivtsi Regional Institute of Post-Diploma Pedagogical Education.

Derrida, J. (1973). *Speech and phenomena.* Evanston, IL: Northwestern University Press.

Derrida, J. (1978). *Writing and difference.* London: Routledge & Kegan Paul.

Dimitriadis, G. (2001). Coming clean at the hyphen: Ethics and dialogue at a local community centre. *Qualitative Inquiry, 7*(5), 578-597.

Douglas, J. D. (1985). *Creative interviewing.* Beverly Hills, CA: Sage.

DuFour, R., & Eaker, R. (1998). *Professional learning communities at work: Best practices for enhancing student achievement.* Bloomington, IN: National Educational Service.

Dyczok, M. (2000). *Ukraine: Movement without change, change without movement.* Amsterdam, The Netherlands: Harwood Academic Publishers.

Earl, L., & Lee, L. (1998). *School improvement: What have we learned from the Manitoba experience.* Toronto, ON: Walter and Duncan Gordon Foundation.

Edmunds, H. (1999). *The focus group research handbook.* Thousand Oaks, CA: Sage.

Erlandson, D. A., Harris, E., Skipper, B., & Allen, S. (1993). *Doing naturalistic inquiry: A guide to methods.* Newbury Park, CA: Sage.

Evers, C., & Lakomski, G. (1996). *Exploring educational administration: Coherentist applications and critical debates.* New York: Pergamon.

Fayol, H. (1949). *General and industrial management.* London: Sir Isaac Pitman.

Feldstein, D. I. (1977). Psychological characteristics of children's collective in the formation of collective qualities of personality of school age children. *Voprosy Psikhologii, 2,* 83-95.

Fine, M. (1994). Working the hyphens: Reinventing self and other in qualitative research. In N. K. Denzin & Y. S. Lincoln (Eds.), *Handbook of qualitative research* (pp. 70-82). Thousand Oaks, CA: Sage.

Fine, M., & Weis, L. (1998). *The unknown city: Lives of poor and working-class young adults.* Boston: Beacon.

Firestone, W. A., & Seashore Louis, K. (1999). Schools as cultures. In J. Murphy & K. Seashore Louis (Eds.), *Handbook of research on educational administration* (2nd ed., pp. 297-322). San Francisco: Jossey Bass.

Fontana, A., & Frey, J. H. (2000). The interview: From structured questions to negotiated text. In N. K. Denzin & Y. S. Lincoln (Eds.), *Handbook of qualitative research* (2nd ed., pp. 645-672). Thousand Oaks, CA: Sage.

Foucault, M. (1980). Two lectures. In C. Gordon (Ed.), *Power/Knowledge: Selected interviews and other writings 1972-1977* (pp. 78-108). New York: Pantheon.

167

Foucault, M. (1982). Afterword: The subject and power. In H. L. Dreyfus & P. Rabinow (Eds.), *Michel Foucault: Beyond structuralism and hermeneutics* (pp. 208-226). Chicago: University of Chicago Press.

Freire, P. (1985). *The politics of education: Culture, power, and liberation.* New York: Bergin and Harvey.

Friend, M., & Cook, L. (1996). *Interactions: Collaboration skills for school professionals* (2nd ed.). White Plains, NY: Longman.

Friend, M., & Cook, L. (2000). *Interactions: Collaboration skills for school professionals* (3rd ed.). New York: Addison Wesley Longman.

Fullan, M. G. (1993). *Change forces: Probing the depth of educational reform.* London: The Falmer Press.

Fullan, M. G. (1999). *Change forces: The sequel.* London: The Falmer Press.

Fullan, M. G. (2001). *Leading in a culture of change.* San Francisco: Jossey-Bass.

Fullan, M. G., & Hargreaves, A. (1996). *What's worth fighting for in your school.* New York: Teachers College Press.

Fullan, M. G., & Stiegelbauer, S. (1991). *The new meaning of educational change.* Toronto, ON: OISE Press.

Furman, G. C. (1998). Postmodernism and community in schools: Unraveling the paradox. *Educational Administration Quarterly, 34*(3), 298-328.

Gall, M., Borg, W., & Gall, J. (1996). *Educational research: An introduction* (6th ed.). Toronto, ON: Longman.

Gall, M., Borg, W., & Gall, J. (2003). *Educational research: An introduction* (7th ed.). Toronto, ON: Longman.

Geertz, C. (1973). *The interpretation of cultures.* New York: Basic Books.

Gerholm, T. (1988). On ritual: A postmodernist view. *Ethnos, 53*(III-IV), 190-203.

Giroux, H. (1994). Slacking off: Border youth and postmodern education. *Journal of Advanced Composition, 14,* 347-366.

Glesne, C. (1999). *Becoming qualitative researchers.* (2nd ed.). New York: Addison Wesley Longman.

Glesne, C., & Peshkin, A. (1992). *Becoming qualitative researchers.* (2nd ed.). White Plains, NY: Longman.

Godon, R., Juceviciene, P., & Kodelja, Z. (2004). Philosophy of education in post-Soviet societies of Eastern Europe: Poland, Lithuania and Slovenia. *Comparative Education, 40*(4), 559-569.

Golarz, R. J., & Golarz, M. J. (1995). *The power of participation: Improving schools in a democratic society.* Sebastopol, CA: National Training Associates.

Greenfield, T. (1984). Leaders and schools: Willfulness and non-natural order of organizations. In T. J. Sergiovanni & J. E. Corbally (Eds.), *Leadership and organizational culture* (pp. 142-169). Urbana: University of Illinois Press.

Gronn, P. (1986). Politics, power, and the management of schools. In A. McMahon (Ed.), *The management of schools* (pp. 45-54). London: Kogan Page.

Guba, E. G. (1981). Criteria for assessing the trustworthiness of naturalistic inquiries. *ERIC/ECTJ, 29*(2), 75-91.

Guba, E. G. (1990). The alternative paradigm dialog. In E. G. Guba (Ed.), *The paradigm dialog* (pp. 17-30). Newbury Park, CA: Sage.

Guba, E. G., & Lincoln, Y. S. (1994). Competing paradigms in qualitative research. In N. K. Denzin & Y. S. Lincoln (Eds.), *Handbook of qualitative research* (pp. 105-117). Thousand Oaks, CA: Sage.

Guba, E. G., & Lincoln, Y. S. (1999). Naturalistic and rationalistic inquiry. In J. P. Keeves & G. Lakomski (Eds.), *Issues in educational research* (pp. 141-149). Oxford, UK: Pergamon.

Gubrium, J. F., & Holstein, J. A. (1997). *The new language of qualitative method.* New York: Oxford University Press.

Hargreaves, A. (1991). Contrived collegiality: The micropolitics of teacher collaboration. In J. Blase (Ed.), *The politics of life in schools: Power, conflict, and cooperation* (pp. 46-72). London: Sage.

Hargreaves, A. (1994). *Changing teachers, changing times.* New York: Teachers College Press.

Hault, K. M., & Walcott, C. (1990). *Governing public organizations.* Pacific Grove, CA: Brooks/Cole.

Heckman, P. E. (1993). School restructuring in practice: Reckoning with the culture of school. *International Journal of Educational Reform, 2*(3), 263-271.

Henry, C. (1995). Postmodernism: The new spectre? In D. Dockery (Ed.), *The challenge of postmodernism* (pp. 34-52). Wheaton: BridgePoint.

Henry, M. E. (1993). *School cultures: Universes of meaning in private schools.* Norwood, NJ: Ablex.

Hodder, I. (2000). The interpretation of documents and material culture. In N. K. Denzin & Y. S. Lincoln (Eds.), *Handbook of qualitative research* (2nd ed., pp. 703-715). Thousand Oaks, CA: Sage.

Holstein, J. A., & Gubrium, J. F. (1994). Phenomenology, ethnophenomenology, and interpretive practice. In N. K. Denzin & Y. S. Lincoln (Eds.), *Handbook of qualitative research* (pp. 262-272). Newbury Park, CA: Sage.

Holstein, J. A., & Gubrium, J. F. (1995). *The active interview.* Thousand Oaks, CA: Sage.

Hoyle, E. (1982). Micropolitics of educational organizations. *Education Management and Administration, 10*(2), 87-98.

Hoyle, E. (1986). *The politics of school management.* London: Hodder.

Hoyle, E. (1988). Micropolitics of educational organizations. In A. Westoby (Ed.), *Culture and power in educational organizations.* Philadelphia: Keynes.

Huberman, M. (1990, April). *The social context of instruction in schools.* Paper presented at the Annual Conference of the American Educational Research Association, Boston, MA.

Huberman, M. (1993). The model of the independent artisan in teachers' professional relations. In J. W. Little & M. W. McLaughlin (Eds.), *Teachers' work: Individuals, colleagues, and contexts* (pp. 11-25). New York: Teachers College Press.

168

Iannaccone, L. (1975). *Educational policy systems*. Fort Lauderdale, FL: Nova University Press.

Iannaccone, L. (1991). Micropolitics of education: What and why. *Education and Urban Society, 23*(4), 465-471.

Janesick, V. J. (1994). The dance of qualitative research design. In N. K. Denzin & Y. S. Lincoln (Eds.), *Handbook of qualitative research* (pp. 209-219). Thousand Oaks, CA: Sage.

Janesick, V. J. (2000). The choreography of qualitative research design: Minuets, improvisations, and crystallization. In N. K. Denzin & Y. S. Lincoln (Eds.), *Handbook of qualitative research* (2nd ed., pp. 379-399). Thousand Oaks, CA: Sage.

Johnson, B. (2003). Teacher collaboration: Good for some, not so good for others. *Educational Studies, 29*(4), 337-350.

Kaplan, A. (1964). *The conduct of inquiry*. San Francisco: Chandler.

Keeves, J. P. (1999). Overview of issues in educational research. In J. P. Keeves & G. Lakomski (Eds.), *Issues in educational research* (pp. 3-14). Oxford, UK: Pergamon.

Keltikangas-Jarvinen, L., & Terav, T. (1996). Social decision-making strategies in individualist and collectivist cultures: A comparison of Finnish and Estonian adolescents. *Journal of Cross-Cultural Psychology, 27*(6), 714-732.

Kolotylo, M. I. (2005, August 26). Introduction of individually-oriented technologies in educational process as the necessary condition for professional growth of teachers and development of students' capacities. *Regional Education (Newspaper of the Department of Education and Science of Chernivtsi Region State Administration)*, p. 4.

Kononenko, P. P., & Holowinsky, I. Z. (2001). Educational reform and language issue in Ukraine. In N. K. Shimahara, I. Z. Holowinsky & S. Tomlinson-Clarke (Eds.), *Ethnicity, race, and nationality in education* (pp. 213-232). Mahwah, NJ: Lawrence Erlbaum.

Krasovetsky, H. (1995). The problems of child collective in the context of school humanization. *Ridna Shkola, 2*(3), 8-15.

Krueger, R. A. (1988). *Focus groups: A practical guide for applied research*. Beverly Hills, CA: Sage.

Kubicek, P. (2002). Civil society, trade unions and post-Soviet democratization: Evidence from Russia and Ukraine. *Europe-Asia Studies, 54*(4), 603-624.

Kutsyuruba, V. (2003). *Instructional supervision: Perceptions of Canadian and Ukrainian beginning high-school teachers*. Unpublished master's thesis, University of Saskatchewan, Saskatoon, Saskatchewan, Canada.

Kvale, S. (1996). *Interviews: An introduction to qualitative research interviewing*. Thousand Oaks, CA: Sage.

Lahusen, T., & Kuperman, G. (1993). *Late Soviet culture: From perestroika to novostroika*. Durham, NC: Duke University Press.

Larson, S. M. (1980). Proletarianization and educated labor. *Theory and Society, 9*(1), 131-175.

Lather, P. (1991). *Getting smart: Feminist research and pedagogy with/in the postmodern*. New York: Routledge.

Leininger, M. M. (Ed.). (1985). *Qualitative research methods in nursing*. Orlando, FL: Grune & Stratton.

Leonard, L. J., & Leonard, P. E. (1999). Reculturing for collaboration and leadership. *The Journal of Educational Research, 92*(4), 237-242.

Leonard, L. J., & Leonard, P. E. (2001). Assessing aspects of professional collaboration in schools: Beliefs versus practices. *Alberta Journal of Educational Research, 47*(1), 4-23.

Lieberman, A., & Miller, L. (1984). *Teachers, their world and their work: Implications for school improvement*. Alexandria, VA: ASCD.

Lieberman, A., & Miller, L. (1990). Teacher development in professional practice and school. *Teachers College Record, 92*, 105-122.

Lieberman, A., & Miller, L. (2004). *Teacher leadership*. San Francisco: Jossey-Bass.

Limerick, D., Cunnington, B., & Crowther, F. (2002). *Managing the new organisation: Collaboration and sustainability in the postcorporate world*. Sydney, Australia: Allen & Unwin.

Lincoln, Y. S., & Guba, E. G. (1985). Establishing trustworthiness. In Y. S. Lincoln & E. G. Guba (Eds.), *Naturalistic inquiry* (pp. 289-331). Thousand Oaks, CA: Sage.

Lincoln, Y. S., & Guba, E. G. (1994). *Naturalistic inquiry*. Thousand Oaks, CA: Sage.

Lincoln, Y. S., & Guba, E. G. (2000). Paradigmatic controversies, contradictions, and emerging confluences. In N. K. Denzin & Y. S. Lincoln (Eds.), *Handbook of qualitative research* (pp. 163-188). Thousand Oaks, CA: Sage.

Lindle, J. C. (1998, April). *Are school boards an effective means of school governance? A micropolitical perspective*. Paper presented at the Annual Meeting of the American Educational Research Association, San Diego, CA.

Little, J. W. (1982). Norms of collegiality and experimentation: Workplace conditions of school success. *American Educational Research Journal, 19*(3), 325-340.

Little, J. W. (1990). The persistence of privacy: Autonomy and initiative in teachers' professional relations. *Teachers College Record, 91*(4), 509-536.

Little, J. W. (2002). Professional communication and collaboration. In W. D. Hawley & D. L. Rollie (Eds.), *The keys to effective schools* (pp. 43-55). Thousand Oaks, CA: Corwin Press.

Lortie, D. C. (1975). *Schoolteacher*. Chicago: University of Chicago Press.

Louis, K. S., Marks, H., & Kruse, S. D. (1996). Teachers' professional community in restructuring schools. *American Educational Research Journal, 33*, 757-798.

Lyotard, J. (1984). *The postmodern condition: A report on knowledge*. (G. Bennington & B. Massumi, Trans.). Minneapolis: University of Minnesota Press.

Madriz, E. (2000). Focus groups in feminist research. In N. K. Denzin & Y. S. Lincoln (Eds.), *Handbook of qualitative research* (2nd ed., pp. 835-850). Thousand Oaks, CA: Sage.

Makarenko, A. S. (1959). *Kniga dlya roditelei [A book for parents]*. Petrozavodsk, USSR: Gosudarstvennoe Izdatelstvo Karelskoi ASSR.

Makarenko, A. S. (1967). *The collective family*. Garden City, NY: Anchor Books.

Makarenko, A. S. (1984). *Pedagogicheskaya poema [Pedagogical poem]* (Vol. 3). Moscow: Pedagogika.

Malen, B. (1995). The micropolitics of education: Mapping the multiple dimensions of power relations in school policies. In D. H. Layton (Ed.), *The study of educational politics* (pp. 147-167). Washington, DC: Falmer Press.

Mal'kova, Z. A. (1988). Education in the country of socialism. *Soviet Education, 49*, 1557-1564.

Mangham, I. (1979). *The politics of organizational change*. Westport, PA: Technomic.

Marshall, C., & Gerstl-Pepin, C. I. (2005). *Re-framing educational politics for social justice*. Boston: Pearson/Allyn and Bacon.

Marshall, C., & Rossman, G. B. (1995). *Designing qualitative research* (2nd ed.). Thousand Oaks, CA: Sage.

Marshall, C., & Scribner, J. D. (1991). "It's all political": Inquiry into the micropolitics of education. *Education and Urban Society, 23*(4), 347-355.

Mawhinney, H. B. (1999a). Introduction to a collection of reflections on micropolitics. *School Leadership & Management, 19*(2), 155-158.

Mawhinney, H. B. (1999b). Reappraisal: the problems and prospects of studying the micropolitics of leadership in reforming schools. *School Leadership & Management, 19*(2), 155-170.

Maxcy, S. (Ed.). (1994). *Postmodern schools leadership*. Westport, CN: Praeger.

McMillan, J. H. (2000). *Educational research: Fundamentals for the consumer*. (3rd ed.). Don Mills, ON: Longman.

Meadows, B. J., & Saltzman, M. (2002). Shared decision-making: An uneasy collaboration. *Principal, 81*(4), 41-48.

Merriam, S. B. (1988). *Case study research in education: A qualitative approach*. San Francisco: Jossey-Bass.

Merriam, S. B. (1998). *Case study research in education*. San Francisco: Jossey-Bass.

Merriam, S. B. (2002). *Qualitative research in practice: Examples for discussion and analysis*. San Francisco: Jossey-Bass.

Messick, S. (1989a). Meaning and values in test validation: The science and ethics of assessment. *Educational Researcher, 18*(2), 5-11.

Messick, S. (1989b). Validity. In R. L. Linn (Ed.), *Educational measurement* (3rd ed., pp. 3-103). New York: Macmillan.

Miles, M. B., & Huberman, A. M. (1984). *Qualitative data analysis: A sourcebook of new methods*. Beverly Hill, CA: Sage.

Miller, L., & O'Shea, C. (1991). Learning to lead. In A. Lieberman (Ed.), *The changing contexts of teaching* (pp. 197-211). Chicago: University of Chicago Press.

Ministry of Education of Ukraine. (1992). *Ukraina XXI stolittya: Derzhavna Nastional'na Prohrama 'OSVITA' [Ukraine of 21 century: The state national program of education]*. Kyiv, Ukraine: Ministry of Education.

Ministry of Education of Ukraine. (1999). *Education for All 2000 assessment* (1990-1999 Ukraine National Report). Kyiv, Ukraine: Institute of Content and Methods of Education.

Ministry of Education of Ukraine. (2004, September). *High-level education for all youth: Challenges, tendencies, and priorities*. Paper presented at the 47th Session of the UNESCO International Conference on Education, Geneva, Switzerland.

Mishler, E. G. (1986). *Research interviewing: Context and narrative*. Cambridge, MA: Harvard University Press.

Monoszon, E. I. (1988). The establishment and development of Soviet pedagogy. *Soviet Education, 20*, 14-98.

Morgan, D. L. (1988). *Focus groups as qualitative research*. Newbury Park, CA: Sage.

Mother of every fifth pupil is working abroad. (2007, November 1). *Doba*, p. 5.

Murphy, J. (1988). Making sense of postmodern sociology. *The British Journal of Sociology, 39*(4), 600-614.

Myts', H. (2004, September 2). From fighting with the teacher to fighting...for the teacher. *Vysokyi Zamok*, p. 5.

Nelson, C., Treichler, P. A., & Grossberg, L. (1992). Cultural studies: An introduction. In L. Grossberg, C. Nelson & P. A. Treichler (Eds.), *Cultural studies* (pp. 1-16). New York: Routledge.

Nias, J., Southworth, G., & Yeomans, R. (1989). *Staff relationships in the primary school*. London: Cassels.

Nielsen, R. (1993). Varieties of postmodernism as moments in ethics action learning. *Business Ethics Quarterly, 3*(3), 251-269.

Novikova, L. I. (1978). *Pedagogika detskogo kollektiva [Pedagogy of children's collective]*. Moscow: Pedagogika.

Ott, J. S. (1989). *The organizational culture perspective*. Pacific Grove, CA: Brooks/Cole.

Owens, R. G. (1982). Methodological rigor in naturalistic inquiry: Some issues and answers. *Educational Administration Quarterly, 18*(2), 1-21.

Palys, T. (1992). *Research designs*. Toronto, ON: Harcourt Brace Jovanovich.

Pascual, C., & Pifer, S. (2002). Ukraine's bid for a decisive place in history. *The Washington Quarterly, 25*(1), 175-192.

Patton, M. (1990). *Qualitative evaluation and research methods*. Newbury Park, CA: Sage.

Peterson, K. D. (1997). The importance of collaborative cultures. *Reform Talk, 10*, 1-2.

Peterson, K. D., & Brietzke, R. (1994). *Building collaborative cultures: Seeking ways to reshape urban schools.* Oak Brook, IL: North Central Regional Educational Laboratory.

Pettigrew, A. (1973). *The politics of organizational decision-making.* London: Tavistock.

Pfeffer, J. (1981). *Power in organizations.* Marshfield, MA: Pitman.

Potter, J. (1996). *Representing reality: Discourse, rhetoric and social construction.* London, ON: Sage.

Pounder, D. G. (1998). *Restructuring schools for collaboration: Promises and pitfalls.* Albany, NY: State University of New York Press.

Pounder, D. G. (1999). Teacher teams: exploring job characteristics and work-related outcomes of work group enhancement. *Educational Administration Quarterly, 35*(3), 317-348.

Putnam, L., & Borko, H. (1997). Teacher learning: Implications of new views on cognition. In B. J. Biddle, T. L. Good & I. F. Goodson (Eds.), *The International Handbook of Teachers and Teaching* (pp. 1223-1296). Dordrecht, Netherlands: Kluwer.

Reeves, D. B. (2002). *The daily disciplines of leadership.* San Francisco: Jossey-Bass.

Religious Information Service of Ukraine. (2006). *Chernivtsi to have own Christian Ethics classes in schools.* Retrieved August 28, 2006, from http://www.risu.org.ua/eng/news/article;11604/

Richardson, L. (1994). Writing: A method of inquiry. In N. K. Denzin & Y. S. Lincoln (Eds.), *Handbook of qualitative research* (pp. 516-529). Thousand Oaks, CA: Sage.

Rosenholtz, S. (1989). *Teacher's workplace: The social organization of schools.* New York: Longman.

Rubin, H. J., & Rubin, I. S. (1995). *Qualitative interviewing: The art of hearing data.* Thousand Oaks, CA: Sage.

Sackney, L., & Mitchell, C. (2002). Postmodern expressions of educational leadership. In K. Leithwood & P. Hallinger (Eds.), *Second international handbook of educational leadership and administration* (pp. 881-913). Dordrecht, Netherlands: Kluwer.

Sackney, L., Walker, K., & Mitchell, C. (1999). Postmodern conceptions of power in educational leadership. *Journal of Educational Administration and Foundations, 14*(1), 33-58.

Schein, E. H. (1985). *Organizational culture and leadership* (1st ed.). San Francisco: Jossey-Bass.

Schein, E. H. (1992). *Organizational culture and leadership* (2nd ed.). San Francisco: Jossey-Bass.

Scheurich, J. J. (1994). Social relativism: A postmodernist epistemology for educational administration. In S. Maxcy (Ed.), *Postmodern school leadership: Meeting the crisis in educational administration.* (pp. 17-46). Westport, CT: Praeger.

Schrage, M. (1990). *Shared minds: The new technologies of collaboration.* New York: Random House.

Schulman, L. S. (1988). Disciplines of inquiry in education: An overview. In R. M. Jaeger (Ed.), *Complementary methods for research in education* (pp. 3-17). Washington, DC: American Educational Research Association.

Schutz, A. (1967). *Collected papers.* (M. Natanson, Trans. Vol. 1). The Hague, The Netherlands: Martinus Nijhoff.

Schwandt, T. A. (1994). Constructivist, interpretivist approaches to human inquiry. In N. K. Denzin & Y. S. Lincoln (Eds.), *Handbook of qualitative research* (pp. 118-137). Thousand Oaks, CA: Sage.

Schwandt, T. A. (2000). Three epistemological stances for qualitative inquiry. In N. K. Denzin & Y. S. Lincoln (Eds.), *Handbook of qualitative research* (2nd ed., pp. 189-213). Thousand Oaks, CA: Sage.

Schwandt, T. A. (2001). *Dictionary of qualitative inquiry* (2nd ed.). Thousand Oaks, CA: Sage.

Scribner, J. D., & Layton, D. H. (1995). *The study of educational politics: The 1994 commemorative yearbook of the Politics of Education Association (1969-1994).* Washington, DC: Falmer.

Seidman, I. (1998). *Interviewing as qualitative research: A guide for researchers in education and the social sciences.* (2nd ed.). New York: Teachers College Press.

Senge, P. (1990). *The fifth discipline: The art and practice of the learning organization.* New York: Doubleday.

Shulman, L. (1989, August). *Teaching alone, learning together: Needed agendas for the new reforms.* Paper presented at the Conference on Restructuring Schooling for Quality Education, Trinity University, San Antonio, TX.

Slattery, P. (1995). *Curriculum development in postmodern era.* New York: Garland.

Spaulding, A. M. (1995, April). *A qualitative case study of teacher-student micropolitical interaction: The strategies, goals, and consequences of student resistance.* Paper presented at the Annual Meeting of the American Research Association, San Francisco, CA.

Stake, R. E. (1994). Case studies. In N. K. Denzin & Y. S. Lincoln (Eds.), *Handbook of qualitative research* (pp. 236-247). Thousand Oaks, CA: Sage.

Stake, R. E. (1995). *The art of case study research.* Thousand Oaks, CA: Sage.

Stake, R. E. (2000). Case studies. In N. K. Denzin & Y. S. Lincoln (Eds.), *Handbook of qualitative research* (2nd ed., pp. 435-454). Thousand Oaks, CA: Sage.

Stolp, S., & Smith, S. C. (1995). *Transforming school culture.* Eugene, OR: ERIC Clearinghouse on Educational Management, University of Oregon.

Strauss, G. (1962). Tactics of lateral relationship: The purchasing agent. *Administration Science Quarterly, 7*(2), 161-186.

Sukhomliskii, V. A. (1981). *Metodika vospitaniya kollektiva [The methods of the collective upbringing].* Moscow: Prosveschenie.

Supreme Council of Ukraine. (1996). *Constititution of Ukraine.* Kyiv, Ukraine: Author.

171

Supreme Council of Ukraine. (1999). The Law of Ukraine "On the General Secondary Education". *Vidomosti Verkhovnoyi Rady, 28*, 230-260.

Sze, M. M., & Wang, M. (1963). *The Tao of painting*. New York: Panteon Books.

Taylor, F. W. (1947). *Scientific management*. New York: Harper.

Townsend, R. G. (1990). Toward a broader micropolitics of schools. *Curriculum Inquiry, 20*(2), 205-225.

Tschannen-Moran, M. (2001). Collaboration and the need for trust. *Journal of Educational Administration, 39*(4), 308-331.

Turner, B. S. (1990). Periodization and politics in the postmodern. In B. S. Turner (Ed.), *Theories of modernity and postmodernity* (pp. 1-13). Newbury Park, CA: Sage.

UNESCO Institute for Statistics. (2005). *Education for All Global Monitoring Report 2006*. Paris: UNESCO Publishing.

Urban, M. (Ed.). (1992). *Ideology and system change in the USSR and East Europe. Selected Papers from the Fourth World Congress for Soviet and East European Studies, Harrogate, 1990*. New York: St. Martin's Press.

van Manen, M. (1997). *Researching lived experience*. (2nd ed.). London, ON: Althouse Press.

von Glasersfeld, E. (1998). Why constructivism must be radical. In N. Larochelle, N. Bednarz & J. Garrison (Eds.), *Constructivism and education* (pp. 23-28). Cambridge, UK: Cambridge University Press.

Walker, J. C., & Evers, C. W. (1999). Research in education: Epistemological issues. In J. P. Keeves & G. Lakomski (Eds.), *Issues in educational research* (pp. 40-56). New York: Pergamon.

Walker, K. D. (2006). Fostering hope: A leader's first and last task. *Journal of Educational Administration, 44*(6), 540-569.

Waller, W. (1932). *The sociology of teaching*. New York: Wiley.

Wanner, C. (1998). *Burden of dreams: History and identity in post-Soviet Ukraine*. University Park, PA: The Pennsylvania State University Press.

Weber, M. (1947). *The theory of social and economic organization*. New York: Free Press.

Weick, K. (1995). *Sensemaking in organizations*. Thousand Oaks, CA: Sage.

White, J. D. (1999). *Taking language seriously: The narrative foundations of public administration research*. Washington, DC: Georgetown University Press.

Willower, D. J. (1991). Micropolitics and the sociology of school organizations. *Education and Urban Society, 4*(23), 442-454.

Zhulynsky, M. (1997). Cultural, educational and linguistic policy in Ukraine, 1991-1996. In R. Weretelnyk (Ed.), *Towards a new Ukraine I: Ukraine and the new world order, 1991-1996. Proceedings of a conference held on March 21-22, 1997 at the University of Ottawa*. Ottawa, ON: Chair of Ukrainian Studies, University of Ottawa.

Wissenschaftlicher Buchverlag bietet

kostenfreie

Publikation

von

wissenschaftlichen Arbeiten

Diplomarbeiten, Magisterarbeiten, Master und Bachelor Theses
sowie Dissertationen, Habilitationen und wissenschaftliche Monographien

Sie verfügen über eine wissenschaftliche Abschlußarbeit zu aktuellen oder zeitlosen
Fragestellungen, die hohen inhaltlichen und formalen Ansprüchen genügt,
und haben **Interesse an einer honorarvergüteten Publikation**?

Dann senden Sie bitte erste Informationen über Ihre Arbeit per Email
an info@vdm-verlag.de. Unser Außenlektorat meldet sich umgehend bei Ihnen.

VDM Verlag Dr. Müller Aktiengesellschaft & Co. KG
Dudweiler Landstraße 125a
D - 66123 Saarbrücken

www.vdm-verlag.de

Printed by Books on Demand GmbH, Norderstedt / Germany